The Satan Trap

The Satan Trap

Dangers of the Occult

Edited by Martin Ebon

Doubleday & Company, Inc.
Garden City, New York
1976

ISBN: 0-385-07941-9
Library of Congress Catalog Card Number: 75-14816

Contents

Introduction:
Delusions and Vanities

The first letter came in April. The writer, a young man living in California, had read one of my books dealing with psychic subjects. He was writing for help. Reading and experimenting in psychic phenomena, mixed with drug-taking, had caused him severe emotional difficulties. Telepathic contact with his girl friend, for example, had become so continuous that, as he put it, "We can't get out of each other's thoughts unless we are driving in our cars in opposite directions." Beyond this, his sensitivity had become so heightened that his mind was almost constantly dominated by nightmarish thoughts and images. What should he do?

A writer in the field of psychic phenomena bears a serious responsibility toward his readers. I therefore answered quickly, urging the young man to end all his experimentation and to stop reading psychic literature, including my own books. He should, I suggested, seek competent psychiatric guidance and restructure his life in a way that avoided the supernatural, no matter how drab, square and all too "normal" this might seem to him.

The second letter came later in the year, around Thanksgiving Day. The young man wrote that he had recovered from his "bout with psychic dangers" and it "seemed very fitting that I should remember someone who helped me in my time of need." Actually, he himself deserved most of the credit. As the contributions to this volume show, dabbling in occult mysteries can develop delusions which, for reasons of personal vanity, are often accepted and cherished rather than fought and rejected. My California correspondent wrote: "Your note to me, suggesting that I turn to mundane matters to recover, was indeed very sage advice."

It is agreeable to be regarded as sage, but I feel that writers on such subjects as telepathy, clairvoyance, prophecy, mind-over-matter phenomena and other psychic practices must constantly be alert to the danger of presenting their subject only in glowing and positive terms. There is another side, a dark side to these phenomena, and in our time this darkness seems to be spreading. On the one hand, scientific study of the frontiers of the human mind is today more active than ever in history. But on the other hand, we are also experiencing a virtual epidemic of irresponsible toying with psychic powers.

Occult powers are not playthings. They open us to influences we do not know, and at times cannot control. One example was given by Francine du Plessix Gray, who described her own experiences in an article on "Parapsychology and Beyond" in the New York *Times Magazine* (August 11, 1974).

She had participated in a dream telepathy experiment in the Division of Parapsychology and Psychophysics in the Maimonides Medical Center in Brooklyn, N.Y. The experimenters seek to communicate images, usually pictures, to subjects who are asleep or in a state of sensory deprivation. The writer's experiences were strikingly positive. She saw pictures of African landscapes, and the slides that had been used to communicate with her telepathically had, indeed, included specifically African scenes.

But Ms. Du Plessix Gray recalled that seeing the slides had caused her "a swell of anguish," followed by a quickened pulse, a serious headache, blurred vision, perspiration, general dizziness and a severe sense of anxiety. She wrote: "Plagued with acute insomnia, I spent the following night mulling over some thoughts that I had shared with many a psychologist concerning the powerful 'catastrophic anxiety' that can result from experiencing psychic phenomena." She noted that people can react with panic when they experience the unexpected: "I build my ego on my perception of what the world is like; when my view of reality is undermined by something so anomalous as a psychic event, I am in a world of chaos in which no place seems safe."

The writer observed that Americans today are "increasingly titillated" with superficial sensationalism in the field of psychic phenomena, but "the experience of having our latent psychic capacities confirmed in a laboratory leads to a deep and primitive anxiety from which we tend to withdraw quickly." Still, an increasing number of people do not withdraw quickly enough, particularly if their experiences are not controlled, not well guarded by laboratory procedures or by skillful guidance.

Scientists draw careful lines that separate acceptable experimentation from harmless nonsense or dangerous foolishness. But most other people do not. And so we have a mixture, in people's minds and in print, of such diverse matters as Satanism, astrology, gods from outer space, prophecy with the *I Ching* or other devices, "black" or "white" witchcraft, reincarnation, hypnosis, palmistry, clairvoyance, various forms of non-medical healing and any number of psychic subcategories. Films such as *Rosemary's Baby,* which popularized witchcraft, and *The Exorcist,* which gave the public a sensationalist version of demon possession, have added to the confusing mixture. The mass media, the newsweeklies in the forefront, tend to exploit these fascinations with their usual mixture of provocative anecdotes, an air of amused abhorrence and a sprinkling of scientifically sounding skepticism. *Newsweek* has said that "interest in the occult, for decades the domain of tiny coteries, has suddenly emerged as a mass phenomenon in the United States." The magazine calculated that there are "increasing thousands" involved in everything ranging from Spiritualism to numerology. In the nation's capital, the Washington *Post* said a growing number of men and women, "from Pentagon officials to housewives," are members of witches' covens, and the number of Washington Satanists is "more than twice the national average."

Even if one allows for overstatements by popular journalism, there is certainly mass involvement with the occult. It cuts across the generations and can be found in all strata of society. It is easy enough to see where all this comes from. One New York psychiatrist, Dr. H. L. Newbold, sees such fascinations as "rebellion against our mechanized, chrome-plated society." The student newspaper *El Gaucho*, on the Santa Barbara campus of the University of California, attributed emotional escapism to "common frustration—born of powerlessness, alienation from one's pre-programmed life and contempt for authoritarian institutions."

Any mixture of frustration, drugs and occult dabblings is explosive, both in terms of individual stability and community survival. Entirely too many experimenters and observers of psychic phenomena have permitted drug-taking to detract them from truly scientific objectivity. At the other end of the social spectrum, young innocents tinker with a Ouija board, which allegedly permits spirits of the dead to communicate, as if it were just a scary toy. Others get involved with witchcraft practices, either for the dark thrill of it, or to "win love" or "take revenge" or to engage in some diabolic parlor game, for instance, to quote a motion-picture title, *Let's Scare Jessica to Death.*

These things may be dangerous for the target person, but they are at least as risky for the practitioner. It all may start harmlessly enough, perhaps with a Ouija board or, one step further, with "automatic writing." The cases are mounting up where men or women follow such "messages" with slave-like obedience. They may move out of a house, break off with friends, engage in erratic financial dealings, decide on marriage or divorce or even be invited by the communicating "entity" to commit suicide to share its life after death.

The Ouija board fad shows a general pattern. Someone will start playing with it "for kicks," and others will join in, with general hilarity. If pot is smoked, the thrill may be heightened. Acid heads for the most part don't need such devices, or only if they are bored with the general run of hallucinations. The Ouija will often bring startling information, telling things that "only I knew," establishing credibility or identifying itself as someone who is dead.

It is common that people who get into this sort of game think of themselves as having been "chosen" for a special task. The Ouija board will often say so, either directly or by implication. It may speak of "tests" that the sitters must undergo to show that they are "worthy" of this otherworldly attention. I have not been able to figure out why this is so, but quite often the Ouija turns vulgar, abusive or threatening. It grows demanding and hostile, and sitters may find themselves using the board or automatic writing compulsively, as if "possessed" by a spirit, or hearing voices that control and command them.

This is no longer rare. I'd say it is now so frequent as to be common. When I was touring a number of towns in the mid-South, a man came to me after a lecture and reported that his wife had become so addicted to the Ouija board that she began to take even its extreme prophecies quite literally. For weeks and months the board told this woman that her mother would soon die. The sitter became more and more agitated, more and more enslaved by these communications. Finally, the prediction became specific: it gave the date on which the mother would actually die. With this information, the woman purchased a reserved plane ticket and packed her suitcase. But the mother did not die. The husband took the Ouija board over his knee and broke it to pieces.

This prediction of death was outside the sitter's power. But what about suggestions of suicide, or even murder? And where does all this come from? Some spiritualists believe that only low spirits, who are earth-bound, are likely to become partners in Ouija board communications, and that these entities may be playful, hostile, fraudulent, misleading or, at any rate, as unreliable as any living persons of doubtful character. But the alternative exists that Ouija board sitters are merely opening the doors to their own subconscious, which operates the board or does automatic writing—without any conscious control by the sitter.

All this is quite mystifying. Even the most experienced parapsychologists, psychical researchers or psychologists cannot tell you what actually goes on. Oh, sure, there is a good deal of learned talk about "emergence of secondary personality characteristics," of "multiple personalities," of "surfacing of repressed tendencies," of "dramatized complementary, compensatory or supplementary facets within the individual." The simple truth is that nobody knows what really goes on, just as nobody knows exactly how and why we dream.

What we do know, however, is that it is dangerous to open doors to the subconscious without proper safeguards. That goes for hypnosis, among other things. A few years ago, a Cleveland high school student, the then sixteen-year-old Cynthia R. Perkins, remained under a hypnotic trance for days and had to be taken to a hospital for treatment with barbiturates. Together with nine other members of the eleventh grade at suburban Berea High School, she had been hypnotized during a science class. While the others came out of their trance quickly, Cynthia could not be awakened. The hypnotist was a seventeen-year-old girl who had learned hypnotic techniques during the summer and was practicing on her friends. Obviously the science teacher was not aware that clinical hypnotists frown on such "stage" demonstration of hypnosis, precisely because no one knows what possible psychophysiological changes may occur under hypnosis, or as a result of post-hypnotic suggestion.

Of course, anyone who looks upon life as one big drag race is welcome to all this—as long as it doesn't affect others. Don Heckman, writing in the New York *Times* on the death of rock star Janis Joplin at the age of twenty-seven, said that "whatever her problems, she dealt in the currency of life, of right-here-and-now-do-it-baby-before-it's-too-late." But two years of "the currency of life" seems a pretty short time. And it is precisely this short-cut mentality that stands behind current occult fads and delusions. Wherever there is this frantic drive to jump from seed to fruit, without a flowering and ripening in between, there we find delusions.

Individual delusion means falling into traps of one's own making; mass delusions, emotional epidemics, are quite another story. I have little quarrel with what people do to themselves, or whatever happens, as the legal phrase goes, between "consenting adults." I do mind messianic stuff. I do mind, very much, the glib dispensation of mystical wisdom, drug-induced short cuts to meditation or the addiction of anyone to anything. There can be, at the very least, solace for the bereaved in a Spiritualist séance, and even serious groping for understanding of man's immortal soul. But there is addiction in constantly running to mediums—just as it is a hypochondriac's addiction, or that of an attention-starved patient, to be forever calling on the family doctor. Occult wisdom, hard to distillate at best, cannot be conveyed whole-sale, and chemical short cuts to nirvana are on the same level as patent medicine cure-alls.

The peddlers of occultism ignore one basic thing: people who are emotionally unstable are their most willing and most vulnerable victims. It may be quite true, as the advocates of "mind-expanding" drugs keep telling us, that only those who are potential psychotics will be damaged by bad "trips." Probably only those who are emotionally vulnerable to start with will fall into the traps of occult self-delusion, will frighten themselves with the notion of malignant telepathy practiced by an enemy or will become as enmeshed in the spells of their own witchery as a kitten in a ball of wool. Granted! But it is precisely for this reason that the promises of "spiritual development," the "instructions in meditation" or "self-hypnosis" be tempered with caution, with an understanding of negative as well as positive potential.

One woman I met in Pennsylvania had developed apparently striking clairvoyant powers. But something was bothering her: "I seem to have developed a heightened sensory perception in my sense of smell. Without apparent cause, I smell something burning, or am pursued by oddly cloying or tempting aromas." Well, now this is something of which we know absolutely nothing. There are thousands of cases of crisis telepathy, for instance, where a message seems to pass from a person in danger, conveyed or channeled through one of the senses: perhaps it is the sound of a voice; it may be in the form of an apparition or the vision of an accident scene. In these cases, audio or visual perception is brought into play. But I do not know any recorded and analyzed telepathy cases that have olfactory impressions as their theme.

But here was a case of consciously developed and carefully guided clair-voyance; and no one could have known that it might have such odd and disturbing side effects. Very likely, this woman would have to give up her newly acquired extrasensory perception if she wanted to avoid uninvited intrusion by curious smells. ESP is much like a drug that has curative qualities but also negative, often unpredictable side effects.

Speaking of drugs: much of the current occult fascination is a post-LSD development. That, in itself, makes personal or mass responses unpredictable and uncontrollable. If there is one thing on which occultists agree, it is on caution, self-protection and care about the safety of others. Certainly, toying with witchcraft and Satanism, possession and exorcism has the same dangers as the drug culture: those who are already delicately balanced emotionally are the first to flock to assorted cults and are therefore most likely to become overinvolved, victims of self-delusion.

There also are violent extremes, cases where fakery, criminality and madness have resulted in tragic events. The most obvious case is the Sharon Tate murder in Hollywood: Charles Manson exercised "hypnotic" powers over his female "family" members. He called them his "witches," while reveling in the idea that he was "Satan." All this took place in a permanent cloud of hallucinogenic drugs.

That such labels as "Satan worshipers" and "witch" may have been used loosely—more respectable Satanists and witchcraft practitioners will correctly denounce all "guilt by association"—illustrates how widespread such concepts have become; like currency in an inflation, terminology has become cheapened and diluted. The epidemic calls for caution, and for a careful drawing of lines. The so-called underground press—where lumping together is also wrong—has in many instances failed to perform the essential task of warning against charlatans and criminals. One example is the *Free Press* of Los Angeles. Following the Tate murders, a wholesale grocer and his wife were also murdered. A knife was found sticking in one of the bodies. The *Free Press*, with its everything-goes enthusiasm, exclaimed in a front-page headline that this was the "Year of the Knife."

Now, let's keep our borders marked off clearly. We must not turn against a thoughtful study of occult traditions, of psychic phenomena and scientific parapsychology, just because these things can get out of hand—just as we can't abandon the use of fire for heat and cooking simply because a match can cause a conflagration. But I am against throwing lighted matches around, and I am against irresponsible occult dabblings. A carefully researched paper on "The Occult Revival in Popular Culture" was presented to the Ohio Valley Sociological Society by Professor Marcello Truzzi of the Department of Sociology, University of Michigan. Professor Truzzi spoke of the "widespread boom in things occult," singling out interests in astrology and in witchcraft-Satanism as "most clearly central" in the occult revival. Next, he said that the study of extrasensory perception and Eastern religious thought, were being used "as bolsters or legitimizing linkages." He said there was a trend to make "generally unacceptable magical elements in astrology and witchcraft-Satanism" more acceptable by emphasizing that respectable researchers are studying ESP and that the East's religious traditions have firm philosophical foundations.

Professor Truzzi sees nothing much wrong with a mass interest in the occult that is purely, as he puts it, "playful and non-serious." In fact, he sees it as leading to a "possible cleansing or purging of the old fears and myths that would quite naturally precede the kind of naturalistic rationalism in line with a more scientific view of the universe." He does not, however, condone excesses that may be practiced by a "small but significant minority." Fire for warmth is one thing; arson is quite another. Thoughtful study and interest is one thing; self-induced delusion is quite another.

I

Prophets, False and Real

Fraud in the Séance Room

MOSTYN GILBERT

*Mediums, who seem to be able to contact spirits of the dead, bear
a heavy responsibility toward the living. Often, those who visit
them are under an emotional strain because someone close to
them has died recently, and in their bereavement they seek assur-
ance and solace. While, as Mr. Gilbert notes, the majority of mediums are sincere in their beliefs and practices, there are and
have been fraudulent practitioners in the séance rooms, in the
United States, England and elsewhere.*

*Mostyn Gilbert, an American who lives in England, is secretary
and a trustee of the Survival Joint Research Committee, an organization exclusively devoted to the study of survival of bodily
death by means of closer cooperation between Spiritualism and
psychical research. Mr. Gilbert, who is not a Spiritualist but has
studied Spiritualist movements and practices at first hand, has
lived in Great Britain since 1958. He was a consultant of the Society for Psychical Research, London, from 1970 to 1973, and as
part of his continued study of the history of mediumship, has also
worked for the Parapsychology Foundation of New York City.*

Mediums often have their first encounters with the spirit world
during early childhood. This was true of the brothers Ira and
William Davenport of Buffalo, New York, who were famous in

the late nineteenth century. The boys, sons of a policeman, were said to have been carried about the house by spirits, even lifted to the ceiling of a room. Another well-known medium, Mary Rosina Showers, daughter of a British general, was observed talking with invisible friends who later materialized as full phantoms (or "ghosts"); her mother noted that solid objects moved inexplicably in the child's presence. The best-known of all American mediums, Mrs. Leonore Piper, recalled that she heard voices while still a small child. She also saw a bright light in her bedroom and felt the mysterious rocking of her bed.

From such childhood encounters, whatever their cause, grew the more spectacular clairvoyant and physical phenomena generally experienced in the séance room. These phenomena include raps on the table, levitation of objects or of the human body, materializations of the dead, and verbal communications through the medium that appeared to be totally outside the medium's personal knowledge. These happenings were regarded either as evidence of spirit power, belief in life after death, or, at least, demonstrations of as yet unexplained paranormal powers.

Scientific inquiry, beginning in the late nineteenth century, tended to confirm reports of the miraculous going back to and beyond biblical times. Of course, much of this evidence was put down to hallucination, misinterpretation, or fraud. Spiritualists, themselves deeply concerned with the "unknown," have been particularly aware of the dangers of conspiracy to defraud investigators or the bereaved, the two principal categories of visitors to the séance rooms.

Psychical research accepts the concept that a medium—a sensitive operating within the discipline of Spiritualism—is a person so gifted as to act apparently as an intermediary between the living and the dead. It is also not disputed that other sensitives, not functioning as Spiritualists, may demonstrate similar power, although these are not necessarily attributable to spirits. Their gifts are sometimes termed the psi faculty, or extrasensory perception (ESP). In both areas, however, opportunities and evidence of fraud are substantial. Usually, the motives seem to be a desire for public acclaim and financial gain.

One complex case of fraud and conspiracy was, in fact, exposed by a U.S. Spiritualist publication, the *Psychic Observer*, whose then editor, Tom O'Neil, arranged for an extended investigation of a well-known center of mediumistic activity, Camp Chesterfield, Indiana. He reported on his findings in detail, noting that he had done so in cooperation with Dr. Andrija Puharich, formerly director of the Round Table Foundation of Glen Cove, Maine, and author of the recent book *Uri* (1974), an account of his experiences with the Israeli psychic Uri Geller. O'Neil had not set out to publish an exposé of Camp Chesterfield, but had hoped that his observations and infrared photographs would document genuine spirit materialization. He wrote in the *Psychic Observer* (July 10, 1960) that his aim had been "not to research, not to investigate, but to record only with the most modern technique of the day, the motion-picture camera, infrared lighting and infrared film."

O'Neil and Puharich employed what the editor described as "the Observer-Scope, commonly called the 'Snooper-Scope' by the Armed Forces," used to "clearly observe the enemy regardless of darkness at a distance of a thousand feet." Ironically, "the enemy" in this case were O'Neil's fellow Spiritualists, who granted him permission to put on photographic record what they claimed as the great truth of "materialization."

The theory of materialization is that a tissue-like substance, sometimes called ectoplasm, emanates from the medium, possibly assisted by the emotional good will of the sitters at the séance. The appearance is temporary, and possesses at some stage human characteristics: limbs, faces, eyes, heads, and even full body forms become visible. The substance may emerge from the mouth or other regions of the body, or form spontaneously in some unexplained manner. At the conclusion of what is obviously a very emotional experience for the sitters, the ectoplasm withdraws back into the medium's body or simply vanishes.

Darkness or near-darkness is generally required for the genesis of this marvel, for it is believed that strong light, particularly, can inhibit the phenomenon and injure the medium. During the various stages of materialization no attempt must be made to touch the ectoplasmic extrusions. Indeed, even when the substance is fully formed into the phantom of a human being, draped in familiar clothing or the white garments of the spirit world, bright lights or seizure must be avoided.

Hans Holzer, author of some forty books on the psychic and occult, described the exposé in an article, "Revolt in Spiritland," in the quarterly magazine *Tomorrow* (Winter 1961). He noted that controversies of this type "go back to the late nineteenth century, when the first scientific tests were applied to 'materializations' by the German physician Baron Albert von Schrenck-Notzing." He added: "Since that time, no other branch of psychic research has been subject to so much discussion, doubt, accusation and unmasking of fraud. The temptation to produce fraudulently the alleged likeness of a 'dear departed' has always been with us. What is new in the current exposure is that a leading Spiritualist periodical has led the movement to expose fraudulent practices and persons, and has sounded the call for scientific tests of physical mediumship."

The medium whom O'Neil and Puharich specifically investigated was named Edith Sitwell (she is, of course, not to be confused with the noted British author bearing the same name). Mrs. Sitwell's "cabinet attendant" and director of the proceedings was the camp's director, Mable Riffle, who was even then in her eighties and has since died. On the first evening of the visit, the motion-picture equipment was not ready but the investigators put into operation the infrared visual monitoring system. The medium sat in front of the cabinet, the curtained-off area which usually serves to protect both medium and emerging ectoplasm from light.

The proceedings began with hymn singing. The "Snooper-Scope" recorded a luminescent glow above the cabinet's curtain. Next, the curtain parted, and a glowing figure emerged, spoke in a male voice, and identified himself as "Brother Benois." He was followed by a female spirit, "Sister Mary."

Until the end of this séance, Dr. Puharich had not noticed anything unusual or suspicious. He wrote in the *Psychic Observer* that when Mrs. Riffle "called a halt to the production of spirits, I noticed that Edith reached around and gathered in the curtains of the cabinet side nearest her, and with the other hand reached out and gathered in the swinging curtain of the door behind her."

Thus, Mrs. Sitwell "made a curtained passageway between the cabinet and the door entering her home," while, above this passage, a head briefly moved from the cabinet to the door. The following day, Puharich trained his equipment on the medium and noted that her "first move was to gather up the curtains" while "we were making noise and trying to get eyes adjusted to the dim red light." Dr. Puharich noted that, at the same time, "I clearly saw the figure of an American 'Indian' enter the room by the door behind Edith, and pass into the cabinet." He was followed by "a female figure."

Next, the "Indian" spirit emerged from the cabinet. The female figure came into the room as well and announced that she was O'Neil's spirit "guide," calling herself "Nita." She disappeared and was replaced by another woman entity who claimed to be the editor's grandmother. Puharich commented that "Grandma" and "Nita" were obviously "the same person."

When the next opportunity arose, the investigators had their camera in readiness. They asked the medium and the camp director to place two chairs in front of the door leading to the medium's room. That night, not a single spirit made an appearance. Puharich and O'Neil were told that their own "lack of faith" had poisoned the psychic atmosphere which made the appearance of discarnate entities possible.

The investigators bode their time. Their patience was rewarded when, at a later séance, Puharich clearly saw an accomplice of the medium manipulate curtains from inside the cabinet, thus shielding another person who slipped into the cabinet from the medium's room. Someone else managed to shift the chairs on the outside, and the spirits quickly presented themselves to the sitters.

The film made of this sequence of events proved fraud so conclusively that the investigators could no longer doubt that the alleged materializations created by the medium were, in fact, impersonators using gauze covered with luminous paint. O'Neil and Puharich received further confirmation from a veteran Spiritualist and publicist, Ralph G. Pressing, the founder-editor of the *Psychic Observer,* who had for several years lived at Camp Chesterfield. Pressing was shocked when he saw the film and was able to identify clearly the alleged spirit entities as "look-alikes to mediums residing on the premises of the Chesterfield Spiritualist Camp." This meant that other mediums were in collusion with Sitwell and Riffle.

Tom O'Neil's disclosures appeared in successive issues of his paper, and they caused consternation within the Spiritualist movement in the United States. Letters to the *Psychic Observer* praised the forthright journalism practiced by O'Neil for having revealed the seamy side of an otherwise honorable movement. Correspondents affirmed that not all materializations were to be regarded as fraudulent, just because fraud had been exposed at Camp Chesterfield; indeed, they noted that evidence elicited by other investigators was sufficiently impressive to have received the support of scientific researchers.

Nevertheless, the exposés harmed the sales and advertising of the *Psychic Observer*. Belief dies hard, and many of its readers were reluctant to face the revelations by infrared photography. A number of Spiritualist groups canceled their group purchases of the paper and canceled advertisements. Tom O'Neil withdrew from the periodical and died shortly afterward. Today, *Psychic Observer*, subtitled "Journal of Spiritual Science," is published monthly, under entirely different editorial direction, in Washington, D.C., although it states on its masthead that the periodical was "Founded in 1937 by Ralph G. Pressing and Juliette Ewing Pressing."

Exposure of fraudulent activity in the séance room has also taken place on the other side of the Atlantic, notably by the experienced and forceful editor of London's *Psychic News*, Maurice Barbanell. In addition to this weekly, Mr. Barbanell also edits the monthly *Two Worlds*. He is the author of several books, including *This Is Spiritualism*, published in England as well as in the United States. Barbanell has been ruthless in his campaign against fraudulent mediumship. Like O'Neil, he is a firm believer in the reality and value of communication with spirits, and thus is particularly bitter about exploitation of the bereaved and of investigators, such as himself. When a medium is caught in fraud, thus harming the Spiritualist movement, he or she can expect little mercy from Barbanell's perceptive and sometimes vitriolic pen.

One case prompted Maurice Barbanell into a particularly detailed exposure and analysis: that of the alleged medium William Roy. Barbanell wrote in *Tomorrow* (Vol. VI, No. 3) that "in thirty-seven years' experience with mediumship I have never met a bigger scoundrel, swindler, liar and rogue" than this make-believe medium. Barbanell was able to speak in such sharp terms because Roy himself had published a series of self-revelatory articles in the London *Sunday Pictorial*, bragging that "by fiendishly ingenious means I deceived even well-trained investigators." Roy admitted that "of all men and women, the most helpless and defenseless are those crushed by grief," whose sentiment he had exploited.

Barbanell noted that Roy's "confessions about his fraudulent séances" had been "read by millions," although the intriguing question remained, "How much of what he has confessed is true?" He noted that running through the whole series was the motif of "how I fooled everybody," which showed "a bragging exhibitionism and a vain desire to bring the whole house of Spiritualism down with him."

Who was this self-confessed fraud? He had been born William George Holroyd Plowright, and began his career as one of a trio of mediums who specialized in joint séances. His co-mediums, or co-conspirators, were Ronald Edwin Cockersell and John Scammel. The first of the two, who shortened his name to Ronald Edwin, published his own confessions in book form under the title *Clock Without Hands;* he also received a prison sentence for housebreaking, at which time the sentencing magistrate called him a "skillful liar." Scammel was found guilty under the British Fraudulent Mediums Act of 1951 and fined the equivalent of $150 plus $60 for costs. The act defines fraudulent mediumship as follows: "Any person who, with intent to deceive, purports to act as a Spiritualist medium, or to exercise any powers of telepathy, clairvoyance or other powers or in purporting to act as a Spiritualistic medium or to exercise such powers as aforesaid, uses any fraudulent devices, shall be guilty of an offense."

William Roy used devices, including electrical and other appliances, and Mr. Barbanell published photographs of them in *Two Worlds* magazine. These, he noted, were "deposited in the safekeeping of Scotland Yard." Roy, in his confession, claimed to have had 100,000 sitters and "to have duped his victims to the tune of $150,000," part of which he paid out as "hush money" to avoid being exposed. Barbanell said that the figure of 100,000 sitters had to be "a wild exaggeration, for it would involve having twenty sitters each day of the week and every week of the year."

Roy had a confederate with whom he quarreled; this confederate first confessed and then recanted. Amid all this confusion, William Roy decided to quit the British scene, give up Spiritualism and go to South Africa. But he soon returned to England, and Barbanell found "the clearest evidence that his séance swindling was being regularly practiced." He is apparently fully active again in Britain, using a pseudonym.

According to Barbanell, cases of tainted mediums are complicated by the fact that they "had, or still have, some genuine psychic powers." The concept that mediums may mix genuine with fraudulent elements has been applied by researchers in the past and present. At times it is suggested that fraud may be practiced unconsciously, or in a state of "dissociation" that includes amnesia; in other words, the medium or sensitive may act fraudulently but not be consciously aware of having done so. This does not apply, of course, to men like Roy who confess that they have kept a system of file cards on sitters that contain detailed data for use by the alleged spirit entities. A medium facing declining powers may consciously fake "phenomena" in order not to lose the regard of admirers. Yet, how apparent tricksters might deceive the operators of laboratory equipment in this age of electronic detectors is not answerable, at least not in a satisfactory way.

The risks of any exposé can be varied, as Maurice Barbanell can testify. Immediately after his exposure of William Roy, the medium's wife visited the editor's office. She tried to assault him with a little riding crop, which, Barbanell recalled, "propelled me into newspaper headlines with exaggerated accounts of an editor who had been publicly horsewhipped." Roy issued a writ for libel against Barbanell, but the suit was soon dropped and the fraudulent medium left the country.

Roy's confederate, according to his confession, "produced appliances . . . to prove that he was telling the truth." He also handed over card indexes "with information . . . relating to people who were regular sitters and those it was hoped would come." From another room the accomplice's voice was "transmitted by means of a microphone and midget loudspeaker concealed by Roy." The confederate admitted that he "did it for the money." It had been a "lucrative racket." Barbanell observed: "Visitors were required to leave handbags, overcoats and other personal belongings outside the séance room. It was his job to scrutinize letters, bills, receipts and other documents. After collecting this information, he conveyed it through a small earphone to Roy in the séance room. A clever feature of their roguery was a completely silent telescopic rod which enabled a midget loudspeaker and trumpet to be extended toward any sitter."

Psychology, no doubt, can answer some of the questions which perplex the investigator in his sifting through the reports of proceedings of this kind. Roy had no difficulty in stating, under oath, that he had never acted as other than a genuine medium. "Yet on the same day that he was admitting his séance frauds" to one newspaper, "he was denying to representatives of other Sunday newspapers that he had ever faked!" On a cautious note, however, Maurice Barbanell related an experience which offers some evidence of a possible genuine psi faculty. Frank Leah, the British psychic artist, undertook a drawing for a stranger. "About this time Leah was invited to visit a séance by Roy at which three other people were present," Barbanell wrote, adding: "Leah was addressed by . . . the guide he had drawn. Speaking through Roy, he told the artist that he had invited him to be present for a special reason. He wanted to warn Leah that his medium was a trickster who preferred to work on his own as a fraudulent medium."

A similar psychological complexity is to be found in Ronald Edwin. There is a body of evidence to show that this medium was a brilliant clairvoyant. He earned a great deal of money and appeared on radio and television. In his autobiography he confessed to faking séances. Yet "when the cameraman, who had photographed . . . his séances, produced the pictures and asked him to say which were genuine and which were fraudulent, he shouted in almost a frenzy, 'How do I know?'" Thus having traveled the road from mediumship to exposer of himself, a journey which included considerable hysteria and backbiting, Edwin's luck ran out and he finally languished in prison, after stealing property worth $4,000. Barbanell commented: "The moral is plain. Possession of psychic gifts is independent of character, mental or spiritual attainment. It is a gift, like the ability to paint, sing, act or write poetry. Its owner is a sensitive who, unless he has strength of character, is tempted into paths that bring about his downfall. It is only when psychic gifts are combined with integrity of character that you have greatness in mediumship."

Since the Golden Age of Spiritualism, from about 1872 to 1887, when the physical phenomena of mediumship were the rage of Europe and the United States, when new truths, so to speak, were being transmitted by alleged spirit agencies through the vocal organs of mediums, confessions, as in the case of Roy and Edwin, or exposures, as in the case of Camp Chesterfield, have besotted the Spiritualist movement. Because a legion of unscrupulous men and women have prostituted their gifts or joined with medicine men of old to fake séances and prey upon the innocence of the bereaved, investigation into these marvels has been difficult. When in 1882 the Society for Psychical Research, London, was established by a group of learned Spiritualists and academics, one of its purposes was to investigate the physical phenomena of Spiritualism "without prejudice or prepossession and in a scientific spirit." Tom O'Neil and Maurice Barbanell have done just that. The possibly genuine nature of materializations, as well as of other physical phenomena, should be easily confirmed once mediums are again prepared to allow séances to face infrared photography. Meanwhile, fear of injury or unjust criticism and lack of familiarity with infrared photography no doubt hold back genuine mediums who would otherwise be willing to submit to tests. It is up to parapsychologists and others to reassure Spiritualists that nothing but common good can come from modern knowledge.

Where Peter Hurkos Failed

WALTER J. McGRAW

Peter Hurkos is one of the Dutch sensitives or, as they are called in the Netherlands, "paragnosts" who seem particularly geared toward solving crimes, locating missing persons and even helping the police to find criminals. Mr. McGraw carefully traced Hurkos's performances as a crime-solving clairvoyant in two celebrated cases: the multiple murder of the Jackson family in Virginia, and the infamous Boston Strangler.

Walter McGraw is an award-winning producer of radio and TV documentaries. A pioneer in the use of taped interviews, he produced "Wanted . . . A Nationwide Manhunt for Fugitives at Large," the first radio series to utilize tapes recorded on location for its principal content. Later, "Wanted" went on TV. His more recent series have dealt with such subjects as narcotics, venereal disease, welfare and science. Crime has, however, been his prime interest, and he co-authored Assignment: Prison Riot, *a book about prison reforms and their failures.*

He appeared on the opening simulcast of NBC's "Monitor" with a continuing segment called "A Day at San Quentin." Also for "Monitor" he began looking into the occult for some of his weekly reports, which led to another book, The World of the Paranormal. *Later, combining his crime and parapsychology interests, he produced a series, "ESP: The Way-Out Frontier," for the Group W stations. Peter Hurkos was the subject of one of these programs.*

Until the thrust into prominence of Washington prophetess Jeane Dixon and Israeli key-bender Uri Geller, the best-known claimant of extrasensory powers in the United States was a Dutchman, Peter von der Hurk, variously called Hurkos and Herkos. He could be called an "accidental" psychic. Until he was a married adult, holding down a job as a house painter, he showed no unusual abilities. Then, when he woke up in a hospital after a thirty-foot fall from a ladder, he discovered that he had both a fractured skull and the power to "see . . . like on a fill-um" secret things about other people. Since then, books and magazine articles have been written in whole or part about his story; TV has not only shown him in person to millions of viewers but has even given us a wild, two-part paraphrase of his known biography; and, seemingly since the beginning of time, Hollywood "is about to do a full-length picture" of his life, usually starring Glenn Ford. Few, if any of these presentations have been impartial in their treatment of Hurkos and his abilities. He has been called "the greatest psychic of the twentieth century" on the one hand and "a fraud, a dangerous charlatan and an opportunist" on the other.

Hurkos is not a fraud. Whether his ability to be right reaches his claimed 80 to 87 per cent is questionable. That his correctness about things of which he could not normally have knowledge goes much, much beyond chance is, to anyone who views him impartially, undebatable. While it is true that professional "mentalists" using shills, "plants" and purely mechanical magic equipment can duplicate many of the things Hurkos does in his public performances, his spontaneous knowledge about people he meets accidentally, for the first time, is an ability that is unduplicatable by a professional trickster no matter what his investigative resources.

While Peter Hurkos's spontaneous ability is the foundation of his fame, it also makes him a basically unhappy man. He cannot stand crowds; touching things bothers him, and he relaxes only when he goes, alone, far out on the water on the excuse of going fishing. In conversation, he is not too coherent, and he apologizes often for this failing, saying he cannot concentrate on the subject at hand. For radio, he is one of the most difficult of men to interview. There is something disconcerting about asking one question and being given the answer to quite another question, one that you have in mind but have not yet asked. Often, his answer to a previous question comes much later. Whenever I have taped him for use on the air, I have had to edit the tape, so that the right answer follows the proper question. Since his English is still flavored with a strong Dutch accent, this is not easy.

As a result of my radio reports, I had several unique opportunities, informally but with minimal controls, to test Hurkos. He contends he works best as a "psychometrist"; that is, that he sees things better when he is holding an object connected with the person or event he is trying, psychically, to find out about. His fingering of objects I gave him that belonged to people who were complete strangers to him, elicited some remarkably accurate and surprising bits of information.

I have also had the chance to do some investigative reporting, complete with tape recorder, on the results Hurkos has achieved in what might be called "psychocriminology." I first recorded his version of the case; later, I talked to others who were actively involved. One of these cases was most impressive.

In a Midwestern city, two parents (who asked to remain anonymous) told me of sending a jacket belonging to their mentally disturbed son to Hurkos in Los Angeles. From L.A., on the telephone, Hurkos described their son to them, told them what he had done on the day he disappeared and gave them information that enabled the parents to find the youth in San Francisco. He was persuaded to return home and undergo needed psychiatric treatment. The parents, a retired policeman and his wife, were almost in tears as they told me of their gratitude to Hurkos, who, for the record, did not charge them for his services.

But in some of his more publicized cases, Hurkos's record is not nearly so impressive. His first great notoriety came when the Stone of Scone, symbol of Scottish nationalism, was stolen from Westminster Abbey in London. Hurkos claims to have been instrumental in its recovery. Scotland Yard has "no comment."

However, there was a great deal of comment on two murder cases in which Peter Hurkos was involved in the United States: the Jackson case in Virginia and the Boston Strangler.

The tragic case of the Jackson family made headlines in March of 1959. All four members had disappeared the previous January while driving from Richmond to their home in Mineral, Virginia. Carroll V. Jackson, twenty-five, and Janet, his seventeen-month-old daughter, were found on March 4 outside of Fredericksburg. He had been shot to death, the baby had been severely beaten but not immediately killed. Death had come to her slowly, after being buried alive, from suffocation and exposure. Seventeen days later, the beaten bodies of Mrs. Jackson and her four-year-old daughter were found. By June of 1960, the case was still wide open.

At that point, Dr. F. Regis Riesenman, then a staff psychiatrist at St. Elizabeth's Hospital in Washington, brought Hurkos up from Miami at $100 per day, to see what he could do with the case. Riesenman felt that the murderer would kill more if he were not apprehended and so he agreed to pay Hurkos out of his own pocket. Long a student of the paranormal, the doctor wanted to see whether Hurkos could pick the guilty man out of the reportedly 1,475 suspects the police forces had questioned by then.

Peter Hurkos went into the case, with a parade of police and reporters following his every move. The fact that he told both police and interested citizens alike about little-known aspects of their lives upon first meeting them was reported in the press with awe. And Hurkos was enough of a showman, consciously or unconsciously, to furnish copy for both A.M. and P.M. editions of the daily papers.

According to the newspaper reports, after two days, during which Hurkos and his entourage had visited the two death scenes in the Jackson case and the site of the murder of a Mrs. Margaret Harold in 1957, Hurkos described the killer: the man had, he told the authorities, a two-tone-colored house with a broken-legged chair outside it. The murderer lived there, Hurkos said, with a sharp-nosed wife who had lost two teeth and wore her hair pulled back. The man dealt in junk or garbage, Hurkos assured the police. The physical description Hurkos gave them sent police high-tailing it to question one of their earliest suspects, trashman John A. Tarmon. The address they had for him took them to a two-toned house with a broken-legged chair out in the yard, but the Tarmons had moved since the police had last interrogated him. When the police caught up with both Tarmon and his sharp-nosed wife at their new home, a search was made and the Tarmons were brought in for questioning. That evening, the couple was released.

The next day Hurkos and Co. went for a chat with Mrs. Tarmon while her husband was away. Hurkos told her what he saw, psychically, about her past and she confirmed his feeling that she had been beaten by her husband some six times and that he had kicked her downstairs when she was pregnant.

What happened after that depends on whom you believe. According to the authorities, Mrs. Tarmon said that previously she had been afraid to talk because her husband had said he would kill both her and the children if she opened her mouth, but that she could not now lie to Hurkos. He knew too much. "Is this man God?" she is alleged to have asked.

She then, according to police accounts, admitted that her husband had been mysteriously away from home at the time of the Jackson killings, as well as at the time of Mrs. Harold's death. After his return, on both occasions, he had acted strangely, pacing up and down and muttering, "What have I done? What have I done?" On the basis of this, Tarmon was picked up again and requestioned. Then, at one-fifteen the next morning he was taken before a sanity hearing and, "at the request of his wife," was sent to the Southwestern State Hospital for the insane for ninety days' observation. Although there was, at that point, no real evidence against Tarmon beyond his wife's testimony (which could not be used in court), it looked as though the Jackson and the Harold cases had been solved, along with some four other killings. Hurkos said he could see nine killings in connection with the Jackson killer, and, indeed, four other open cases showed patterns similar to the Jackson and Harold killings. Hurkos finally predicted that there would be another big break in the case in fourteen days. On that score he was 100 per cent right.

Exactly two weeks later the FBI arrested Melvin David Rees, a piano salesman who, with the help of his diary describing Mrs. Jackson's death, was convicted and sentenced to death. He was questioned about and suspected of nine different murders: the Jacksons, Mrs. Harold, and two other double murders.

Meanwhile the American Civil Liberties Union had asked some pointed questions about the middle-of-the-night sanity hearing that one newspaper called "Crystal Ball Justice"; Mrs. Tarmon accused the police and Hurkos of wearing her down until she made "erroneous statements"; and the again-free Tarmon instituted a $25,000 suit (which he later dropped) against three state policemen and a county detective for "false arrest and false imprisonment." He charged them with "rough treatment . . . a severe blow on the head . . . repeated threats of prosecution for murder." Curtis Fuller, publisher of *Fate* magazine, wrote that the happenings in Virginia could "only reflect unhappily upon public attitudes toward psychic phenomena" and theorized that Hurkos had been influenced by a "telepathic cross-over" from the thoughts of one of the policemen who had questioned Tarmon previously.

Riesenman (interviewed in Washington, D.C.) admits to being puzzled by this strange mixing of facts concerning the unlucky trashman, Tarmon, and Rees, the piano salesman who was tried and sentenced to death. Riesenman's version of the story differs little from that reported in the press, save that his is much more detailed (he literally kept minute-by-minute notes on Hurkos's visit) and that his point of view is less cynical. He subscribes to Fuller's "telepathic cross-over" theory and has even tabulated how many of Hurkos's activities could be attributed to pure telepathy and how many to clairvoyance.

Dr. Riesenman was impressed with Peter Hurkos literally from the first moment of their meeting. When Hurkos walked over to the doctor after debarking from the plane, Riesenman accidentally dropped a photograph. Hurkos picked up the picture, which had fallen face down, and without looking at it, told Riesenman about the subject: the doctor's eighty-two-year-old father. He detailed not only four auto accidents the old man had had in the last two years but predicted that, within six months to a year, Riesen-

man's father would die in his sleep of a stroke. Eight months and
two days later, this prediction unfortunately came true.

Hurkos also detailed accurately the story of Riesenman's
mother's death and funeral. At the Riesenman home he met two-
and-a-half-year-old Mary Alice, who had never walked. He told
Mrs. Riesenman her daughter would walk on her third birthday
and would, a few days later, walk over to a Christmas tree. Sure
enough, six months later, on her birthday, December 21, Mary
Alice took her first step, and on Christmas Eve, she walked over to
the tree to get her presents.

As for Hurkos's handling of the Jackson murder case, Riesenman says that Hurkos had actually talked of three different men.
The first was a "Mike," who was never described physically and
has never been found to have any connection with the case. The
first physical description Hurkos gave of the man he saw as the
murderer came far closer to that of Rees than of Tarmon, even
though the men were not too dissimilar in appearance. Next, he
described the murderer's wife. Unfortunately, there are thousands of women who fit the description of having a pointed
face, pulled-back hair and two missing teeth. And, by coincidence, both Mrs. Tarmon and the woman with whom Rees was
living at that time not only fit that description, but, according to
Riesenman's investigations, both had recently dyed their hair, as
was also specified by Hurkos.

According to Riesenman, Hurkos had impressed the police by
describing elements of the various crimes involved that had been
carefully hidden from the press. He mentioned a piece of brown,
insulated wire that only the police knew about; he described the
committing of the various crimes with details never printed in any
newspaper; he said that Mrs. Harold had suffered a miscarriage
six months prior to her death, which fact had also not been
publicized; and he gave a graphic description of how Mrs. Jackson had been forced to perform fellatio and then been killed. The
police were amazed that his descriptions accounted for all the evidence they had found and tallied completely with their own
reconstructions of the crimes. Only after that, Hurkos got into a
police car with detectives who had questioned Tarmon as one of
the hundreds of suspects in the neighborhood. Then, and only

then, according to Riesenman, did Hurkos's description begin to change and to fit Tarmon. He mentioned two scars on the murderer's leg, a tattoo on his arm and a recent haircut. The police knew about Tarmon's house, description and tattoo, so Hurkos could have been reading the minds of the men alongside him. But, while it was true that Tarmon had scars on his leg and a recent haircut, this could not have been telepathy which "crossed over," because the police did not know either of these things.

Dr. Riesenman hypothesizes that the combination of the police telepathically sending details of the man Hurkos saw as the murderer and the actions of the Tarmons when under questioning misled everyone. He points out that Tarmon even admitted to telling his wife he had killed, although he did not admit to the police that he had killed at all, much less killed the Jacksons. Further, according to Riesenman, the midnight hearing developed from not only Mrs. Tarmon's fear for her life, but Tarmon's quickly developed relationship with Dr. Riesenman himself. He had, at the time of the hearing, become the doctor's private patient, and when the suggestion was made that he be committed, his reaction was that it would be "a good idea."

Riesenman still thinks he was right in bringing Hurkos into the case and that, given the same circumstances, he would do it again. He feels Hurkos was at least 80 per cent right and that he has the documentation to prove it. Riesenman, with a record of over twenty years in the medical service of the U.S. government and his continuing activities as a psychiatric adviser to both federal and Virginia courts, is a hard man to challenge. He is used to presenting evidence that, literally, has to stand up in court. He feels his version of *l'affaire* Hurkos would do just that.

Peter Hurkos, interviewed in Milwaukee, agreed to the "crossover" theory and claimed he had named two possible suspects but that the police decided to go after the trashman first. He quit when the police seemed satisfied they had their man. Hurkos still seems reluctant to separate the trashman entirely from the nine killings that go to make up the Jackson case, saying that the trashman was involved, if only by coincidence, with scenes pertinent to the murders. He claims the trashman's army I.D. bracelet was found close to one of the graves and that both the trashman and the piano salesman had lived in the same house, though at different times. He feels "the vibrations may have crossed" there.

It was largely as a result of the publicity Hurkos received in the Jackson case that he became involved in that of the Boston Strangler. Hurkos said that the "attorney general of Boston" had brought him into the case, for which he received no fee, only expenses. Actually, it was a friend of the then Massachusetts attorney general, now Senator Edward W. Brooks, Jr., who suggested that Hurkos's help be enlisted. The suggestion was turned over to Assistant Attorney General John Bottomly, who was in charge of the Strangler investigation for the state. The feeling had been that the case, involving as it did several jurisdictions, needed state coordination under the attorney general's office. This had not been too popular a decision with some of the local police, so Bottomly felt he had to tread carefully in his job.

He and his staff checked on Hurkos with much care. As far as the Jackson case was concerned, a member of Bottomly's staff secured verification from the State Police in Virginia that, in their opinion, Hurkos "had identified the correct murderer . . . and that, as a matter of fact, the State Police of Virginia had dispatched a representative of their department to arrest the particular individual involved [the piano salesman] who was in another jurisdiction."

Despite the fact that the FBI had picked up the piano salesman first, the Virginia authorities felt "Hurkos had made a definite contribution to the solution of that rather difficult crime, in terms of solving it." Bottomly's staff also checked with the FBI, who said "Hurkos had made no contribution to the solution of the crime."

Assistant Attorney General Bottomly confirmed Hurkos's statement that he had insisted on there being no publicity about his trip to Boston and that he had renounced any claim to the $10,000 reward. He states that Hurkos was paid a $1,000 fee, over and above his expenses, by the attorney general's friend. After determining that no public monies would be involved and that the police investigations would in no way be "disrupted" by bringing Hurkos into the case, Bottomly arranged for a press black-out on news concerning the psychic's trip while he was in Boston. Hurkos was sneaked into a suburban Boston motel.

From here on, both Bottomly's quiet description, recorded in Boston, and Hurkos's earlier dramatic recounting of the events are in substantial agreement. Just as in the Jackson case, Boston officials assigned to work with Hurkos were amazed by bits of intimate knowledge he kept dropping about them. But, as in the Jackson case, they were most impressed by his knowledge of details concerning the crimes that were known to only a few of the police. Also, since the stranglings were basically sex-oriented, the newspapers had voluntarily left some of the gorier details out of their reports. Hurkos was not so inhibited. His knowledge seemed to be sure; his language, direct.

The first day he was in Boston, he was brought a large pile of photographs, each inserted in an unmarked individual manila envelope. These had, that very morning, been taken out of the office files and put into the similar envelopes, also obtained that morning from the main stationery supply room of the attorney general's office. According to Bottomly: "He selected certain of these pictures without opening the envelopes, then proceeded, to the astonishment of those assembled, to describe in rather minute detail what was on the picture without ever having seen it. Then they opened the envelope and, lo and behold! it was what he said it was. I can't explain that."

Two things about that morning session were mentioned by both Bottomly and Hurkos. One had to do with one of the first envelopes fondled, but not opened, by Hurkos. This, he indicated, was a picture from another, already solved murder. Upon its being opened, Hurkos was found to be right. One "phony" picture had been put into the group as a control. Hurkos in no way resented this. "The police got a right to be suspicious," he said.

The second incident concerned the murder of what was then thought to be victim number eleven, one Mary Sullivan. Here was by far the most grisly of the crimes, so many of the details had not been made public. Among the envelopes given Hurkos, thirty-six of the enclosed pictures concerned this case. Hurkos picked out five of these and said they concerned the same case. He then went on to describe the victim's final moments, including the fact that she had grabbed at "some kind of drapes . . . to save her neck." Bottomly described them as "one of those collapsible-type doors . . . almost like drapes only they're heavier." No information had been made public that these had been pulled from their runner in what must have been the victim's death struggle. One of the photographs described, but not seen, by Hurkos showed this runner. "This," said Bottomly, "rather surprised and impressed some of the Boston police from homicide who were there."

"He then went over there," Bottomly went on, talking about the envelopes lying on the motel bed, "and he spread these pictures on the floor and did some more thinking or receiving . . . whatever you want to call it . . . and everything that he said was put on tape . . . and he gradually came around to describing a particular type of person . . . a general description."

After the session at the motel, Hurkos had the police drive him around Boston, where he pointed out some buildings where he said crimes, but not necessarily stranglings, had been committed. Invariably, he was right. Then, at the staff offices, he "would take a file of letters or documents . . . documents dealing with these crimes . . . and he would leaf through the letters . . . not flat out on the desk to read them but as if they were standing on edge in a file . . . and then select a letter to say that this had a particular interest to him." He did this and selected a letter which the department had earlier received from the authorities of Boston College, located in Newton, through the chief of police of Newton. The letter writer, who represented himself as an alumnus of the college, asked for a list of the students in the Boston College School of Nursing in 1950, saying he was interested in matrimony. Because of the crimes, the Boston College authorities decided to forward the letter to the Newton police. An investigation into it had begun a few days before Hurkos arrived. Bottomly added:

"That investigation had revealed that the writer was a door-to-door shoe salesman. He had a previous mental history; he had previously been committed to a mental institution. I personally had conversed with his doctor, who had said that he was mentally disturbed, but he thought perfectly harmless, and a very pitiable figure . . . a sort of a lost soul in this modern society in which we live. He found it very difficult to cope with it. He was a bachelor and had twice attempted to become a priest and had been unable to, apparently, cope with the discipline of either a monastery or a seminary. He didn't like to have any particular associations with other people. He disliked very much ever having people touch him. In fact, he had, for a number of years, worked as a dishwasher in a restaurant but he had quit because a waitress brushed against him in the corridor, and he felt very upset about it and left. He was really a hermit in the midst of a large city.

"Well, Hurkos felt this man was somehow involved in the stranglings. He did *not* fit the previous physical description. Nevertheless, Hurkos thought he was of interest.

"About this same time it had been decided that the local authorities ought to go and talk to this fellow anyhow, in view of what his doctor said about him and his history, so we sent over a State Police detective, a detective-lieutenant, and a local Boston policeman, and a doctor, and a representative of this office. They convinced him on their second visit—the first visit he wouldn't open the door—they explained who they were and the doctor asked if he could come in and talk to him? And the gentleman said yes, he could.

"So they went in and talked for ten or fifteen minutes and the doctor then signed what they call a 'ten-day paper' . . . a procedure in Massachusetts under which a doctor can recommend to the superintendent of the state mental institution that a person be committed for observation for ten days. The next step is for the person to go down to the mental institution and have an interview with the superintendent, who felt that he showed very strong symptoms of deep-seated paranoia and thought that further tests and observation would be appropriate. At no time was he accused of any crime. He was not incarcerated or put under police guard in any way. His family was notified about where he was and why he was there. One of his brothers advised me that for many months he had been trying to convince the individual to voluntarily commit himself for tests and observation and treatment. The other brother said that he wasn't the least bit surprised.

"The result of this was that I and one of my assistants went over and talked to him. We told him why he had been brought to our attention; told him about the letter and he readily admitted signing it.

"We had learned from one of his brothers that he had also joined a number of marriage clubs within the past two years and all this conduct seemed totally inconsistent with a man who for fifty-odd years had been a celibate.

"It developed that he was not at all comfortable in any of his relations with the opposite sex. He was a man, I think, who was a very talented person. Really he is a very *kind* person, but just unable to cope emotionally with the society in which he found himself."

I asked, "You don't think he was responsible for any of the stranglings?"

"No, I do not," replied Bottomly. "I think the only good thing that may have come out of this, interestingly enough, is that it brought that family closer together. His brothers and his sister, perhaps, came to understand a little more the difficulties that their brother was having in his life and, perhaps, became a little more sympathetic and a little more helpful to him, so maybe it all happened for the best."

But Hurkos had said of the shoe salesman: "That is the murderer." Later he hedged a bit by saying that the Boston police had another suspect, also a shoe salesman, who fit the same description. Hurkos seemed a bit uncertain that all the murders had been committed by the same man. He was, however, certain that there had been more than eleven victims.

It was in November 1964 that one Albert DeSalvo was arrested on sex and other charges having nothing to do with the stranglings. It was not until March 1965 that, to his lawyer, F. Lee Bailey, he confessed his involvement in not eleven, but thirteen deaths.

And Hurkos may have been correct on more counts than that. Thirteen months prior to DeSalvo's confession, according to Bottomly, Hurkos, while in the motel room with the photographs, had described the strangler as "somebody with dark hair; about five foot ten; large, pointed nose, tattoos on his arm; trouble with one of his thumbs; scars on the inside of his arms; dark hair with a widow's peak, a very handy man, very capable of fixing anything around the house; customarily dressed in sort of casual, informal clothes rather than in a formal business suit; around thirty to thirty-five years of age."

DeSalvo is five feet eight and a half inches tall, has scars on the inside of his left arm and has held jobs as a maintenance or handy man. He did a good deal of work on his own and other people's houses. Partly confirming Hurkos's identification of the strangler as being given to wearing informal clothes was his habit of wearing green slacks. At the time Hurkos was in Boston, DeSalvo was in his early thirties. Looking at a picture of DeSalvo, the two features that register most are the widow's peak of his dark hair and the large, pointed nose. While at the time Hurkos gave this description one of the police officials called it "a description of 'Mr. Average American'" and Bottomly felt "it had no particular value," *post facto* Hurkos seems to have been coming fairly close to DeSalvo's description before becoming involved with the Boston College letter.

What was Bottomly's evaluation of Hurkos's contribution?

"None of us who were associated with Mr. Hurkos, or his coming here, expected that he was going to point to Mr. X and say, 'He is the strangler,' and expect that on the basis of Mr. Hurkos's statement anybody was ever going to be arrested or accused of something, let alone convicted.

"The most that had been hoped for was that he might develop some information that had not previously been developed, which, in turn, could lead to further investigation, which would develop objective facts that would be the type of evidence that would be ordinarily placed before a court to prove a crime. Nobody in this department (or anywhere in law enforcement in the United States that I know of) is under any illusion that the testimony of a psychic is of value in a criminal trial. But for that matter, neither is a polygraph [a lie-detector test], but on the other hand, I think almost all law enforcement agencies now make use of the polygraph as a part of their interrogation technique.

"I also thought that, at the very least, Hurkos would perhaps stimulate others involved in these investigations and would open up areas of thought . . . possible theories of the case . . . that had not previously been considered. And I think in that area he did make a definite contribution."

But to this broadcast reporter who has largely concentrated on law enforcement, the use of psychics in murder cases is not an idea whose time has come. It is refreshing to find some of our police who are open-minded enough to want to try ESP in murder cases, but there are a good many arguments against it, over and above the fact that, in two cases now, innocent if admittedly emotionally troubled men have suffered what, at the very least, could be called embarrassment. Perhaps it would be wiser to wait until more is known about ESP before making it a regular tool for police work.

To which suggestion I can hear frustrated police officials saying: "Yeah, but by that time the Supreme Court will probably handcuff us by deciding that police use of mind readers is a form of 'bugging.'"

3

The Edgar Cayce Cult

MARTIN EBON

The late Edgar Cayce is undoubtedly the most widely publicized psychic sensitive of this generation. His "life readings" in reincarnation and his clairvoyant diagnoses of diseases have brought him hundreds of thousands of followers. Mr. Ebon, editor of this volume, seeks to put the current "Edgar Cayce cult" into the over-all framework of the actual life and work of Cayce, in the hope that the image of the "sage of Virginia Beach" or the "sleeping prophet" does not become excessively mythologized.

The name of Edgar Cayce is a household word in the United States and many other countries. The Association for Research and Enlightenment has branches all over the United States, devoted to the study of Cayce's work and to related psychical phenomena as well. As books about him have become more numerous, study groups have multiplied, lectures and workshops have grown in number, it has become increasingly difficult to keep the real Edgar Cayce in focus—an essentially modest man, soft-spoken, rather puzzled by his unusual gifts and by the attention they aroused in his lifetime.

It took some twenty years after Edgar Cayce's death for public attention in his achievements to reach a loud, and at times confusing, crescendo. Sounds from the periphery drown out words uttered at the center; a flock of writings, ranging from solidly responsible to noisily opportunistic, have proliferated in recent years. I sometimes have the shocking impression that this excited multitude resembles a circle of wild-eyed dancers who aren't really celebrating Cayce's memory but burning him at the stake.

Edgar Cayce should be best known for his inexplicable ability to diagnose illness clairvoyantly and to prescribe unorthodox but effective medications. He also forecast the progress of an illness, of cure or other personal changes; many of these anticipations were accurate and served to give him the label of "Prophet." As part of his effort to help troubled people, he used to give them "life readings" while he was in a trance-like state, telling them about their identities, professions and experiences during previous incarnations.

All this is amazing enough. Edgar Cayce was an astounding person, and we're far from finished with the job of studying his life, personality and puzzling abilities. I don't think this task has really been helped by the flock of books that have mined the Cayce records, kept with admirable care at the Virginia Beach headquarters of the Edgar Cayce Foundation, and have assembled his observations on everything from Jesus to organic food. To be candid, much of Cayce's talk was rambling to the point of incoherence, often trivial, and certainly not to be treated as Gospel on every subject.

The Cayce family has been administering his legacy efficiently and with the kind of common sense respect his memory deserves. They seem engaged in a losing struggle to keep a "Cayce cult" from flourishing. I know that this dilemma has been particularly troubling to one of his sons, Hugh Lynn Cayce, who is most prominently identified with the Foundation and the A.R.E. Together with his younger brother, Edgar Evans Cayce, he has described their father in *The Outer Limits of Edgar Cayce's Power* (New York, 1971).

Sons of prominent fathers usually find it troubling to live with the looming shadow of the man whose name they bear. The Cayce sons are no exception. These are decent, sensitive people. Don't think for a moment that being, to put it crudely, "in the Cayce business" has hardened them against the oddity of it all.

"Is the whole Edgar Cayce story a mammoth hoax?" they ask. Here is a man who for some 43 years used to lie down and lose consciousness twice a day, gave readings, influenced the lives of thousands, and apparently practiced a nearly unique gift of healing and guidance.

The two Cayce sons believe that their father was much too involved in everyday living, too unconcerned about what people thought about him to have been able to "consciously manufacture the more than ten million words of which the readings were composed." Their childhood memory of their father is that of a man who was handy with tools, a good photographer, not much of a reader—in other words, an engagingly average head of a very average American household.

The brothers supply impressive statistics concerning Edgar Cayce's diagnosis-plus-healing results, based on written reports. Of 150 people sampled, 43 percent reported positive results, 7 percent were negative, and half did not reply. The Cayces assume the ratio between positive and negative is likely to be the same in the non-reported instances. They feel that they can project a total negative ratio at 14.4 percent, with 85.5 percent positive.

All I know about such statistics is what they write in the public opinion polls: when people don't report, they don't report; statisticians, a quarrelsome lot, would probably disagree about the way the Cayces make assumptions about those who did not reply to their questions. Their sampling is pretty limited, considering they have 14,246 readings on file. Of course, many of those who had successful readings are now dead. In fact, the Cayce brothers report separately on "Readings for the Dead." In one case, Cayce's long-time secretary, Gladys Davis Turner received an unnerving phone call. She was advised that Edgar Cayce had given a reading on a woman who "was in her grave at the time the reading was given." The brothers wonder, "If the patient had been dead at the time of the reading, why didn't Edgar Cayce say so? Why didn't he know about the woman's death?" They explain that the letter containing a request for Cayce's "reading" and advice had not been given to him until after the death, that in his unconscious state he "was able to view the past, present and probable future of one's life and communicate this information to the one seeking help and understanding through his psychic abilities."

Of course, many, many Cayce readings were strikingly on target. Cases such as this after-death "reading" are cited because they are characteristic of the candor shown by his sons. Edgar Evans Cayce and Hugh Lynn Cayce note that "a significant number of Cayce's psychic readings seem to have been verifiable and helpful," but analyze "the relatively few that seem to have been misleading and downright wrong."

There is good reason to examine shadows, rather than light, now and then. The Cayces are quite right to say that apparently inaccurate "readings" may throw light on the "limitations and validity of psychic data." Every psychic experimenter should keep a record of, and when possible publish, those tests that failed to come off. The Cayce brothers go further. They believe that what was true of their father may also be true of other psychics—mediums, clairvoyants, people practicing telepathy or precognition (prophecy), and all those who, more or less successfully, follow in Cayce's footsteps and offer "life readings" that are supposed to reveal someone's previous incarnations. They state this concept as follows:

"An obvious criterion of the validity of data of any sort is its source. Where do psychics obtain information? Where did Cayce, in particular, get his information? How important are the motives for seeking and giving psychic information in relation to its accuracy? The answers to these questions are, we think, the keys to how accurate psychic information is likely to be. Unfortunately, the answers are not simple. What makes them complex is that there is really no one answer because on different occasions Cayce seemed to obtain data from various sources. To compound the problem, several factors certainly determined not only the source, but also the manner in which Cayce contacted the particular source and relayed the data to be transcribed. What applies to Cayce may undoubtedly apply to some degree to all other psychics and the exercise of their abilities."

Exactly; and very well said, too. The Cayce sons believed that their father's sources of information may have included these categories: Unconscious Memory, things he knew consciously but had forgotten; Clairvoyant Observation of Psychical Data, obtained by traveling out of his own body or similar extrasensory means; Telepathic Communication between Edgar Cayce's subconscious or superconscious mind and that of other individuals, living or dead; Communications, with the minds of dead individuals. With so much possible difference in focus, it is hardly surprising that the "readings" differed in emphasis, viewpoint and even quality. Where a request was motivated by greed, a response might be particularly lacking in quality. When an answer sounds "inane," maybe the questioner got precisely what he deserved. At one period of his life, Cayce gave "readings" to treasure hunters. There is a long-standing occult tradition that psychic powers should not be used for material gain—although some sort of gain is surely involved in even the most detached practice of psychic powers.

Hugh Lynn writes about the "Elusive Treasure of White Hill," which was selected clairvoyantly not only by his father, but also by the famous dowser Henry Gross (who bore a remarkable resemblance to Edgar Cayce). It was a long and frustrating effort, involving voluminous correspondence, travel, assorted hopes and disappointments. It all had started with a reading, on April 9, 1931. Cayce had been pestered by a wheeler-dealer, and the dialogue in this case ran as follows:

"Q: What is the amount of the treasure?

"A: This is sufficient to use the real effort for locating same! For it will be more than a million—see?"

Twenty years later, after much backing and filling, on July 11, 1952, the treasure hunters left on a boat for White Hill. They used pumps, they dug in a bay, but "the results were entirely negative —no gold, no silver, no jewels." There were similar would-be adventures following the Depression, which had wiped out Cayce's own hopes and made him the target of prospectors. The stories of digging at Kelley's Ford and "the lost Dutchman Mine" are tragicomic in all their frustrating detail.

Then, too, oil located clairvoyantly by Cayce was supposed to finance psychic research. Four drillings, in 1952, came to nothing. Similarly, a search for "Indian gold" in Arkansas was a wash-out. Presumably, in such efforts Edgar Cayce was out of his depth. His sons state that his gifts were simply beyond the normal range of knowledge, just as "dogs hear sounds beyond the range of our ears" and "there are insects whose sense of smell makes our nose a very coarse instrument indeed." They ask, speaking of their father's powers, "Is it so strange to find now and then an individual whose perception extends beyond what we consider normal?"

The Cayces do suggest that motivation and other human qualities may affect results. Just as electronic devices may be jammed, so may psychic powers suffer interference: "Selfishness, ego, negative thought patterns, littleness of purpose, wrong suggestions, bad settings, are the static which seem to block and distort psychic perception."

It is astonishing with what Phoenix-like strength the work of the man has survived his person. The Edgar Cayce Foundation was formed early in 1948. The vast number of readings were microfilmed. Hugh Lynn Cayce began to direct the Cayce-oriented Association for Research and Enlightenment. But the effort of guarding Edgar Cayce's work from becoming the center of an uncritical "Cayce Cult" remains an uphill road.

4

The Guru Syndrome

ROBERT H. ASHBY

Mr. Ashby has observed the phenomenon he calls the "guru syndrome" from his position as Director of Research and Education for the Spiritual Frontiers Fellowship. He holds degrees from Kenyon College and Duke University, and has done postgraduate work in history and psychical research at the University of Edinburgh. Mr. Ashby has been a teacher for fifteen years and formerly served as Research Officer of the College of Psychic Studies, London. He is the author of A Guidebook to the Study of Psychical Research.

Following my lecture before a large group in an eastern city, a well-dressed lady approached me. Stylish, attractive, and vibrant, she seemed a typical well-to-do suburbanite. Putting out her hand, she exclaimed, "Oh, Mr. Ashby, I would go anywhere to hear you speak, no matter what you said!"

I smiled and shook my head. "I'm afraid you haven't even listened to what I said tonight, or you wouldn't make such a foolish statement."

Somewhat taken aback by my rather churlish response to her genuine compliment, she looked hurt. But then she too smiled, and laughing with some embarrassment, said, "You mean the 'guru syndrome'? Touché!"

As I do in virtually every engagement, I had included in my address a rather strong warning against the tendency I term the "guru syndrome," and yet, this intelligent lady had unwittingly demonstrated some of the very characteristics I had described: an uncritical acceptance as fact of what is but honest opinion; an unbridled admiration for anyone with apparent credentials, such as Rev., Swami, or Sri before his name or Ph.D. after it; a misplaced faith that being the author of books or articles necessitates Illumination; an erroneous conviction that to be psychic is to be spiritual; an absolute homage to whatever is vaguely paraded as "scientific findings"; a thorough confusion of simplistic for simple; and a thoughtless acceptance that someone has "the Truth" for once and for all and has the singular right to dispense this to his humble followers in return for goodly fees in dollars, time, and/or devotion.

It is hardly surprising that such a state of mind should have become so common among those interested in the paranormal and the occult, because these fields—and it should be noted that the two are not synonymous—are so confusing and confused, the data are so contradictory, so little is firmly known about them, so few scholars have given such faculties and occurrences the time and effort they deserve, and because they are areas that lend themselves with tragic ease to exploitation of the unwary by the unscrupulous. Furthermore, there is such an innate fascination with what is loosely termed "the psychic" that it can, and does, for some become an obsession, a sort of cosmic fanaticism that leads the devotee to spend all too much of his time in the misty realm where careful research and blatant superstition merge in so complex a fashion that it seems impossible at times to disentangle them.

With such a fixation comes the strongly felt need to have or to be a guru, a teacher, a leader. Some are mere followers until their "inner voice," "ascendant master," "Christ consciousness," or "spirit guides" assure them that they are destined to be teachers of truths too long suppressed by a materialistic establishment, and a messianic strain of the flagrant kind emerges. Ego runs rampant in the name of spiritual humility; all vestiges of intellect are shoved scornfully aside for the sake of "enlightenment"; astonishingly extravagant claims for unique insight into the "true" nature of God, man, and the universe are freely made; equally amazing denunciation of all those who either disagree with the revelations or who also claim such revelations lead to bitter inter-sect fighting; incredibly bizarre demands are made upon follow-ers (one group in a major city held a "Psychic Bizarre" with a welter of booths offering occultist titillations of every sort!); and, very often, after a certain period of time, there is a schism and some new guru announces "the true" revelation, gathers a few followers about him, and starts the costly process all over.

So it is that all over the United States there are such one-man or one-woman shows with dutiful adherents convinced that their guru has *the* way to "spiritual unfoldment," "enhanced aware-ness," "psychic development," "tapping the cosmic power," "fulfillment of human potential," etc., *ad nauseam*. If the reader doubts this, merely leaf through occult and spiritualistic periodi-cals and tally up how many such "teachers" advertise their psychic and astral wares to the naïve. Note how many books there are that promise to teach the "secret of the ages," how to "visual-ize whatever you want and it is yours instantly!", and this incredi-ble faculty is available for only $5.95 postpaid, even though the volume is the fruit of the experiences of "many lifetimes," "world-wide travel," and "study with leading Masters." One wonders why the author is trying to sell books if he truly has such a gift at his command: his altruism is quite staggering.

This is not to say that there are no genuinely spiritual leaders in the occult and spiritualistic communities, for I know some per-sonally and have good reason to accept that there are numerous others; but they do not garishly parade their ideas or brashly push their personal organizations. They feel that those who are ready and who need their particular teachings will find a teacher when the time is ripe. Far from being money-conscious, such real guides on the path to wisdom give no more thought to finances than is absolutely necessary in a pragmatic world; and, most im-portant of all, the touchstones of true spirituality are genuine hu-mility together with open-mindedness and generosity toward those who view things differently. If those seeking guidance will apply those standards to prospective gurus, they will be on much

firmer grounds than if they use only the self-proclaimed ascend-
ance of a guru and his devotees.

During the last several years, my heavy correspondence and
my experience in speaking before all sorts of groups across this
country have brought to my attention some very clear and sometimes tragic instances of how dangerous the guru syndrome can
be. In November of 1971, I was telephoned by a friend who was
most disturbed over what had occurred to a young woman of her
acquaintance. This person, we shall call her Nancy, had a history
of recurrent depressions, a persecution complex, and other psychiatric disorders. She had spent several months in a mental sanitarium earlier in 1971 and had been dismissed from resident care
only in October, but was still consulting a psychiatrist weekly. I
had met Nancy at the meeting of a local group and had noticed
her nervousness, compulsive speech, and obvious fascination with
personal experiences of an apparently psychic nature. Among
those present that evening was an ardent graduate of a course of
the mind control type, whom we shall call Mary. Mary spoke at
great length with Nancy about the remarkable ESP abilities developed by this training and, as I later learned, urged her to attend an introductory lecture on it. Nancy subsequently enrolled
in the course. After the second training session, Nancy became
quite upset, claimed to perceive all sorts of fantastic images
"through ESP," gave endless details in a rather boisterous
manner, and ultimately was unmanageable by the teacher of the
course. She was driven home, her mother reached the psychiatrist, and within forty-eight hours, he deemed it necessary to return Nancy to the sanitarium, where she had to remain for several
weeks. There was no refund of her fee. Nor is this the only case
brought to my attention of an obviously unbalanced person being
encouraged into and accepted by such a course.

Here we have the dangerously misplaced enthusiasm for
proselytizing by the follower of a movement without due consideration that such instruction is not necessarily valuable for everyone, and without understanding that, indeed, any increased sensitivity on the part of a person whose personality is not well
integrated may be most deleterious. Also, we find a disturbing
lack of screening of prospective students to determine whether

they are psychologically stable enough for such a course. It is precisely because so many people have been psychologically harmed by this type of instruction that a large number of psychologists, parapsychologists, and psychiatrists are vehemently opposed to them altogether.

If adherents were to examine the cause of which they are so enamored with any degree of detachment, they would be more likely to see its weaknesses as well as its strengths. Please note that I am not arguing that no one has ever benefited from a course of the above nature; but it is most unwarranted for such a person to assume that everyone will obtain similarly beneficial results. This is one of the major errors made when a person is completely imbued with the guru syndrome: his ego, which had at first been submerged in the following of a guru, reaches a point where it is convinced of the "rightness" of its commitment to the teacher, the uniqueness of the specific "truth" given by this guru, and needs to substantiate its commitment by persuading others of the "truth." Beyond this step lie blind, uncritical conviction, evangelism, and ever growing intolerance of the unenlightened who do not recognize the one and only revelation.

An equally distressing case came to my attention in the spring of 1972. Following a television interview in a large Midwestern city, I received a call from a lady in tears. Her story was that she had a friend who had been toying with a Ouija board for some years and had, in her opinion, contacted various deceased relatives, friends, and eventually an "ascendant master" who revealed "higher truths." As a Christmas present, the friend gave this lady's seventeen-year-old daughter, Linda, a Ouija board and urged her to try her luck. Linda and a high school friend, Wendy, began sitting with the board the week after Christmas and within a few days, the pointer began to move and spell out some coherent messages amid the usual gibberish. To their question, "What is the name of the communicating entity?" the board spelled out "Joe." Intrigued by this, the girls began a daily practice of going to Linda's room as soon as they arrived home from school and spending two or three hours "communicating" with "Joe."

As is typical in such instances, Joe proved to know correctly details of a family nature about the two girls, much to their amazement; from this, Joe became witty and the girls thought him really clever; from his innocuous witticisms, Joe moved on to slightly off-color suggestions which tickled Linda and Wendy further. His next stage was frankly sexual propositions that soon had the girls disturbed; but when they asked that he stop this, the messages became threatening, the warnings including something Joe termed "psychic rape" if they did not comply with his wishes. At this point, Wendy was so frightened that she stopped sitting at the board. Linda, however, was so "hooked" that she felt it more dangerous to stop than to continue, for Joe ordered her fiercely to keep on with the ritual. Eventually, the climax arrived when Joe told Linda that she must drop out of school and stay home all day to communicate with him, for they were, he assured her, "soul-mates" from former lives. The punishment if she did not do his bidding was serious physical disfigurement or even death at his hands.

By this time, the mother was aware that Linda was in serious psychological trouble, and tried to persuade her to discuss things with her counselor, but Linda refused. She now threw the Ouija board away, but was afraid to go to school because of Joe's threats. Linda became a recluse, unwilling to seek psychiatric help (Joe had warned her against that), afraid to continue school, and sinking steadily into a desperate mental state.

Her mother asked if I could help. I assured her that I was eager to talk with Linda and explain how the Ouija board works generally, but that psychiatric care was obviously essential and that I was not a psychiatrist. She telephoned later in the afternoon to say that Linda refused to see me because Joe had whispered to her that he would kill her if she did. I do not know what has happened to Linda. I can only hope that her parents succeeded in getting her psychiatric help soon enough to prevent a complete mental breakdown.

The pattern outlined above of "messages" proceeding from evidential to witty to suggestive to obscene to threatening is all too common in Ouija board experiences. Whether the source is really some "entity" or the subconscious of the operators (which is by far the more likely), such material is disturbing, frightening, and often harmful. While living in London, I found that many students of the paranormal, including researchers and ministers concerned with the paranormal and Christianity, were urging the prohibition of the sale of Ouija boards, especially to children and adolescents. Each of those involved in this campaign had his own store of heart-rending accounts to tell, similar to Linda's experience above. The Ouija board is not a toy; it can be a channel for true paranormal information, and there are some data that lend themselves strongly to a discarnate source as the most viable explanation. But set against this very small segment of the total that is worthwhile is the overwhelming majority of cases that consist of gibberish, nonsense, or damaging obsession. Except for trained researchers, the game is not worth the candle, in my opinion.

In such instances, the guru syndrome manifests in the *tool* as an unfailing source of truth beyond itself. A similar state of mind is engendered by another dangerous practice in which the syndrome is attached to a *method:* automatic writing. I have received dozens of letters from automatists, mostly women, who have been instructed by their "teacher" or "master" to write me about arranging for the publication of the automatic writings which contain truths the world has been too long without. The pattern in such cases is also remarkably consistent. After reading about it, the person decides to try automatic writing, and after quite a few abortive attempts, the pen, pencil, or typewriter starts to write "by itself." Like the Ouija board, at first the sentences make no sense, but gradually they take form and coherent passages are written, correct answers are given to questions, the handwriting seems quite different from her normal script, and the automatist is convinced that she could not possibly be the source of the material. It is rare for the communicating "entity" to give a name as yet, but it hints strongly at some famous spiritual, philosophical, or literary figure, or someone from an exotic civilization such as Egyptian, Mayan, Aztec, Persian, or Atlantean. The messages now become increasingly general, with religious and philosophical overtones; but such statements are rarely anything more than glaring platitudes, clichés, and truisms. To the automatist, however, they smack of real revelation, and she is puzzled as to why she has been chosen for such important teachings. The source, who now reveals himself to be Christ, Buddha, a saint, a famous medium like Arthur Ford or Eileen Garrett, one of the Kennedys, Martin Luther King, Jr., or some other martyr, solemnly informs the automatist that she has been chosen because of her unusual psychic gift, her spirituality, her sensitivity, her innate ability at communication, her devotion to disciplined growth; moreover, she is assured that she has been trained for this role over a long period of time, guided into the psychic field, and gradually brought to this form of communication as the chosen vessel for revelation.

Her role, she learns, will be that of a teacher, lecturer, and writer; such work will take her to many places before large audiences; fame and money will come to her as a matter of course if she follows the communicator's instructions. In order to fulfill this vital mission, she must recognize her latent talents, be more self-confident, mingle more socially, express herself more forcefully, become more sensitive to the needs of others, and generally emerge as a charismatic leader, for all these qualities are hers, as witnessed by her having been chosen by the spiritual masters.

Clearly, much of this latter advice is psychologically sound. Many, if not most, of the automatists I have known are women with: too much time on their hands, a feeling of being too little needed by their families, a keen interest in the psychic, a basic sense of personal insecurity, futility, or unfulfilled promise, often an inferiority complex, a tendency to fantasize themselves in prominent positions of leadership and recognition, a frustration toward writing, a talent that they are sure they possess, etc. Whatever the source, if such suggestions lead them toward fuller realization of their true potential, such admonitions can be therapeutic. The problem, however, is that the writing becomes obsessional with many; they are so utterly certain that they are in touch with higher teachers and that what they obtain via automatic writing must be true, that anyone who disagrees with the concepts is completely wrong. They tend to move from a very unsure person to a dogmatic one in a single step. As a surrogate for some great soul, they assume the mantle of a missionary to proclaim the truth to a recalcitrant world and thereby claim for themselves the status of a guru.

Such a transformation can put in jeopardy a marriage, family relationships, social connections, close friendships, and even mental balance itself. If fed by a band of followers, an automatist can develop an egocentrism of the most virulent sort, all in the name of spirituality and humility. It is not unusual for other automatists to develop among the devotees, and if their messages diverge from the orthodoxy of the guru, they either submit to the authority of the leader as the arbiter of truth or leave and found their own splinter group.

Like the Ouija board, automatic writing can be a vital channel and method for veridical paranormal information. Some of the most impressive evidence in psychical research has been produced by famous automatists like Mrs. Piper, the superlative Boston medium discovered by William James; Mrs. Willett, the British sensitive investigated for years by leading experts; Mrs. Verrall, a distinguished Cambridge classicist who was both an excellent psychic in the cross-correspondence material and a thorough student of the paranormal; and Geraldine Cummins, the Irish automatist of undoubted integrity whose works over a forty-year period comprise one of the most important bodies of survival data on record. However, these ladies worked under the supervision of carefully trained and scholarly researchers who knew a good deal about the dissociative states most conducive to quality automatic writing. They did not allow the practice to dominate their lives; they retained balance and a proper priority of values in terms of their family and friends. They did not proclaim themselves as oracles of eternal verities, and they avoided the common pitfalls of egoism. With proper supervision and a sufficiently detached attitude, automatic writing can be a profitable research tool into the nature of the paranormal; without either, it can lead to mental disorder, misplaced values, and obsessional behavior.

It was a sunny, crisp day in June of 1971, shortly before I left London after two years there. I had a sitting appointment with a well-known medium whom I shall call Mrs. Smith. When I entered the library where one waited until the medium was free, the secretary told me that Mrs. Smith was about forty-five minutes late in her schedule, a most unusual situation for this meticulously prompt lady. She apologized and shook her head. "Mrs. Wilfredson simply had to have a sitting this afternoon, and she has disrupted things, I am afraid."

"Why today especially?" I asked.

"Well, she has been sitting weekly with Mrs. Smith for over eight years now, and she won't decide anything of a financial or personal nature without communicating with her discarnate husband, Stephen. Something very important has come up, and she begged Mrs. Smith to fit her in today rather than at her regular time on Friday."

"Weekly for eight years?" I asked in amazement. "But why does Mrs. Smith allow it? She isn't one of those parasite mediums after every pound she can drain."

The secretary, an elderly lady with wispy gray hair, removed her horn-rimmed glasses and smiled wistfully. "I know. She has tried to persuade Mrs. Wilfredson to stop, or at least to reduce her sittings to once a month. For a while, she did come only twice a month, but she was so unhappy and felt at such loose ends that she pleaded most pitifully to be allowed to come back weekly. I'm very much afraid that these communications have become a real psychological crutch for her. Whether we can ever 'wean' her now is doubtful."

Three quarters of an hour later, Mrs. Smith came downstairs with a thin little lady whose red eyes showed that she had been crying. She was holding tightly to the medium's hand, like a small child grasps its mother's for security. Mrs. Smith came over to the secretary's desk and said, "Mrs. Wilfredson won't be needing another sitting for six months. She will write us about the date and time." She patted Mrs. Wilfredson on the shoulder. "You'll be fine now, dear. Remember that Stephen has said so."

Nodding slowly, the lady turned and ambled out, seemingly in a daze. The medium turned to me and waving toward the stairs, said, "I'm so sorry to keep you waiting. Shall we go up?"

When we were comfortable in the small parlor, although somewhat hesitant to ask the question, I decided that I knew Mrs. Smith well enough, and plunged in. "I hope that you won't think this is prying into confidential matters, but as you know, I am very interested in the problem of sitter dependency upon a me-

dium. What about Mrs. Wilfredson? Why has it taken you so long
to break her of this weekly habit?"

She sighed wearily. "I don't mind telling you, because there is
no secret about this particular case. It's a long story, but briefly it
is a rather common situation. Her husband Stephen was a very
successful financier who kept his wife in complete ignorance of
his affairs. He dropped dead of a heart attack in the underground
eight years ago, leaving a considerable estate, rather involved
affairs, and his widow with not the slightest idea about managing
things. Then she came to me through a mutual friend; we contacted Stephen, and during the past eight years he has guided her
in her business dealings. Once she was convinced that Stephen
had survived what we term "death" and that they would meet
again, she seemed unable to let him go on, even when he urged
her to hand over her affairs to a competent trust executive, which
she eventually did. Both my control and Stephen advised her to
come less frequently, and so did I in a waking state, but I found
that she was so lonely—they had no children and she has very few
friends—that for her this weekly hour was the high point of her
life. This has been the most difficult 'weaning' I have ever had.
But today, Stephen apparently really told her off firmly but with
love; and when I awoke, she was in tears, but did say that he had
ordered her not to return for six months. I am really relieved!"

A similar and perhaps even more astonishing pattern was one
of the many fascinating practices I encountered during a three-
day stay at a leading Spiritualist camp, Camp Chesterfield in Indiana, in August of 1973. I found people who had been coming to
Chesterfield for ten, twenty, even thirty years for a large part or
all of their vacation. They had sittings with the same mediums
year after year, received basically the same messages from their
loved ones, and found these steadily comforting. When I pointed
out how easy it would be for mediums to present the evidential
material when they had sat with them dozens of times, they
disagreed that this lessened the validity of their "communications." Of course, for them proof of survival was no longer
in doubt, and such messages were merely confirmation of their
loved ones' continued interest and love. Moreover, I learned that
many of these habitués insisted that any error made by a medium

was due not to a faulty faculty on her part, but to "bad vibrations" brought into the circle by a doubting sitter or by mischievous "earth-bound entities." For them, neither the medium nor the communicating discarnates could make a mistake.

Such dependence upon both a medium and an unseen source of information is a compound of various facets of the guru syndrome. First, there is the assumption that a psychic taps sources of truth unavailable to ordinary people. The more separate from the medium the source seems, the more impressive it is and the more validity it carries for the sitter, possibly because this remoteness seems to lessen the likelihood of contamination by human fallibility. This may be one reason why many find trance mediumship so much more impressive than waking psychic impressions. Second, there is the suspension of critical standards, partly because one feels that to be skeptical is to reduce the odds of obtaining evidential material (and there is both experimental and anecdotal data supportive of the inhibiting nature of disbelief on psi), partly because most sitters have no standards or experience by which to judge ostensibly paranormal information, partly because the confidence of the medium can be intimidating to many, especially when the purported communicators are loved ones or some great historical figure. Third, the mixture of "spiritual" advice and guidance gives an aura of authoritativeness both to the communications and to the medium which impresses the sitter. Consequently, dependence seems both warranted and safe. Once developed, it becomes a psychological "crutch," as my British friend put it, a mental habit which is difficult to break, almost impossible without the cooperation, indeed, the initiative, of the medium. If the medium, for reasons of ego and/or money, is unwilling to aid in such an ending of a relationship, she casts herself in the role of a guru and in that capacity can develop in the sitter a steadily stronger tie. The unhealthiness of this over a prolonged period is too self-evident to warrant belaboring.

There is a particular type of book that can readily engender the guru syndrome and can do so in a fashion that is very insidious, even though doubtless unintentional on the part of the authors. These are, first, the "optimism unlimited" works that preach not only positive thinking, but the certainty of success if the formulae to be revealed are followed as per instructions. A large number of these volumes argue that there is a "cosmic reservoir" of power to be tapped merely by learning how to image one's desires. The fact that success is generally less than spectacular by the purchaser makes these works less effective in establishing the author as having a direct pipeline to the supposed source of all that makes the good life. Still, I have heard adherents of such systems argue that any failure lies in application of the principle, not in the principle itself, a circuitous reasoning which is strangely comforting to such individuals.

Second, there are those books that deal with prayer and how it can bring whatever one wants if utilized properly. The problems with such easy statements are first, that the naïve reader assumes that God's role is that of some limitless giver and that there is little if any obligation on the part of the pray-er; and second, that the implication that no prayer ever goes unanswered is all too rarely coupled with the suggestion that the answer may well be in a form different from that imagined or desired; thus the answer may not even be recognized as such. (I leave aside the even more important question of considering prayer as basically a petition for something rather than a communion with God, which makes the very premise of these works highly dubious in my view.)

In the late 1950s, when these sorts of books were very popular, a close relative of mine, Alice, became convinced that the promise of prayer always being answered as she understood it from authors like Collyer and Clark meant that sincere prayer would inevitably result in that prayed for. Her beloved sister-in-law, Doris, was ill with terminal cancer, and Alice began a regular prayer schedule for Doris's recovery. She asked friends and clergy to join in prayers for distant healing, contacted prayer groups around the country, and bent every effort at directing prayer power toward Doris's cure. When despite all of this, Doris died, Alice was stunned. Her faith was shattered when she realized that what she had prayed for so long and so sincerely had not occurred, that her prayers apparently had been ignored by God, and she was completely disenchanted with all religious groups, all organized churches, even Christianity itself. They all seemed a sham. For a decade, Alice went through the "dark night of the soul" totally without spiritual moorings, and only after much meditation and counseling could she come to a deeper and more valid understanding of a true prayer life.

I am not suggesting either that Alice's interpretation of these books was correct or that the authors intended to suggest that whatever one prays for will materialize exactly as one has visualized and prayed for. But such reservations were not so clear or so convincing as they needed to be for a layman; and thus was activated the guru syndrome of accepting as valid what was written in such an authoritative fashion by writers with impressive credentials, and this led to the suspension of critical acumen and the failure to weigh carefully such assertions. Writers, like lecturers, need to be most mindful of the impact of their ideas as expressed in such a scholarly format that they carry conviction to the non-specialist, and to be certain that the reservations which they, as specialists, recognize as inherent in every generalization are also manifest in their exposition for the reader and listener.

There are other sources of the guru syndrome, such as astrology, upon which millions depend to some degree. My personal experience with the various horoscopes which have been cast for me without cost by astrologers seeking to convince me of the validity of what they consider a science has been quite unimpressive. But I am the first to admit that some very intelligent people I know are quite certain, after much study, of the importance of astrological signs in establishing life's potential patterns, and also that one must not, in all fairness, characterize all astrological experts by the grossly absurd drivel of two-line newspaper daily horoscopes. Further, I realize that really competent astrologers of integrity urge their clients to realize that careful consideration and free will are essential ingredients of a fruitful life and utter dependence upon astrology is foolish. The fact remains, however, that untold numbers of the credulous do so depend, blindly and regularly.

It is obvious that practitioners of various divining processes such as palmistry, numerology, Tarot cards, tea leaves, scrying, or phrenology all have the essential ingredients for triggering the guru syndrome, depending upon how persuasive they are as psychics and dynamic as leaders. Satanism and witchcraft—black far more than white—are particularly dangerous routes to such a situation.

What of the various Eastern gurus who now abound in the United States? Some of those whom I have met and heard are truly remarkable men with indubitable psychic gifts, charisma, and real spiritual messages; and as noted above, gurus of this stamp are genuinely humble pilgrims on the spiritual way whose counsel and teaching can be of very great benefit to others. I have already mentioned the touchstones of humility, open-mindedness, and ready tolerance of opposing beliefs as sound criteria by which to judge the quality of such a leader. With the best of these, however, the guru syndrome is often rampant among their followers, despite the advice to the contrary by the guru himself; indeed, such sincere humility may merely compound the disciples' conviction that this holy man is worthy of reverence and complete acceptance of his views.

As an example of this, in a Midwestern city in 1973, a chapter of a national organization was split and virtually destroyed by the insistence of a local member who heard a visiting guru lecture that an ashram to follow his teachings must be established. Even though the Indian teacher told her that she could just as readily pursue her studies of his yogic discipline within the existing organization, she was determined to prove her devotion by leaving that group and starting one committed solely to his teachings. It is remarkable that here the syndrome was so strong that the devotee actually contravened the revered teacher's advice in order to demonstrate her total devotion. Such is the strength of this tendency.

Perhaps the most distressing instance of such unthinking acceptance I have yet encountered took place at the Boston airport in July of 1973 while awaiting a plane. A handsome young man, dressed in faded but clean dungarees, with a gray canvas bag over his shoulder, approached and sat down beside me. He smiled, handed me a magazine from the bag, and asked, "May I talk with you about . . ."

I recognized the name as that of the adolescent guru whose following had mushroomed fantastically into a large movement. I nodded, "Certainly."

He then began a presentation of the guru's views in a manner
so rote that it was clear that he had delivered it dozens, even
hundreds, of times. The most striking claim made for the guru
was that while Krishna had incarnated before in great religious
leaders like the Buddha, Moses, Lao-tse, Jesus Christ, and
Mohammed, this young man is the greatest of all such incarnations; he is sent as the savior of the world if people will but recognize him as such. I discussed this with the young man at some
length, pointing out how such a stance was flatly contrary to the
most basic beliefs of the major religions and how frequently similar claims had been made for lesser-known leaders. I asked
whether it was not more reasonable to assume that his guru was
but one of many good spiritual leaders rather than claiming such
a unique status for him.

"No. He is the greatest and the only present incarnation of
Krishna, sent to save the world from destruction. You have no
right not to accept this until you hear *sansi* from the beloved
guru."

My interest more aroused, I noticed how vacant and even
glazed his blue eyes were. My arguments, while apparently listened to politely, had not reached him at all. He was surrounded
by an impenetrable shell of belief. Concerned over this in such a
bright young man, I urged him to study the writings and
teachings of other spiritual leaders and compare them. He shook
his head vigorously. "There is no need to study what anyone else
says. Guru says all that is true; what others say is of no importance to me. I know that he is the savior of the world. Come, hear
sansi and you, too, will know."

"There really would be no point," I replied, "since I cannot accept at all his belief and yours that he is the greatest religious
figure of all time. No doubt I would agree with many of his
ethical principles and practices, but I cannot possibly adopt that
extravagant claim."

He smiled wistfully and without a word moved on to someone
else in the airport lobby.

Here was the guru syndrome in its fullest and saddest flowering. What a damning comment upon our intellectual and spiritual
establishments that such a gifted and questing young man should

have to turn to this sort of movement to find moorings for his life!
If he is to blame for abdicating his God-given common sense and
judgment, how much more are those in positions of leadership
who have refused to recognize the real needs of millions of young
people like him and have provided, in the name of "truth" (for
which read "orthodoxy"), nothing but a vacuum when they have
desperately sought anchorage, nothing but a deaf ear when they
have pleaded for a hearing, nothing but indifference when they
have asked for love. Possibly more than any other single facet of
the so-called occult revolution, the guru syndrome carries with it
the most stinging denunciation of the sterility of our contemporary religious institutions.

The final example of the stunting stance inherent in the guru
syndrome lies far outside the psychic community. It resides in the
very citadel of the establishment, science itself. Here it takes the
form or a worship of methodology, an assumption of impossibility
without any examination of the data, a philosophical commitment
to materialism, and an unequivocal denial that anything can be
established as factually true except by those methods of experimental physical science. Quantification is the supreme arbiter of
truth, controlled experimentation the only path, and replication of
experimental measurements the essential criterion. This syndrome
is the most bitter foe of psychical research, for it sees in the poten-
tialities of psi a factor that seems diametrically opposed to the
entire structure of reality which the physical sciences have so
carefully and impressively constructed over the last century and a
half.

When psychical research commenced as a disciplined examination into the paranormal in the 1880s, it was undertaken precisely
because, on the one hand, spiritualists were claiming that man
possesses a non-physical facet that could telepathize, clairvoyantly perceive, foresee future events, move physical objects in
a non-physical way, and demonstrate conclusively the survival of
death by the individual personality, while on the other, scientists
were arguing that man is solely a biological organism, that consciousness, memory, idiosyncrasy, all that we mean by thought
and personality are utterly dependent upon the brain and that
with death the brain disintegrates; thus survival is naught but

desperate wish fulfillment. Telepathy and types of psi were labeled fraudulent, coincidental, or delusory. The great scientist Helmholtz categorically said that he would not be convinced of the reality of telepathy if all the Fellows of the Royal Society testified to it, for it was clearly impossible.

The early leaders of the discipline insisted then, and competent researchers insist now, upon investigation of as impartial and objective a nature as is possible. But despite the fact that today, almost a century later, the data are monumental, running into thousands of pages in learned journals in several languages, and into thousands of books, many by some of the greatest scholars of our era, most scientists dismiss the entire case as "unsubstantiated," by which they mean that they will not waste their time examining the evidence since what the evidence purports to support is untenable at worst and so unlikely at best that it warrants no such effort.

Can one honestly say that such a position is truly scientific, that it is any more critical or objective in its argument than the most credulous Spiritualist or the most avid occultist? Indeed, if one considers carefully the insistence upon repeatability of experimental results, one finds that the underlying reason is basically that the scientist must see for himself what another scientist claims to have established factually before he is willing to plump for its factuality. Is not this ultimate subjectivity rather than objectivity, as they believe? I am not suggesting that such procedures are pointless or worthless, for they are clearly most valid within certain disciplines; but to assume that *all* facets of reality must conform to such methodologies or forever be relegated to a limbo labeled "unproven" is a belief assumption of a most glaring sort.

During my twelve years of involvement in the field of psychical research, I have never met anyone who doubted the reality of ESP who had studied the data thoroughly. Nor do I exempt from that statement people like Hansel, Rinn, Scott, Christopher, or Rawcliffe, who have written debunking works about psychical research, for anyone who reads their books critically will find that they have not studied the evidence carefully, but from a standpoint of selectivity in order to substantiate their negative hypothesis. (I am not arguing that some of their criticisms are not valid, but that their general conclusion about the reality of psi is unfounded and biased.)

It is encouraging to note a changing climate in academe with reference to the pervasiveness of this syndrome. A growing cadre of physical, behavioral, and social scientists plus members of other disciplines are expressing belief that psi is worthy of careful, objective scrutiny. One cannot ask any more than that, but one should not expect any less from science if it be true to its goals.

While there are various other routes to the guru syndrome, enough has been shown to warrant the reader's coming to some conclusion, however tentative, as to the validity of my argument. On a personal note, I find that, like any lecturer, researcher, or writer in the field, I too will be cast in the role of guru if I am not constantly on guard to prevent it. The flattery, the boost to the ego, the encouragement in one's chosen profession that such unbridled admiration evokes are heady and difficult foes to keep in check. Yet, for the sake of the student and for my own mental and spiritual well-being, such vigilance is, I submit, essential.

How does one avoid the glamour of this syndrome? I suggest that one does so by steadily using one's critical acumen, by maintaining a balance in the role the psychic plays in one's life-style, by recognizing that no one knows the definitive answers in this area of inquiry. All are on the path, and if someone seems a bit ahead in one aspect of study and wishes to share the insights he has gained, such should be considered for precisely what they are: honest opinions, not revelations from on high. That great pioneer of psychical research, F. W. H. Myers, once termed the psychic dimension "the labyrinth of the unknown," and that it surely is. If, in one's personal exploration of that labyrinth, one decides to sit at the feet of a guru, I urge that, both literally and figuratively, each one remember how to get up and walk away.

5

Teachers of Delusion

MARGARET GADDIS

Biofeedback, mind control, mediumistic development, sensitivity training, advanced witchcraft—these are among the subjects being advertised and taught throughout the United States. But how qualified are the sometimes self-styled experts who introduce a fascinated but at times emotionally ill-prepared audience to the world's psychic phenomena and pseudo-phenomena? Mrs. Gaddis, whose knowledge of the subject matter is matched only by her common sense, examines this question with candor. She has been a professional writer since the 1940s, and her interest in psychical research dates back to that period. Margaret Gaddis is the author of five mystery novels and of numerous short stories and articles.

"Truth is heavy, therefore few wish to carry it," says the Talmud, the Hebrew book of ethics. And when, as in the contradictory realms of parapsychology, the "heavy" is also nebulous, in what butterfly net can it be captured? Yet, interest in all its myths and marvels is growing so fast that classes are starting in public schools all over the country, both in adult education and at high school levels. Just what is being taught, and who are the teachers?

They range from the informed and dedicated whom we ourselves encountered, to those who are secretly recruiting for dubious gurus or bringing witches and Ouija boards to class for group journeys into the dark. We have been spared the latter type of instruction and usually enjoyed good speakers and fine films. However, my personal feeling is that sweetness and light are overstressed and too little emphasis is given to the dangers.

Those who wish to sensitize themselves should be informed that they are thereby opening themselves to *both* good and evil potentials. If they are neurotic and unbalanced, a gentle meditation on an opening flower is not going to prevent the emergence of a worm. They should hear also of the sometimes horrifying cases of poltergeists and hauntings, and of the disasters that have followed dabbling in black magic, hypnotism and "mind control" classes. In criticizing the latter we are treading on the toes of Big Business, for some of these courses are very costly indeed. Yet two scientific studies of their graduates gave negative results, and in another, a psychiatrist taking the course reported to the Menninger Clinic that four students out of thirty became psychotic, two being hospitalized.

A medical student, learning how food is converted through anabolism into living tissue, is not kept ignorant of the opposite process of catabolism and excretion.

Here are just a few of the many courses offered recently.

The Denver Free University required a $10.90 surcharge for its course on the theory and practice of witchcraft "to cover the costs of candles, bats, blood and other items needed for the practice part of the class."

Elsewhere a class was taught by a disciple (Grade OT7) of the founder of dianetics and scientology, L. Ron Hubbard. One of this cult's ministers, addressing the class, tried to pulverize orthodox psychologists, and was told by the students to "put up or shut up!" They could become "clears"—freed of conscious and unconscious complexes—by an expenditure of over $1,000, yet Hubbard himself is so far from "clear" that the British deported him. At another meeting of this class, a male witch of a nude Temple of Isis spoke on the grave dangers of Ouija boards. Yet, the next week class members were to bring their own Ouija boards for a group journey into the beyond. All these students have received promotion material by mail.

Another class, on UFOs, is quite obviously an attempt to form a cult revering a man who was exposed, long before his death, as a charismatic phony. When this teacher was shown books by levelheaded investigators of the field, his scathing put-down was: "Of course *these* writers have never ridden on a saucer!"

However, there is hope. At the University of Wisconsin, Professors David C. Lindberg and Robert Siegfried taught a course on the occult and pseudo-sciences whose objective was to develop informed skepticism.

"What we do," says Lindberg, "is to raise a different kind of question than the popular press and TV . . . We hope to show students that the senses cannot be trusted—that the capacity for self-deception is nearly infinite."

In the San Francisco area, author Gina Cerminara, Ph.D., who lectures on parapsychology and semantics, mentions that some courses rather naïvely require pledges to be signed, promising that the powers conferred will be used only for good. Is it likely, she asks, that such promises confer instant integrity, or that those who are unstable, immature or malevolent will be any less so than before?

"I have known a goodly number of psychically talented people," she says, "who patently were using their gift for self-inflation (hardly anything can match the heady feeling of being regarded as omniscient!) . . . to enrich their bank balances, or to meddle, on occasion, in the lives of others . . . *Every new power of the mind must be accompanied by a new power of the heart*: by compassion and concern for all forms of life. Otherwise the psychic revolution could well become a disastrous component of a debacle of our civilization."

Newcomers to this study should at least be informed that dangers do exist. Meditation exercises, aura readings and visits from mediums should be balanced by surveys of case studies that deal with the darker side of psychic phenomena and the danger of accidental contact with dangerous, evil forces. Even objects may become malevolent. No one knows why, but the "magnetic fields" of objects may explain haunted houses. And, indeed, if rocks and crystals are "alive," why shouldn't personal belongings retain intangible powers from past owners?

The story of a haunted voodoo stick owned by Wilhelmina Pickering Stirling is such a case. Mrs. Stirling, an English aristocrat of the last century, wrote several books on the psychic experiences of the titled and wealthy in British society.

The stick had been sent to her mother from Jamaica, where it had belonged to a witch doctor. Made of polished red wood, it had at the top a hand with long, tapering fingers, the outside of it black, while inside carefully formed nails were red.

"Only the thumb (will power) is absent," she wrote, "indicating this is a magic stick which the right person can rule. Along the stem are two snakes, one in red wood with scales, the other black and shiny. At the base kneels a grotesque little figure with upraised arms."

One day she met a celebrated palmist who asked if she might see the stick. They held a séance and the stick announced that it disliked Mrs. Stirling because she was not powerful enough to rule it. If only it could return to its original home, ancient Egypt, where it had been used for "raising the devil"!

After the séance she left the stick out on a tapestry chair which had a narrow wooden rim curving around the top. That evening her husband remarked that he wanted a book he had left up in her sitting room.

"Take a candle," she suggested, but he said the moonlight was so bright and he knew just where he had left the book.

Within moments he came racing down the stairs, very white. He had gone straight to the book, clearly revealed by moonlight streaming into the room, but turned around on hearing strange knocks.

"There in the moonlight I saw distinctly a stick resting on the seat of your tapestry chair, waving backward and forward, and hitting the wooden back of the chair as it swung to and fro!"

"He knew nothing about the séance," Mrs. Stirling wrote, "and didn't even know that I possessed a witch's stick, so what produced in his brain an impression of the stick waving and hitting the chair?"

A story difficult to believe, yet any reader who had earlier encountered a description of Mrs. Stirling's ancient lineage in Burke's Peerage would be unlikely to call the lady a liar.

There are many instances of inanimate objects being invested with strange powers. It makes one wonder if having witches, Satanists and "clears" addressing school-sponsored groups is really harmless entertainment.

In Norwalk, California, psychologist Dr. James D. Lisle, director of the Helpline Youth Counseling Center, says he has come in contact recently with several young persons involved in witchcraft and Satan worship.

"You can never be sure a person involved in this won't step over the line into infant sacrifice or cannibalism," he says. "We have evidence that it happens. The people who get involved in a thing like witchcraft have a developing tunnel vision about the world and life. It is a continually narrowing thing that cuts them off from what is going on around them."

He has found people who substitute the occult scene for the drug scene, or combine them, and says there are strong parallels in the psychological factors drawing these people to witchcraft and Satan worship, and those that move them from occasional marijuana usage to heroin addiction.

"In both instances," he says, "the person is likely to be suffering from powerlessness and seeking power; seeking to gain control over his own life and sometimes the lives of others; engaged in primitive, magical, childish thinking; or seeking to escape some reality problems in life."

Kenneth Grant, an authority on ritual magic, tells in the encyclopedic *Man, Myth and Magic* (Issue 74) that the late actress Jayne Mansfield was a practicing Satanist. In 1965 she began to attend Anton La Vey's Church of Satan in San Francisco. "La Vey became very friendly with Jayne," Grant writes, "and she began to accompany him on his trips to investigate haunted houses and other allegedly paranormal phenomena."

This friendship angered Sam Brody, Jayne's attorney and lover, who feared that it might become known and harm her public image. Brody then threatened La Vey with damaging publicity. The Satanist told Brody to "publish and be damned" and ritually cursed the attorney. A few days later Brody was injured in an auto accident. Later, in June 1967, La Vey telephoned Jayne and said he had received an "occult message" that Brody and possibly

Jayne might be injured in a second accident. She ignored the warning. On June 29, two weeks later, near Biloxi, Mississippi, Miss Mansfield's car collided with a truck in a heavy fog. Jayne was decapitated. Sam Brody and a chauffeur were also killed.

The investigation of haunted houses has great fascination and certainly need not lead to psychic disaster. But students should be aware that it, too, has sometimes been dangerous. One such experience happened to the family of a chaplain in the Marines who later served in Korea. He confirmed the facts in writing, as given in the *Journal of the American Society for Psychical Research* (October 1951) under the assumed name of De Leau. In 1930 the family had moved into what seemed a pleasant house until "something" began to share it with them. Even their little boy felt it.

"It grew in intensity and awfulness," Mrs. De Leau wrote, ". . . until finally . . . at 10 P.M. exactly it would be in the hall waiting. As the intensity of its animosity grew, the more clearly could I 'see' it without seeing it—a tall, dark, faceless, shrouded presence, utterly evil, utterly vile. Just waiting and waiting and hating there in the hall."

The presence came earlier on the night her husband had to leave for a three-day convention. In terror she began calling out mentally to him for help. He got the message and arrived before dawn. When they compared notes they found that both of them had grown conscious of "a presence . . . evil, vile, and increasingly threatening and dangerous." The minister had not wanted to confess such superstition to his wife, but now they began packing hurriedly.

Boxing books that day, he suddenly stopped and rushed downstairs. "My God!" he gasped, "that damned thing came into the study just now!"

Mrs. De Leau ended her report: "If I tried to convey the ghastly loathsomeness of the terror, I couldn't. But this is the way it was."

Not all apparitions take human form. Among the many ghosts in the Tower of London, a weird transparent cylinder appeared to the keeper of the crown jewels one October night in 1817. "Like a glass tube . . . its contents appeared to be a dense fluid, white and pale azure." It moved around the table while the family sat at dinner, terrorizing them before it disappeared into a recess.

This story is peculiar but other non-human shapes have been seen. They take their place among the many queer things which tantalize the puny minds of men and explain our fascination with the supernormal.

Dr. Shafica Karagulla, a neuropsychiatrist with an outstanding background, is a member of the Royal College of Physicians in Edinburgh, the highest medical qualification in England. Later she worked in Toronto with Dr. Wilder Penfield, one of the world's top neurosurgeons.

About a dozen years ago she became interested in man's supersenses, and is now Director of the Higher Sense Perception Research Foundation in Beverly Hills, California. Her first book, *Breakthrough to Creativity*, is required reading in several colleges and universities. Her wide knowledge of the physical body as well as its higher octaves of perception make her warnings authoritative. These studies have convinced her that man survives death, and that unwise tampering with hidden forces has at times led to possession by other entities.

ESP can certainly be developed, she says, but "if you try to force it, you disturb one aspect of the body which results in an unbalanced energy system and the problems which accompany this . . . People should realize that it's not important to have these abilities. It's what we are that's important. Once we realize this, we go ahead—where we want to be and what we want to become. Then these things automatically become part of our experience."

The educational system will be completely changed, she thinks. Now the emphasis is on competition. It should be on cooperation. "Life doesn't compete with itself, it cooperates. And so must we."

Even psychic healing has dangers, she says; " . . . most people don't know that a healer can overcharge a person with energy . . . We sorely need research centers to . . . [observe] how different healers work and their effect on patients. We could also tell them at what point to stop."

Dr. Karagulla is adamantly opposed to hypnosis and states that it is extremely dangerous both to the one who's being hypnotized and to the one hypnotizing, for two reasons. "In hypnosis if you remove symptoms, you haven't restored the area to health, you have blocked it by inhibiting its experience by the patient . . . the hypnotist is depriving the person he's trying to help of his free will. I believe that whenever the free will of a human being is blocked when he is in an unconscious state there is a basic disturbance to his total integration as a human being. Also, both of these people, by linking their fields, may pick up each other's illnesses.

"If a man is to grow and become a creative individual, he must retain his integrity and separate individuality from all other human beings—whether from an entity on this side or the other. He must grow on his own."

Certain people are energy sappers "pulling from you through the solar plexus, the eyes, and the voice. Distance doesn't matter . . . most of these people are self-centered . . . they want to take pre-digested energy from someone else for their own use."

Today's systems of mind control and mind dynamics appeal popularly as supposed short cuts to genuine growth. Dr. Karagulla thinks that they are really using mass hypnosis. "People have to be awakened to the fact that there are dangers in these things because they disorganize the fields of energy. This is like opening the door to your mind which can be influenced by other intelligences, some greater than your own. In such a passive state, an entity can get in and obtain control of you."

Such disturbances are not always from the other side; at times they are purely physiological. "However, if you disturb the three fields I've discussed [energy, emotional and mental vortices which act like transformers] . . . and tear them apart by doing abnormal things to yourself [before you are spiritually ready] then their integration is not complete and another entity can squeeze in and take over your physical body. That's how possession occurs."

Or there may be instead the lesser problem of obsession, where an entity is within your field but cannot take complete control. Naturally both states are highly undesirable possibilities when tampering with "powers."

Back in 1850 it was discovered that hypnotized persons could be made to experience "community of thought"—that is, if mustard, pepper, sugar, etc. were put into the hypnotizer's mouth, they sensed it, or knew if the hypnotist pricked himself with a needle. Some subjects have done "astral traveling"—gone out of the body to report back, accurately, what was happening at that moment at a distance.

It is not true that people cannot be hypnotized against their will or influenced to commit crimes. If the subject is convinced first that the gun is not loaded, or that dangerous substances are harmless, they will be used to injure. On the good side, these powers have been of use to the police in solving crimes.

Considering these facts, does it seem advisable to bring hypnotists into classrooms or put on stage performances?

Also considering these facts, as disclosed by Dr. Karagulla and others, does "sitting for development" of mediumship seem a desirable pastime? At best, mediumship is a dubious blessing, usually deteriorating the health, and severely straining integrity when powers fluctuate in financial crises. The finest mediums are born, not made.

This immensely complicated subject is soundly presented in the books of Phoebe Payne, an incorruptible English medium, and her husband, Dr. Laurence Bendit: it is not possible to acquire *positive* psychism without first training the self to live in an all-round way through austerity of character and discipline.

Negative psychism is confused and erratic. Sitting for development and hatha-yoga carry man back along the evolutionary path; the ego is surrendered and the confusions of the sitters are picked up and "replayed."

Today everyone talks only about the good effects of psychism, but there is now so much money, ego-tripping and prestige involved that the negative potentials are suppressed.

Training in control of "alpha" has been greatly oversold and probably does little more than create pleasant feelings and relaxation, though self-suggestion can be planted in that state.

Unfortunately just as hysteria following sloppy and wrong use of the hallucinogens brought rigid government controls to end genuine research there, so the current hysteria of irrational belief in anything far out is hampering research by antagonizing hard-nosed seekers.

Some experiments in voluntary sense deprivation have led to remarkable, though subjective, results. A device known as the witch's cradle, long used by jungle priests to get themselves into trance states, has been refined into an "altered state of consciousness device." Hanging in a swinging cage in a soundproof room, the subject wavers and sags. Robert Masters and Jean Houston, at the Foundation for Mind Research in Pomona, New York, reported one reaction:

"I am expanding, expanding. I can see images, beautiful images, mathematical images. This is the source of life. It is as if my mind merged with the mind of God. I am one with Him and with His understanding." The man reaching this transcendental experience is a professor of theology, and during it, to the observer, his face convulsed as if in pain, his eyes rolled up and his breath whistled. But he left the cage unharmed, with an altered view of reality. Not all results from various devices are so happy.

But as Professor Charles Tart at the University of California, Davis campus, says, we make lousy use of our five marvelous senses, and developing a sixth gives just one more source of information to add distortions to! Work first at eliminating the distortions!

Apparently it is even possible to create ghosts to order:

In *Psychic* magazine (October 1974) Allen Spraggett, who reports on such matters for the Toronto, Canada, Society for Psychical Research, says that their group did just that.

The experiment was monitored by Dr. A. R. G. Owen, former professor of genetics at Cambridge University, and now director of a Toronto foundation. Dr. Owen is the author of *Can We Explain the Poltergeist?* and co-author of *Science and the Spook*.

Spraggett said: "Eight persons agreed to meet once a week for an hour or more conjuring a wholly imaginary ghost they named Phillip. Before they were through the mythical phantom was communicating with them in a variety of eerie ways. Dr. Owen said that the experiment had remarkable implications. The ghost apparently exhibited the qualities his creators gave him. We have shown that in some manner we don't understand, a group of people can create a thought-directed force which can be expressed in a physical way."

Rosalind Heywood, one of England's most distinguished investigators, has had many psychic experiences. She says, "I think if parapsychology can establish the fact of subconscious interaction between all men, perhaps we could understand that the biblical statement, 'We are all members, one of another,' is a statement of scientific fact."

It is just because we do "pick up" intangibles from one another that it is of utmost importance not to rush enthusiastically where angels fear to tread.

Instead, approach psychics, healers and gurus with caution. A small gift of mind reading, such as knowing what we were doing recently, does not qualify anyone to advise us in the most crucial areas of our being. If we could really "look beneath the covering" as the ancient mystery schools advised, we might see vanity and desire for power looming far larger than sanctity and smiling charm.

This is especially true of the healers, where misplaced trust can lead to devastating grief. A case in point is taken from a letter signed by Ms. Dagne Crane of Danbury, Connecticut, which appeared in *Psychic* following an article on miracle gurus.

Ms. Crane, grieving for a godson paralyzed after an accident, went to India in desperate hope to the noted healer Sai Baba. She had to wait almost three weeks to see him, meanwhile watching a stream of the blind and crippled, none of whom seemed to be helped.

When she finally got an audience with the master, "he promised unequivocally that the boy would be *totally cured and walking in fifteen days*. [All present] cried and kissed his feet, as I did."

She returned home eagerly, carrying an amethyst ring the master had "materialized" with instructions to hold it against the boy's severed spine. Uncertain if he should know of the master's promise that he would be cured by God within fifteen days, to her everlasting regret she told him. His agony on finding that promise false was just one more hideous crisis. He took the failure as rejection by God. But halfway around the world it was business as usual for Sai Baba—and news of this "marvelous cure" was widely spread!

"Sathya Baba did inadvertently teach me a great spiritual lesson, which I wish I had known before I bought all my expensive travel arrangements and unleashed all that misery for my godson. I should have stayed at home, the better to understand those simple words from the Bible, 'The Kingdom of God is within.'"

After sharing over thirty-five years of personal study, my husband and I are enjoying our second year in adult education classes. We have been uncommonly fortunate in our instructors, but as we checked on other schools, we conclude the employment of teachers is hit or miss.

Also results depend on the character of the seekers. As Carlyle remarked a century ago, there is always an overplus of those who hunger and thirst to be bamboozled. Some are filled with vanity, lust for the limelight; or hostility, greed and self-pity, and these tempestuous imbalances will corrupt any psychic channel on this two-way street.

Only the crippled soul hungers for power. You have no right to control over any sane adult—except yourself. Meditation, group or private, can help one survive turmoil, and an exploration of the powers of the unconscious can be a humbling and illuminating experience. It is the flaws within us that suck in the dangers. And there are far more stories than space permits to prove these dangers real.

An English photojournalist, Serge Kordiev, found out the tough way. Like Jayne Mansfield, he and his wife joined a secret cult at a Black Mass with robed and cowled figures, then signed allegiance in their own blood.

The fee had been high, but immediately checks and assignments from magazines poured in. But they became uneasy and before the final ceremony they broke away and left London. Their recantation ended their run of luck abruptly. Kordiev was nearly bankrupted by a lawsuit and his wife had a breakdown.

One night they returned to their country place in Kent to find an enormous toad waiting on the doorstep, which shattered Mrs. Kordiev's poise completely. The studio was separate from the house and securely locked with barred windows bolted inside.

As they went to bed the wind howled off the sea as in a horror film. "We seemed to be asleep only minutes when we both sat upright . . . Outside came the sound of maniacal laughter—absolutely terrible!— . . . then the sound of glass smashing." Kordiev was worried about his expensive photographic equipment but his wife did not want him to go out in the dark.

Next morning he found their dog cowering in the kitchen and the studio almost demolished. "Drapes and furniture had been torn down and strewn everywhere . . ." The window was shattered and "the glazing bars had broken under the weight of someone or something bursting out [not in], for the lawn and path were littered with broken glass."

Ten years later the Kordievs still have no explanation and it took them a long time to feel free of sinister influences. The studio had been empty when he locked it, and there were no signs of how anyone got in. "I still think that somehow the incident was caused by an evil power in revenge for our breaking away from the Satanist group."

He says that he agrees completely with the English writer of thrillers on black magic, Dennis Wheatley. Wheatley, who has studied witchcraft for over fifty years, is thoroughly afraid of it. Some of these people can take your money, your wife, your mind, he says. There are only a few, but these are enough!

Wheatley knew ritual magician Aleister Crowley; Montague Summers, a famous authority on witchcraft; and the investigator of the poltergeists at Borley Rectory, Harry Price. These people were experts, Wheatley warns, yet Crowley landed in an asylum for six months after trying to call up the devil, and the other two men faded into eccentric old age. Wheatley concludes: "Even with their great knowledge, they weren't safe. So how can anyone else be?"

Stewart Edward White, who received books through the mediumship of his wife Betty, about forty years ago, was one of the first to popularize the study of the unknown. In *The Job of Living* he, too, has something vital to say about forcing growth.

Can we force progress, or gain wealth through ritual, he asks. Yes. But will the results be the right kind, suiting our current development? *Nothing is free.* Here we will have bought a pig in a poke. In a store we compare merchandise and prices. "With occult practices, we do not see. But, someday, we pay. Powers are by-products. Do not strive for them. Let . . . the ability to make rabbits come out of hats take care of itself." You build your rabbit machine, he concludes, by building yourself—by the exercise of decision, moment to moment—not by ventures into instant bliss.

Another scholar has come to a different and sadder conclusion. Eric J. Dingwall, the distinguished British investigator, has abandoned the study of parapsychology after sixty-five years' acquaintance with most of the great researchers.

He says that he cannot name half a dozen who are objective and honestly wish to discover truth. Instead they wish to prove personal opinions.

"We are drifting back into the Dark Ages," he states, and tells how often priceless papers have mysteriously disappeared from society offices, apparently because they disproved someone's pet theory.

"The general public is led to believe that the paranormal can be observed almost anywhere at any time . . . skepticism is deplored and . . . anybody who throws doubts . . . is [supposedly] sunk in a morass of outdated materialism. Little do they know what lies beneath the surface of the new occultism and the new witchcraft. Anyway, I have finished with it." A sad closing of a dedicated career.

But perhaps we can avoid such tragic disillusionment if we study the bad with the good without fear, without involvement with gurus.

6

Inside the Psychic Jungle

Wanda Sue Parrott

Like Alan Vaughan, Susy Smith and other contributors to this volume, Wanda Sue Parrott speaks of the dangers of overinvolvements in the psychic and occult from direct personal experience. She brings to her presentation of facts and ideas the skills of several years as a reporter and columnist on the Los Angeles Herald-Examiner (*1968–73*), *where, as she says, she "refused assignments that would not give the readers information or methods to lead fuller, happier lives." Ms. Parrott now lives in Tempe, Arizona, and is writing books and participates in the production of motion pictures. Her book* Understanding Automatic Writing (*1974*) *will soon be followed by* Auras; *she is now completing self-help instructions on* Mental Magnetism. *Wanda Sue Parrott has contributed widely to magazines, including* Fate.

What is the greatest threat to human well-being in the world of psychic phenomena? I would say, from experience, *fear.* Fear of losing one's sanity and self-control are nearly as common as fear of losing one's soul!

There is really little difference between the fears "normal" people experience and those "psychic" people know. After all, psychics were "normal" before their consciousness expansion began! Once they are "expanded," however, the superconscious psychic's fears may become superexpanded. A nightmare becomes a bout with demons, a pinched nerve might be the result of a distant person sticking a pin in a voodoo doll. Heaven and hell become supersized in the psychic's mind, depending on religious fears he carries over from childhood.

The greatest danger *zone* in psychic circles is the God groups. They often defeat the purpose of psychic development study, which should be the quest for expanded love. Impersonal love, however, is often lost when students in psychic "work" discover their own personal power. Condemnation, censorship and judgment of others' souls is their forte. My own soul has been on the God-group chopping block for nearly as long as I can remember.

In the beginning, my grandmother used to admonish me, "If you don't join the church and accept Jesus as your saviour, you'll go to hell." At ages two, three and five I had no concept of what she meant. My parents had moved to California to get away from the Bible Belt and its Fundamentalism, so my grandmother didn't really scare me. Instead, she planted the seeds of thought in my mind.

"How can a person accept Christ?" I used to wonder, when I was a little older and her letters contained reminders that Jesus was man's savior. "If Jesus was a man who died two thousand years ago, how can I possibly ask him to come into my heart now?"

Several uncles were ministers. Ministers of God. One of our neighbors was also a minister. Of God. I used to wonder, "How can anyone claim to be a minister of God when he cannot see God? What is God? And, if God does not have a body, how could Jesus be his son?"

Once I tried asking our neighbor-minister this question. I was told, "If you don't become baptized and saved from hell, you'll find out more about Satan than God."

Because I was given no religious training, and therefore was raised in no church, the minister forbade his children to play with me. They, of course, were fascinated with me and they sneaked across the street to my house. "You're a real sinner," one girl whispered. "I never knew one of them before."

"What's a sinner?" I asked.

"I don't know," the girl shrugged. "It's a person who plays cards and whose mother smokes and who goes to movies, I guess."

My mother did all those things. I did them also, but I only smoked in secret. And then, I only smoked when I had collected enough tobacco from my parents' cigarette butts to fill a corncob pipe. My friend Gerald and I would smoke in the garage.

Gerald was also considered to be a sinner. We were, to the minister, nearly but not quite as bad as the Catholics who lived on the corner. The ministers' children would also sneak into the back yard of the corner house. Forbidden fruit always tastes best to humans, even when they are only ten years old.

"Why is Cherie a sinner?" I asked the minister's daughter.

"Oh, the Catholics gamble. And that's a sin," I was told.

"Why is Gerald a sinner?" I asked.

"Because his mother is divorced," the minister's daughter said.

Ironically, Gerald and I both grew up and became professional journalists—a field of work in which a good reporter uses both his psychic and intellectual abilities to draw out the spiritual core of a story. Perhaps if we had been praised as saints during our young years we would be standing on ivory pedestals somewhere today. But because we were the sinners of Emery Park, we took our freedom and had a fine time exploring life.

Around the corner lived an elderly, dignified retired school principal, the pillar of propriety. Our parents feared Miss J.! She was stately, calm and self-possessed. She was kindly, wise and a disciplinarian par excellence. Bullies and little beasts in pigtails did not rip up her lawn or climb her trees. Miss J. could send them scattering merely by standing still and looking at them.

Gerald and I, oddly, did not fear her. She lured us to her premises with homemade taffy and deep purple grape juice. And at night, with the heavy blinds shut and the velvet drapes drawn closed, Miss J. and her aged friends brought out a card table that could dance, float and "talk."

Perhaps Miss J. needed the energy of youth to help her conduct séances. Or maybe she saw in us a vital spark that surely would be extinguished before it burned. And she made it her project to fan the flame. She never said, "We are conducting a session of com-

munication with the spirits." Instead, she said, "We would like
you to play the Up Table game tonight."

My parents, believing I was getting an evening of proper education from this spinster, let me go freely to Miss J.'s. They even
invited her for dinner at our house. They never knew the dessert
Miss J. served on the table at her house.

We placed our fingertips lightly on the table. Soon, the table
would quiver. Then it would rise, fall, rise, fall, and rise until it
stood on one leg. On several occasions the table actually levitated
and moved horizontally across the room. Once we "upped" a
heavy wooden dining table. It was a table with massive legs,
hand-carved of beautiful oak. It levitated as easily as the card
table.

Generally we used the card table for our parlor game. It would
rise on one leg. Then the ladies would ask questions. The table
would bump up and down, tapping out a code which Miss J. converted into letters. The letters spelled out words. It was a slow
method of spelling and none of the messages interested me. It
was the attention, feeling of love and acceptance, and the grape
juice that I liked.

By the time it was discovered that I was sinning, it was too late.
I was already on my way to hell! Cessation of séances did not halt
the candleflame of spiritual consciousness within me from burning. I would awaken into a semi-sleep state, into the presence of a
group of "beings" whom I recognized to include Abraham Lincoln and other political forefathers of America. Together, as
equals, we worked. Those experiences are still wonderful memories, for love was their essence.

One night I woke to find a man standing by my bed. I told my
parents. That was the beginning of the dreadful knife of fear, as it
cut me into intrinsic psychic pieces that remained invisibly glued
as if into a whole being.

"There was no one there," I was told. "It was just your imagination."

The next time a man appeared in my room, I screamed. Ghosts
had arrived to haunt me. I screamed and screamed until my father woke. He took me through the house, assuring me there was
nothing there.

The next time someone appeared in my room I yelled again. And again my father was awakened. Irritated, the tone of his voice let me know I was not to bother him again. And I did not. Instead, I held my breath, dived under the pillow and lay awake all night in dread, chilly terror. Whoever or whatever was in my room never came again after that.

Even now, despite years of education and research into—as well as experience in—many various psychic-spiritual zones of being, I react with shock when a soft breeze brushes my cheek or a very real, but invisible, body seems to sit beside me. With my eyes closed I can "see," but I have a deep psychological block against "seeing" the invisible world from mortal eyes. I have learned to use logic, to overcome fear quickly, even to send thoughts such as, "If you are here to communicate with me, make yourself more dense so I can see you as if you are physical. Or, communicate solely on a thought level so I can receive your ideas from within my unconscious mind-level. But don't scare me!"

I was raised relatively free of the hellfire-brimstone fear that religion implants in people. What suffering must those upon whom religious psychic persecution was forced be enduring?

I meditated on this question, and the answer came as a thought: *They freeze fear so deep within themselves that they do not know what they are enduring. They live out their lifetimes like puppets, neither knowing who they really are, nor what they really could become. Fear freezes the soul on ice, leaving only the shallow surface waters of self to flow.*

Hot water will always melt a block of ice faster than a block of ice will cool hot water.

In the human being, one brief conscious encounter with the flame of spiritual self-reality can start the symbolic ice of self melting, so soul-force is released to flow.

Frequently this happens through a psychic experience, a seeming brush with death during an illness, or by spiritual illumination that comes during an emotional crisis. However consciousness expansion happens, whether naturally or through a drug-induced experience, the "inner self" seems to begin flowing through cracks in the ice (subconscious repressions and blocks) to mix with and expand the "outer" self.

If an individual has a beautiful psychic or spiritual experience, it becomes religious in nature. Even if the experient does not practice religion, the sublime feeling he has known becomes religious in essence.

Other people might experience the opposite. The opening of their psychic channels may be so frightening that in order to quell their terror they seek the answer, "What happened and how can I avoid it in the future?"

Both types of expansion—of discovering the deeper self—send people running to psychic circles. Most men and women who become actively involved in psychical research or development groups are like travelers on their first safari. They don't know a jungle from a forest. All they know is: trees grow in both.

The most common feeling among persons taking their first psychic safari is, "I will find company, guidance, help, wisdom and safety among people who have been here a long time." Innocently, honestly and peacefully, the newcomers enter the psychic jungle in the mistaken belief it is a placid forest. Peace and love are symbolic of such a place.

Unfortunately, they may soon find themselves feeling hanged by invisible vines! There is no sense of choking harder to cope with than that of being spiritually stifled! Yet this often happens in the psychic world, because the men and women who run the jungle are also victims of fear.

They, too, fear losing their sanity, their self-control and their souls—which most of them have found and expanded through psychical development! They transfer their pre-psychic fears to post-expansion expressions. But now that they have discovered the "power" within them, they mistakenly act as if they were among God's "chosen ones"—prophets, who foresee man's future, are profuse. And ironically, those who foretell of doom often grow the richest! People pay these prophets to cast their souls into veritable forthcoming hell, believing that their "love donations" are helping spread Truth and prevent Armageddon—or its psychic counterpart, such as a West Coast earthquake.

I say these people "mistakenly" act as if they were God's chosen ones. Perhaps they are. In my opinion we all have spiritual equality. Some of us know more than others, but does this constitute being chosen by God? I have yet to meet a human who has convinced me he knows who or what God is. In fact, those who talk the most usually know the least about love! Kathryn Kuhlman, the healer, is an exception. She glows and flows with love, while talking about Christ and God as if they are sitting on her shoulder. Rev. Paul Wilkinson of Asbury Methodist Church in Phoenix also glows with love. He teaches of Christ so that his congregation may experience the Light. Neither of these teachers demands homage be paid to them. They share truth to set others free. They spread love. They do not spread fear.

Many people never get out of the psychic jungle. They are trapped there by fear. Fear multiplied begets more fear. Where fear is power, love cannot flow. Many of the most unloved, unloving mortals comprise the psychic jungle's population. And many have come out of the jungle, far wiser than when they entered.

"I found that psychic is not the same as spiritual," says a young mother of three whose psychic safari lasted three weeks.

A Los Angeles writer says, "I entered to listen to the silence, but I couldn't hear it because of the din and clatter around me."

A West Coast actress claims, "I thought my guru was God's next of kin, until I discovered he made my girlfriend pregnant at the same time he was sleeping with me."

At a mass flying saucer sighting at Twentynine Palms, California, two women rolled in the dust, hitting one another and pulling hair, because both claimed to be reincarnations of the Virgin Mary. "I didn't know what was worse. Those two women or myself," a middle-aged seeker of truth confesses. "The group thought I was a princess from Venus! I went to the gathering because I thought I might discover something valid about communication with intelligence beyond the earth plane. It was a side show, complete with freaks. One man babbled about his contacts with saucers. He was raging drunk."

In Westwood, California, however, Dr. Thelma S. Moss of UCLA conducts psychic research groups in an entirely different manner. Her approach is intellectual. I spent an evening in a soundproof chamber in the lab at Neuropsychiatric Institute. I was able to "hear" the words of Elroy Schwartz, on the outside. A student aide confided that people loved Dr. Moss, but the work might be more fulfilling "if it was more spiritual."

Across the United States, intellectual parapsychologists, as well as non-intellectual emotionalists, vie for the psychic limelight. "Everyone wants to be top dog," the ex-leader of a psychic discussion group told me. "When the egos started fighting, I got out."

Throughout human history, men and women who have experienced "the light" have shared their illumination with others. Sharing and caring, natural extensions of spiritual illumination, become a loving experience. That is, the man or woman whose mental ice blocks melt and in whom spiritual effervescence flows becomes a channel through which cosmic energies stream. The greater the flow, the more uplifting and harmonious the "feeling" is of "I am at one with All-Being; I am loved; I AM love." Kindness and sincere desire to share this miracle with men leads the illuminati into circles where they can share with others the wonderful enlightening experience so others, too, may become channels for the "Godspell." But a loving experience can turn into a nightmare when one's "gift" is rejected and, often, hurled back angrily.

If you are involved in psychic study groups or spiritual development organizations, you should learn the difference between "psychic" and "spiritual." This knowledge can save you unpredictable grief, wasted time and psychic circling on paths leading deeper into mental mazes.

Psychic. Psyche is a Greek word meaning soul; it also was and is used to mean "inner" mind. A psychic person uses his mental abilities, generally in non-physical means of communication, to obtain information dealing with man, the physical-mental being. Love, wealth, health and position on a social scale, family level or in the work force usually become prime topics a good psychic discusses. A subject's inner secrets pertaining to his relationship with others on earth are the subject matter a psychic shares with his followers. One's personal future is discussed; often a person's past or "past lives" become the foundation for "being as you are today." A spiritual psychic is one who teaches his followers how to act and how to acquire persons, places or things for himself. A non-spiritual psychic, but a powerful one, is a person who makes others dependent on his advice. Psychics include mediums who communicate on a one-mind-to-one-mind level, whether such communication is with people on "this plane" or "from the other side." Aura readers, palmists, Tarot card readers, crystal ball gazers, automatic writers and many healers are "psychic" rather than spiritual. Those who start religious movements around their psychic "powers" often become the central figures upon whom devotees depend. Covens in witchcraft groups, which depend on the high priest or priestess, are often more psychic than spiritual— whether they claim to practice "white" or "black" magic.

Spiritual. Spiritual individuals are those who have undergone a form of mental, or conscious, growth not yet widely experienced by the mass of humanity. They see, hear, smell, taste, feel and *know* beyond ordinary sensory perception. Being sensitive to other humans' vibrations is part of one's spiritual development, and thus these people are usually psychic; however, they are seldom concerned with what tomorrow holds for physical man.

Canadian physician Richard Maurice Bucke experienced the illumination; his book *Cosmic Consciousness* is a classic work detailing "the light" that is available for man to experience, although humanity is unaware of the radiant cool flame until mortal centers of perception are capable of perceiving it. Bucke compares man's spiritual development of consciousness to his ability to see color. Early man saw three colors, red, black and white. The vibrations of color were present but man was yet unable to perceive them. Shortly before Jesus's birth, the Greek philosophers who wrote of color had not yet developed multiple color vision, according to Bucke. The multicolored spectrum, he claims, has become perceptible to the majority of humans only in the past two thousand years.

Man takes for granted that which comes easily; thus, mass color consciousness is not respected as a wonderful sign of human evolution or expanding consciousness. The forerunners of today's color-conscious generation must have had a terrible time trying to share the splendid rainbow they saw with those who knew not of what they spoke. The same is true of individuals who have the ability to see, and explore, regions of light, life and love beyond

ordinary human conception or perception. In this light all healing, love, peace and wisdom pervade the energy realms available to man. Spiritual man wishes to share the cosmic kingdoms
with others, so they may know from whence they come and to
whence they go.

Those who attain unity with the light become instantly transformed by love and wisdom for which there is no written human
language. Spiritually enlightened men and women desire no more
than to share this loving experience.

Psychic people and spiritual people look just about like everyone else. The only way really to determine whether you are involved in a psychic group or a spiritual one is to *feel*. If you feel
better after working with a teacher or a group, then you have
probably had a spiritual experience. Spirit is energy, and if it is
loving spirituality in motion that gives your group impetus, then
your vibrations are being raised.

If you feel worse after being with a teacher or group, then you
were probably being psychically drained, or a deep-rooted mental conflict has arisen because of your involvement. If you feel
trapped, worn out or sick because of your involvement, get out! If
you don't get out, you may become another victim hanged by the
invisible jungle vines.

Carlos Castaneda, author of the drug generation's Bible and
appendices, *The Teachings of Don Juan* and subsequent books,
once told me, "Most people spend their lives trying to recapture
their first love affairs. It cannot be done." If you joined a psychic
group to gain mental power, you may not suffer in the psychic
jungle. If you joined in search of love, or to recapture the rapture
of a loving experience, beware. What you seek is communion
with others on a spiritual level, and though psychics often pose as
enlightened people, they will go to any lengths to force you out of
their scene! Love IS the greatest power. Psychics who are not
channels for the love-spell, which I call the Godspell, don't want
you. You frighten them! Therefore, they will do what they can to
scare you—and because they do it frequently in the name of God
they may fool you into believing they are sincerely "the chosen
ones."

True leaders, or teachers, be they in the psychic field or in the "outside" world, share with Abraham Lincoln the wisdom and understanding of these words: "We the people . . . in order . . . to form a more perfect union . . ." True teachers, men of wisdom and enlightenment, know the two important words here are "in order."

There is orderly human history and distorted, disorderly human history. Each human life rewrites history. Generally, our histories follow a path of orderly physical, mental and spiritual development. An enlightened teacher leads his students into understanding of this history of self, then lets the student develop freely as his body and mind enter the various natural stages of human growth. A bad teacher will try to make the student over into an image of himself. This is where criticism, judgment and casting a student's soul into hell is most common, for unenlightened men and women automatically criticize those who think or act differently from themselves.

Unenlightened teachers or leaders simply desire the people to form a more perfect union by living as they dictate, and to hell with the natural order of things!

My own life story reads as a perfect example of distorted history. I tried to be anyone but who I was, and only after I revised my own edition of self did my Book of Life take on any semblance of order or meaning. I was a lucky one who reclaimed my soul from the people's devil, and also dared face their "vengeful God" and found love instead. I am no longer a victim in the jungle, psychic or "outside." This was not always true.

As a baby I projected out of the body nightly after Mother kissed me and tucked me into bed. I merged with golden light, traveling at a great speed, to a plane of intelligence where we had no bodies but we had a perfect union of sentience. We were pure energy, pure light. Descent back into the body was like a slide down a colorful scale of light. My spiritual self was like a traveler checking into a hotel; my body was the hotel. But it was not home.

I never discussed these early experiences, these cosmic excursions. They were as natural and normal as breathing is. Perhaps this is why I do not suffer "infant amnesia" as most people do. Because I never made an issue of my spiritual soul travels, no one condemned me or filled me with infant fear. Most humans, however, can remember nothing before their sixth or seventh year of life. Could this be because fear forced them to forget their I AMness so they could survive in their I AM not-ness as members of the "human social order"?

After I entered school and began intellectual programming, I ceased having conscious recall of projections into the realms of light. My exposure to the hellfire-brimstone mass consciousness had begun. Deep-seated guilt and fear formed, preventing me from expressing such simple awareness as, "My fingertips are not points in space where I end. I extend beyond the flesh." I knew it, but dared not speak of it. And, in time, I began doubting my own sanity. With no one to talk with, fear became a psychological superlative! The more I was told "do this" or "be that," the greater became the terrifying feeling that my soul belonged to everyone but me. Greatest of all chastisements, I believe, was the admonishment, "You are different from everyone else. What's wrong with you? Why can't you be a decent person like everyone else?"

At age nineteen, after earning a degree in business, I took an apartment. I was chasing the soul that so elusively lured me. But I was blind, deaf and dumb as to what I was pursuing. I simply followed, like a leaf blowing in a wind. I had tried clinging to the tree of life, but when the wind blew strongly the leaf became disengaged.

I fell in love. Love left me. Programmed to be a loser, I pondered, "What is wrong with me? Why am I unfit for love?" This, perhaps, was my natural "order" for I fell so deep into depression I passed out my own dark side. At age twenty I re-entered the Light. I have been traveling through space, both here on earth and through the galaxies, ever since. Now I know that falling in love is not the same as rising in love. Where the mortal soul rises in love there can be no fall. There can be only effusive joy, wealth of spirit beyond description and light where darkness prevails in the limited human misconception.

I consider re-emergence with the light as a spiritual form of baptism. It was the most joyous union I have ever known, so joyful that I ran out to share the good news with my friends. They looked upon me as if I were crazy. Even worse, several of them said, "You? It couldn't happen to you! That's got to be the devil's work!" There were also a few persons who saw my transformation from a different viewpoint. They believed me an automatic angel! On one side were my friends and relatives who were ready to cast me over the brink, to get me out of their immediate circles, and on the other side were those ready to form a religion around me!

I entered the psychic jungle to learn what had happened to me and why. Wisdom had come as a spiritual influx, but I now needed knowledge for gaining of human understanding.

Instead of finding friends, however, I discovered more criticism than ever. I couldn't seem to please anyone, not those who supposedly were masters of esoteric knowledge, nor those on "the outside." I have never known such pain as that of deep loneliness, loneliness that is begotten when a person tries to share love with a world that cannot accept it. Love then becomes twisted, forming invisible vines that become knots in which the lover hangs alone.

I left my suicide note when I was twenty-three. It compared the lover to life's artist. It said:

> Above the rest, whom do they uphold,
> And pay great tribute
> When centuries past are dust that is re-kissed?
> Is now, was then, and forever will be
> Upheld and made immortal—the artist.

The note also revealed the tragic truth: the artist is often scorned while he lives. His tribute comes only after death. I told myself my death would be a noble act.

I managed to get out of the body. But once "on the other side" I realized this was merely a great escape, not an ascension. I chose to come back, for escape is no excuse for evolvement. Luckily, I was able to check back into the "human hotel" in which I will continue living until the order of life determines it is the right time to go.

I nearly died because no one in "the jungle" wanted me. How many others have had the same sad experience? The psychic jungle can be treacherous. It is also the most exciting place and plane on earth! Therein, you will meet previews of the forthcoming race of *Homo sapiens.* You will swap stories that beat anything you will ever see on film because truth is, indeed, far more exciting than fiction. If you are lucky enough to make friends, they will be friends for life. They will not only like you, they will love you.

If you make enemies, some of them will remain enemies unto the death—be it physical or purely the death of a relationship. There really is no lukewarm relationship in the jungle; you will either run hot, as spiritual energy, with people, or you will run cold, like freezing ice water.

The greater your "talent," the higher you will be elevated; and the farther down you will fall when that smashing moment of descent comes. There is no escape from the natural "order" of psychic-spiritual evolvement. Once your mental ice blocks begin melting, you will reach symbolic mountain peaks and valleys darker than you can ever imagine. When you are "high" you will want to stay there. When you are "low" you will be almost frantic in your quest to rise again.

The joyfulness of expansion is indescribable. The misery of expansion's reverse side is hell. But as long as love is the light, literal or merely symbolic, that leads you on your safari into the psychic jungle, you can count on coming out the other side with wisdom, enlightenment and blessings I won't begin to predict.

If you can bypass the God people who will cast your soul into a hell you might not even believe in, and can live in the shadow of fear without letting it obliterate you; and if you can bite your tongue when you feel yourself tempted to judge others, the psychic world may be your stairstep to heaven.

If you arrive at a point where you can defend the point of view of the man who is trying to undermine your own security, you will already have passed through the jungle, even though you might still be active in its groups.

My own life is filled with encounters with the devil's advocates. I have learned a lot about God because of these encounters. Now I think, "I have given them my time in hearing their sides. Lord, when will they return the same courtesy to me?"

I am neither rude nor crass. But I no longer have time to spare in getting my soul saved. If I have learned one lesson only in all these years, it is this:

From spiritual dust I come; to spiritual dust I will return. We are all part of the vast union known as God, and therefore we have our beginnings, middles and endings in God's spirit-energy body. Therefore, what is there to be saved from if we are already where we were and where we are going? So relax and enjoy life while we have it.

I do not fear God. I do tend to tremble, however, if an unexpected ghost pats me on the shoulder. Hell, fire, demons and brimstone are as much a part of the psychic jungle as God, Christ light, love and spiritual affinity with All-Being are part of the spiritual forest.

II

The Mind in Danger

7

Innocent Witch

Ruth Pauli, as told to Daphne Lamb

This narrative deals with personalities and a period that seem to be getting rarer, as both the seductive qualities of hallucinogenic drugs and an aimless search for occult-sexual fulfillment have lost some of their glamour in recent years. Yet this story, told pseudonymously, is sufficiently typical and gripping to be representative of a generation, or at least a group, of young and idealistic women—Ms. Pauli calls herself a "white witch"—who sought insight and found degradation.

When I was a sophomore in college, some years ago, the university theater mounted a production of Marlowe's *Dr. Faustus.* I went to see it and then returned twice more, fascinated. Faust, as you may recall, sold his soul to the devil in return for magical powers and privileges. These he enjoyed to the hilt, even summoning Helen of Troy from her centuries-long sleep to make him immortal with a kiss. When it came time for the payoff, Faustus, like all men, was shocked and horrified to discover that the price of all his earthly pleasures was indeed to be his soul. Mephistopheles had made it all quite clear from the start, but who ever believes he'll really be called to account? Something in his plight during that last hour on earth moved me terribly—I must add that I believed in neither God nor the devil, and that my agitation over poor Faust's plight arose from humanistic rather than religious roots.

The idea of a human being going "further" than he is meant to go—whether in the role of bank robber, madman, or black magician—is an enticing one, but it is also pitiable since it is not within our natures to accept the results of our actions. We all, I suspect, believe we are immortal. And how shocked—how absolutely offended we are when it turns out we are no different from anybody else. I, like Faust, practiced magic. I believed, without believing in God, that there was a center of power in the universe and that, if it could be penetrated properly, everything else would fall neatly into place. I also believed the only thing holding me back was my own lamentably conventional approach to life. To this end I practiced the sort of solipsistic magic all children favor: ("I'll be elected president of the fifth grade if I can think of ten cities starting with *B* before recess") and worked really hard at breaking down my middle-class reserve. By the time I entered college it was almost second nature. I told my fortune with cards, willingly reading for others and acquiring a modest reputation as a "white witch." Anything to do with the occult was wildly fashionable on campus that year, and I was one of the first to become embroiled in astrology, studying my horoscope and babbling to like-minded friends about my "sign." We were quite ecumenical in our practices: we read Tarot cards, threw the *I Ching*, cast mild spells with locks of hair, burned incense and black candles in the dorm while listening to *Carmina Burana*, held séances, and talked earnestly of the need to find a substitute for the old God who—as we all knew—was dead. What it was, basically, was fun masquerading as deep involvement and alienation from the current preachings of the Establishment. I was more than ready to meet my Mephistopheles, but when he did come on the scene I failed to recognize him.

Antony—he never used a last name—appeared on our Midwestern campus in the spring of the year. He was a striking figure and news of his arrival traveled quickly. What was he doing here? Who was he? He was older by four or five years than the rest of us, and there were rumors to the effect that he was either a jaded veteran of the immoral war in Vietnam or the son of an aristocratic Eastern family bumming his way across the continent. I was very flattered by his attentions and found him extremely attractive. Antony was tall and very dark with glittering, charismatic eyes and an oddly innocent smile. He always wore a pendant of some dullish, woven material around his neck, and he was, as they say, "into" witchcraft and astrology and all the things I found so intriguing. He guessed my sign (Scorpio) immediately and pronounced it his favorite sign in a woman. He was cultivating me so carefully that I barely resented the attentions he paid to my friend, Liz. He divided his attention between the two of us so expertly that neither of us knew which he preferred. Liz was a rich and rather casual Southern girl who far outstripped me in her easy acceptance of drugs and experimental sex. I was basically, despite my "sorceress" role, a Midwestern puritan child who had only just learned to stop blushing visibly.

Liz and I often went with Antony to his room, where we smoked marijuana with him and talked. He never laid a hand on either of us, which only served to increase our fascination, but he did surprise us by confiding that marijuana was no more potent to him than a slug of tomato juice. He was used, he said, to better things, which he possessed in great abundance in his California "summer theater." He hoped that we would join him there when school was out and help to participate in a great experiment. This experiment was never clearly defined, but Antony said it had to do with living communally, as a unit, and joining ourselves to nature until we had learned to extract the latent power from the universe around us.

If we decided to join him at this cosmic summer theater, located somewhere between San Francisco and Big Sur on the Pacific coast, we must tell no one of our whereabouts and we must come prepared to be utterly free and open. He would make great actors of us, and superior human beings. He seemed very confident that we would accept, and of course we did. We told our parents that we would receive college credits for joining a "life experience" group in California and headed for the West Coast as soon as school was out.

The "theater" was a disappointment, since it consisted of several very rough cabins scattered over a hillside overlooking the

ocean, but the view from the nearby bluffs was beautiful and I
resolved to make the most of the summer and profit from Antony's
wisdom. The group, or "The Unit" as Antony called it, was even
more surprising than I had imagined. It consisted, as far as I
could tell, of Antony, Liz, myself, a silent young man named Lars,
and two other girls. The youngest, a timid little creature named
Dorothy, seemed scarcely older than sixteen and actually stam-
mered when you spoke to her. She was plump and pallid and appeared to serve no other purpose than that of an unpaid servant.
She fetched and carried exactly like a faithful dog. Antony told
me she was a runaway whom The Unit had taken in, but it was
hard to imagine Dorothy doing anything as definite as running
away from home. She had no will of her own—even her large, pale
eyes reflected nothing but devotion or, if anyone spoke to her
sharply, hurt.

The other girl, Martina, was her polar opposite. Martina went
so far as to refer to herself in the third person, as if she were
legend: "Martina doesn't like to get up early," she once told me;
"it makes her sick." For some reason Martina always reminded
me of the Roman empress in a movie I had seen as a child; she
was the sullen beauty who languidly tipped her thumb in a
southerly direction, thus condemning to death some righteous,
sweating Christian. She and Antony were lovers; they stalked
about the forest like a lion and its mate. You must understand that
at first I felt several cuts above this odd assemblage. Martina was
selfish and rather stupid—her earnest references to "The Unit"
embarrassed me. Lars spoke so rarely, he might have been a lobot-
omy, poor Dorothy was a rabbit, and only Antony seemed to
have some sense of purpose.

The first night we were there, Antony announced that a small
party was to take place so we could get to know each other better.
When Liz and I arrived, we were welcomed by Martina, who
embraced us formally, planting a kiss on our foreheads and waving us into the room. Lars was there, staring morosely into the
fire, and Dorothy sat far back in the shadows, as if trying to
nullify herself. Martina gave us wine and lay back on a cushion,
assuming her empress pose while we drank in silence. Then she
passed around a bowl of cigarettes, assuring us they were the

finest hashish money could buy, rolled in Antony's special papers, and insisted that we each have one. Presently Antony arrived, smiling benevolently and taking a seat in front of the fire. I felt absurdly pleased when he looked at me so approvingly. Hadn't he singled me out—smiled more warmly at me than at Liz or Dorothy or even Martina?

The hashish had done its work, and far better than any grass I had smoked during my college days. My whole body felt warm and tingling and *alert;* it seemed my consciousness was gaping open for the first time in an almost frantic desire to absorb and share with these wonderful people. I became aware that Antony was speaking, and willed myself to listen to his every word with as much intelligence and will as I could muster. "This theater can be the most meaningful experience of your lives," he said, "if you will resolve to open yourselves up completely to it. Here, at The Unit, we are not separate entities, but one living, breathing, powerfully loving being. We are all one person. Antony is Martina, Martina is Lars, Lars is Dorothy—" The others had taken up the chant in a mumbling descant that seemed very beautiful to me. Martina had twined her arms in mine and was encouraging me to join the litany. "I am Antony," I ventured, and Martina nodded encouragement.

I knew that I was very high and not in control of my impulses, and it felt wonderful. I was happy for the first time since coming to California. Antony embarked on a long discussion of theater as life experience. There had never been, he said, a group of actors who could perform as an entity, could breathe life into plays in a way never before known because they were outside themselves. The Unit would accomplish this, but it would take many long weeks of work before we were ready. We had to seek the aid of powers outside ourselves, unattainable at present.

It all seems ridiculous gibberish in the recounting, but at the time it made perfect sense. Martina stood up at some point and spoke of the woodland spirits that inhabited the forests of the Pacific northwest. She was one of them—a wood demon. Each of us spoke for a time, even Lars, who roused himself to a brief statement about the death of God and the rise of dark spirits more suited to man's needs. A bowl of some sort of stew was passed

around which we shared, eating with our fingers and washing
down the gluey mess with more wine. We smoked companionably
in silence for a time, and at last Antony stood up, sweeping the
room with his eyes. "Martina," he said imperiously, "come with
me." Martina did not stir, and we watched while he crossed the
room to Liz. "You are Martina tonight," he told her softly, "we
are all one." Liz followed him to the small bedroom. The door
clicked, Martina smiled and yawned, and I felt a sensation of
purest anguish. Liz had been chosen, while I had been cast into
outer darkness . . .

When I wakened the next morning I was still on the floor of
Antony's cottage. All around me lay the members of The Unit, in
various stages of drugged somnolence. Dorothy appeared soon,
bearing steaming mugs of tea, which she deposited near us
silently, like an efficient valet. Martina rose to her feet and read a
schedule of the day's activities: we were to troop down to the
beach and bathe in the ocean. Then we would work on some
improvisatory themes, designed by Antony to facilitate our most
intimate knowledge of our psyches. We obeyed her, shivering in
the cold water and feeling that something important was about to
happen. The morning was very beautiful.

The "improvs" took place on the beach itself. Antony would
outline a situation and then we would act it out, each of us having
a different motivation unknown to his partner. I, for example, was
told that I was a virtuous woman trying to prove my fidelity to my
suspicious and jealous husband, Lars. Lars was told that he had
already received specific proof of my infidelity; thus while I
improvised dialogue for myself in which I acted the loving, innocent wife, Lars was bent on punishing me. It was all great fun
at first. The others watched gravely while Lars and I went
through our paces. Then, suddenly, it became quite serious.
"Lying bitch!" Lars screamed, planting a stinging blow on my
cheek that sent me reeling. I was amazed that he would go so far
in an effort to appear realistic, but I was determined to play
along. "No!" I screamed, and then Lars was all over me, pummel-
ing me with his fists and twisting my arm behind my back until I
was sure I would lose consciousness.

After what seemed an eternity, Antony nodded and smiled, and

Lars loosened his grip. "That was very good, dear," Antony said softly. Sensing my indignation and fear he added, in a whisper, "You must be willing to stretch yourself to new limits. You must trust us."

For the rest of the morning I watched, rather numbly, while the others underwent similar tests. Dorothy's was the worst. Antony himself was her partner, and before they began he whispered long instructions in her ear, nodding and caressing her dull hair with his hands as if gentling a beast. Then they took their positions on the sand. At first nothing seemed to happen, but then Antony began to bark out instructions. Dorothy obeyed with alacrity, turning somersaults in the sand, removing her blouse to expose her babyish breasts to us, and at last walking into the ocean without a pause or backward look. There was a slight surf, and Dorothy, as we knew from our morning ablutions in the sea, could not swim. Nevertheless she continued, the water rising to her shoulders and occasionally slapping up over her head.

Liz stirred uneasily and plucked timidly at Antony's arm. "Call her back," she pleaded in a shaky voice, but Antony was silent. Dorothy had all but disappeared from view when he called her name. At the sound of his voice she pivoted and struggled back through the water, climbing up on the beach and sitting down at his feet like a sodden, shivering retriever. "Dorothy," said Antony informatively, "was told that she was hypnotized by me. If I hadn't called you, Dorothy, you'd be out in the ocean now, wouldn't you?" Dorothy nodded happily, and Antony smiled. "More than any other member of The Unit," he said, "Dorothy has learned trust. Study her. She is your example."

"I will never allow anything evil to happen to you," Antony said to me that evening in his cabin. "We are all one here." Once more the whole group was convened to lie about drinking wine and smoking the potent grass. Martina confided that it was opium mixed with hashish. "A beautiful combination," she said dreamily. I was again flooded with a sense of well-being and allowed Lars to rest his head on my knee, although he repelled me in my soberer moments. Even the little impromptu show (which might have been entitled "Dorothy Shows Her Trust") impressed me as

a glorious proof of the commitment we shared and moved me
almost to tears.

Dorothy allowed Antony to place a live coal in her hands and
held it there until he told her to drop it. She seemed unhurt, although the following morning her hand was wrapped in a crude
bandage, and in my drugged state I longed to show some sign of
my own good will. You must believe that the tenor of life at The
Unit was schizoid; in the morning one could hardly believe what
had gone on the night before, but nobody seemed the worse for it.
I was disturbed by the force of my own sexual feelings for Antony, who had not "selected" me, but I determined to bide my
time and give myself totally to The Unit's principles.

Little by little, small revelations were made. Antony's pendant
was made up of locks of hair from each member of the group.
They were braided and twisted into a small knot; a strand of Liz's
bright red hair was already incorporated in the amulet but I was
presumably still a probationary member and would remain so
until Antony himself had initiated me. Liz would not talk about
her initiation—she had grown quiet and contemplative. The Unit
was short on funds and there was very little to eat, aside from the
haphazard communal stew we shared in the evenings. Then, of
course, made placid by the wine and opium, we had so little ap-
petite it didn't seem to matter, but by morning I was always rav-
enous. I felt short-tempered and grouchy as the day wore on, with
only my morning tea to fortify me, but nobody else seemed to
complain. Twice a week Dorothy drove a battered van to the
nearest town, but her main expenditures remained a mystery. Antony told us this discipline was good for us. Americans were
overfed, he explained, and a more rigorous diet would keep us at
our creative best, opening us to more visionary experiences.

Gradually I lost my desire for the food I had known and no
longer dreamed of cheeseburgers and fried chicken. I might have
been with The Unit for a week or two months when my hunger
receded—we did not bother with time and it had no meaning in
the context of our spiritual lives.

On the night that I was finally chosen to bed with Antony, he
spoke at length to us about the need for new forms of religion.
The old Judaeo-Christian ethic had proven meaningless, he said;

God had turned his back on his children and things like the war in Vietnam and the starving people in Biafra were sure signs of his abandonment. We must act as the peasants did in the Dark Ages, and choose a new God to worship. If God were our sworn enemy, then it stood to reason that God's archrival, Lucifer, must be our champion. The life of rigorous discipline and semi-starvation we lived at The Unit helped to prepare us for new revelations; we were, maintained Antony, living a medieval exist-ence so that we might adapt to medieval forms of worship.

At the conclusion of this speech we removed our clothing and chanted a hymn to Astarte. We went through the ritual of taking each other's names, and when our voices had died away into the deep night silence, Antony beckoned to me. I followed him to the small bedchamber, euphoric in the knowledge that I had at last been made one of them. I was made to stand by the side of An-tony's bed, where he handed me a large, gleaming shears and in-structed me to cut a lock of my hair. When I handed it to him he solemnly braided it around his wrist, chanting in some guttural language and staring deep into my eyes. "Knowest thou who I am?" he breathed, and when I had nodded he placed me on his bed. "Repeat after me," he whispered. "I am the Antichrist, prophet of Lucifer . . . I am thy Lord and Master . . . Whatso-ever I tell thee, thou wilt do . . . My star is rising." Eagerly, I re-peated the words. It seemed a marvelous game to me; the sensation I had was one of drowning in a sea of custard.

When Antony made love to me, however, I felt nothing. It was as if my body had become numbed to all feeling, and my disap-pointment only made me more eager to prove myself. "They are Satanists," I thought to myself as I drifted down into my drugged sleep, "*We* are Satanists." That night I had a dream, and it was horrible to me. In it I was back in the Midwest, attending a Lu-theran Sunday school. The minister was familiar to me—he had belonged to the Rotary Club along with my father. When it was time to approach the altar for communion he raised his hand as if in greeting, and then the robe fell away from his wrists and I wanted to scream. His arms were covered with scales, his hands clawed and repulsive. I tried to shriek myself awake, but the dream was of the paralytic variety and nothing I did could force me to come up from under. This seemed to continue for hours, and when I wakened near dawn I was drained and exhausted.

The perverted mass of which I had dreamed became a reality soon enough, and, strange to tell, I loved it. In my lightheaded, semi-mad state it seemed the most complete test of our allegiances to one another. It is hard now to recall exactly how many of these celebrations we held, but there may have been half a dozen. We began by simply holding informal parties in the forest, emulating our medieval idols by running naked through the brambles and dancing around huge fires. I always, when recalling them, imagine I can hear a thin, high piping, but there were no musical instruments and the sound must have taken place inside my own head. We rubbed our naked bodies with earth and clasped each other, chanting and plunging sticks into the fire to make torches. It's a wonder we didn't set fire to the whole Pacific northwest coast, but somehow we wakened in the morning around the smoldering remains of our celebration, exhausted but unhurt.

On Midsummer Eve (or what Martina said was Midsummer Eve—we had no way of telling) we held our first mass. We scorned such conventions as the bent-back body of a virgin for altar; none of us was a virgin in any case, and we were all one entity. We pledged everlasting allegiance to Lucifer, made manifest on earth by Antony, and we drank wine mixed with whatever our leader chose to put into the chalice. Once Antony killed a cat which had come snooping around the van Dorothy drove to town, and offered it up to our Master.

I had always loved animals, but the murder of the cat did not disturb me in the slightest. Antony crushed its head with a large stone, and then drew signs on our foreheads with its blood. Dorothy became morose and wept a bit, and she was punished for her lack of faith by being instructed to fling the cat's body over the cliff and into the sea. It was the first time she obeyed a command reluctantly; for a moment it seemed she might rebel, but eventually she hurled the limp creature over the brink and returned to sit at Antony's feet. When she lifted a hand to brush back her disheveled hair, she left a long streak of blood on her childish forehead. That night she was chosen.

Something had been plaguing me for some time, and I was afraid to tell Antony for fear of incurring his displeasure. Liz had whispered to me of leaving, of trying to run away from The Unit. I was terrified of the consequences and would not listen to her. "You're as crazy as the rest of them," she hissed, and for a moment I knew a jolt of pure terror. Then I accused her of jealousy—of wanting Antony to herself. That stopped her, but I knew she was planning something foolish. When she made a run for the van one day my heart almost stopped. Antony caught her easily and dragged her, kicking and screaming feebly, to the smallest of the cabins. Here she was locked in and told to "examine her loyalties." Dorothy took food to her, and tea, and Antony himself visited her once a day, at sunset. I had always suffered from claustrophobia, and the thought of Liz, locked in the gloomy little shack, was more than I could endure. By the third day I begged Antony to let her go, but he said he was preparing for a revelation and could not waste time with traitors.

I suppose Antony was planning to summon Satan and I have a feeling that one or more of us might have come to some physical harm, but as it turned out the revelation was not slated to occur. Liz scotched our revels by escaping, and nobody knew until hours after she had gone. She had managed to coax Dorothy inside the cabin, and hit her with a large rock. Dorothy was not badly hurt, but something seemed to give way in her sad little soul. She sat, rocking and holding her head, on the threshold of the cabin. She told Antony that Liz had left much earlier in the day, and looked to him for comfort. When he merely cursed her stupidity she wept openly. Martina lost all patience and slapped Dorothy repeatedly, and then an amazing thing happened.

For the first time, Dorothy acted. With a speed and agility that was incredible, she bolted for the van and scrambled inside before Antony could even take in what was happening. He ran after the departing van, shouting and cursing in distinctly non-medieval fashion, but Dorothy drove off without so much as looking back. Antony insisted we spread out over the surrounding cliffs and find Liz, but it was a hopeless task, and we knew it. What happened next was beautifully simple. I was ordered to go inside and prepare something to eat while the others conferred. I stumbled around the little kitchen, putting together a half-edible concoction of vegetables and rice, and when I went to tell them it was ready, they were gone. Antony, Martina, and Lars—all gone without a trace.

I was alone, and instead of feeling lost and frightened I felt my whole body go slack with relief. All that evening I sat looking out to sea and trembling uncontrollably. I badly wanted to return home, and I would not let myself think of the alternatives. Someone would come to help me. Liz, even in her weakened condition, would return. I was literally too weak to walk very far, and my reflexes were so shattered that the mere thought of striking off on my own seemed a task of Herculean proportions. Even to move was a chore. Late that night the police came for me, and they were very kind. Liz had managed to make her way to the main road and thumb a ride, and she had told them about The Unit and begged them to rescue me.

I found that I could barely speak to anyone for the next few days. I wanted to cry when they told me about Dorothy, but even my tear ducts had ceased to function. Dorothy had wrecked the van and gone off the cliffs five miles up the coast. The police didn't think it was suicide—it was just that she was in no condition to drive so fast. Liz and I were found to be suffering from malnutrition and the effects of the multiple drugs we had taken. Opium, LSD, mescalin, and whatever else had been given to us left their marks, and we suffered from a mild form of withdrawal from the laudanum.

Our parents, of course, had to be notified. We were returned to our homes, where the greatest punishment—at least for me—was yet to come. My parents were so utterly bewildered by what had happened, and I so unable even to begin to describe the charms The Unit had held for me, that it created an unbreachable rift between us. I had nightmares about Dorothy which were so vivid and horrible I thought I might lose my mind if they continued. My gums were infected, my skin jaundiced, and I had lost twenty pounds. The idea of Antony haunted me. Who had he been, and where was he? For a long time I feared that he would hunt me down and return me to The Unit where I would be punished for my infidelity. When the grisly story of the Manson family exploded into the nation's consciousness I felt the parallels so acutely that I shudder to this very day. Antony has never been found, so far as I know, and may be posing as the head of a new Satanic Unit at this very moment. Or he may, like so many fragmented and evil personalities of that time, have been absorbed back into the framework of normal society and look back on his Lucifer days with astonishment.

I spent, as I later discovered, almost two months in that "commune" on the Pacific coast, and the effects will last for a long, long time. I'll trade my nightmares for yours any day of the week.

8

ESP or Madness?

Albert W. Potts, Jr.

The Reverend Albert W. Potts, Jr., is a Methodist minister who has had parishes in Iowa, Vermont and Connecticut, the last during his student days at Yale Divinity School. He now makes his home in Iowa City, Iowa. His observations on the psychological risks of psychic involvement are based on firsthand observations among parishioners and others who have come to him during the course of his ministry. This contribution originally appeared in Spiritual Frontiers (*Summer 1972*).

"I haven't told people of my experiences because they might think I was insane." I've often heard this statement when I've led developmental sessions or counseled beginners in the psychic. Some of these budding sensitives, like a woman I will call Leila, worry that their paranormal experiences actually are symptoms of mental illness.

I told Leila that I consider this a healthy worry. It put her on guard against the real dangers in psychic development. No one is free from inner conflicts and at least minor neuroses. The newfledged psychic will find symptoms of these mental difficulties masquerading as clairvoyance and spirit communication. Whoever cannot recognize these disguised symptoms is in danger of having them destroy and replace his true psychic powers without his knowing about it. If you are trying to develop your psychic ability, for your own sake and the sake of being able to help others, you need to learn to distinguish between true paranormal messages and pseudo-psychic delusions.

This is the advice I give to help people keep their psychic development free from unhealthy elements:

1) *Put full trust only in what you can verify by checking facts.* Several years ago, one of the most impressive mediums I have ever met, Mrs. Phoebe Carpenter, of Colchester, Vermont, told me that when she gives a message service she always waits for the person's response to see if the message was on the track and can be confirmed. She has a good approach. Unprovable messages and visions, no matter how vivid, may be mere flights of fancy originating in unconscious problems. The true psychic is a doubter. No matter how many years he has received verification of his psychic powers, he hesitates to believe anything not confirmed by facts.

The more dogmatic a person is about his spirit communications, the more likely that they are unconscious deceptions. One woman wrote me a six-page letter to convince me that "buggers," federal thought-police, and invisible criminals watched all that she did and interfered with her life. She added, "God knows this is *all* true." This "the-whole-world-is-wrong-and-I-alone-am-right" attitude is typical of people who are perfectly sincere in their belief, but who have let their inner world become a substitute for reality. So they see no need to check their "spirit communications" against the facts.

2) *Experiment with the psychic only when it has a helpful, positive effect on your life.* Leila was receiving fascinating but strange "messages" by automatic writing, purportedly from her mother in her mother's handwriting. Each day Leila was spending more and more time alone, obsessed with this writing. She sensed the danger and asked for my advice. I suggested that she stop automatic writing and join a developmental group. She could then try to get messages about the others which she could check with them. And they could point out to her any weird material. Leila did join and quickly proved to have good clairvoyant skill. Her husband, Ronald (I'll call him), was not particularly psychic

himself, but he encouraged Leila and joined the group with her. Their daughter, Nikki, also turned out to have psychic ability. They all attended lectures and workshops together, tried to receive messages about each other throughout the day, checking them with each other at dinner. Leila is now working with good success in healing. The paranormal had opened up a whole new world of discovery and family activity for them. After the initial detour into automatic writing, it had an entirely beneficial effect on all of them.

But another young couple, whom I will name Ben and Anne, living a few miles away from them in a lonely farmhouse, were getting deep into trouble through their psychic experimenting. Ben and Anne had a semi-hippy life-style and had experimented with drugs. They had had verified paranormal experiences, but they had let their guard down and become too absorbed in the occult. They believed anything and everything. Alone, Ben went into a dark room during the evenings and tried to communicate with spirits. With other young people, they went to a graveyard and used bizarre rituals to call back ghosts. They mistook every gastric pain for the sign of a spirit's approach and blamed all their problems on spirit tampering. The psychic world, once so exciting to them, had become a mess of malevolent ghosts, fears of possession, mind readings, and a source of fear, gloom, and real danger. They both had jobs, and their work was declining in quality. Their marriage was showing strain. Their psychic experimenting had only a destructive effect. But after they had taken my advice to cut back on their involvement and believe only what they could prove, they told me that their lives had improved.

On a table in their living room had been the skull of a cow. Although they did not use this in their rituals, such a symbol could not help but have had a detrimental effect on their minds. This brings up the next point.

3) *Avoid charms, weird rituals, black magic, witchcraft, and uses of the psychic aimed at self-interest or producing spectacular effects.* I suppose that every teenager sometimes plays with an Ouija board or tries to levitate or uses a silly chant to bring back a ghost, and no harm is done. But a person who seriously tries to

make sustained attempts to create spectacular effects or explore the psychic out of morbid curiosity is doomed for trouble.

4) *Develop your psychic powers only insofar as they provide fun, exciting and happy experiences.* Anyone who thinks a sensitive should be a lonely, eccentric, otherworldly person would never suspect that Gary Fischer would be a most promising psychic. Gary is a brilliant mechanical engineer, a former star long-distance runner who still jogs three miles a day, a cheerful and friendly man who was once president of his church's men's club, a man outgoing and liked by everyone. In one developmental session, Gary, in great detail, successfully described a man's office by clairvoyance, when Gary did not even know what the man did for a living, much less what his office looked like or even if he had an office. The whole developmental group was thrilled.

In another session, a second member of the group, Chet Pryor, predicted that Gary would take an airplane trip, have a worrisome problem about his wife at take-off time, fly through a snow storm, and return safely. At the predicted time Gary did fly to a meeting where he gave a speech. His wife was to meet him at the airport to say goodbye, but she was caught in a traffic jam and neither could get to the airport nor explain to Gary why she was not there. The plane took off through an early fall snow flurry. Gary was so excited about these predictions coming true that he could hardly wait to tell Chet and the rest of the developmental group, all of whom were delighted by the confirmation of powers at work among them. This is the attitude of joy and eagerness proper to the ESP field when it is healthy and free of neurotic elements.

5) *End your psychic experimentation if your "messages" become demanding.* A man I will call Dale was hearing innocent-seeming voices correctly predicting shifts in the stock market, telling Dale when to buy and sell. As Dale listened more, the voices began to say, "We are testing you. If you obey our commands exactly, we will give you a job of great importance to do." Flattered and impressed, Dale did obey the voices, which gave him bizarre tasks and shouted at him angrily. Dale began to black out and wake up in strange places. His voices were drowning out

other people talking to him. The job assigned Dale by the voices turned out to be protecting the world from an invasion of tiny Martians living in his stomach. Dale had no idea that all of this was insane, but obviously he had to be hospitalized.

The strange messages which Leila had received by automatic writing, supposedly from her mother, were similar to Dale's. Leila was "especially loved in heaven" and would be given an important job if she could obey. The only thing to do was cease paying any attention to such messages. Never ask a spirit to help you make a decision. If you have trouble about decisions, see a counselor.

6) *Discount any "messages" which make too much of you personally.* One man wrote me that Jesus Christ gave him a personal call to establish a political party and become ruler of the world until Jesus' Second Coming. Another man wrote that he had been given a divine commission to organize an expedition into the center of the earth to look for the Ten Lost Tribes of Israel. These men could argue, "this idea couldn't be from my own mind because I never would have thought of it myself." And they are completely sincere. They do not recognize their delusions. Other people hear voices shouting that they are worthless and evil. This is the other side of the same coin, the opposite of delusions of grandeur.

Be cautious. The proper use of psychic development is for understanding of the spiritual realm, glorifying God, learning to lead a more positive, satisfying, and happy life, and being more helpful to others. Properly used, psychic development will have all this in store for you.

9

Vampire and Demon Lover

RAYMOND VAN OVER

The author, while member of the faculties of the School for Continuing Education, New York University, and of Hofstra College, on many occasions acted as adviser to men and women seeking to deepen their knowledge of psychic and occult practices; some of these efforts, as Mr. Van Over observes, led to dangerous aberrations. Raymond Van Over was editor of the International Journal of Parapsychology *and has edited several anthologies, including a two-volume work,* Eastern Mysticism, *as well as* Psychology of Freedom *and* Psychology and Extra-Sensory Perception. *He is the author of* Unfinished Man.

Most people one meets in the occult will nod and smile knowingly when you mention how many nuts there are in the field, and then proceed to tell you of their contact with a Venusian who popped out of their hard-boiled egg that morning. Now this is a gross generalization, but my personal observations (which span over twenty years in studying the occult and meeting people with varying degrees of interest in it) bear out the conviction that unstable personalities dominate the occult population.

During the years I have worked in parapsychology I have been visited by many people attempting to make sense of their personal encounters with the psychic. Some of the events did seem to

contain evidence of ESP phenomena. But in most cases the line
between the stark visitations that beset the mentally disturbed
and what appeared to be ESP was extremely thin. It was
precisely this confusion between the fear of madness and the
hope that the disturbing experiences were only a trick of the
mind, or perhaps even genuine psychic phenomena, that forced
people to seek advice. But the search for rational advice came
only upon the heels of a crisis. The individuals had become involved in uncontrollable and even dangerous events before they
felt the need for critical, rational examination of what was happening. Most do not seem to want any form of discriminating
analysis when it comes to occult phenomena until they get out of
hand. These are people who have gravitated toward the occult
field because of its otherworldly attractions. In the occult field, no
less than in parapsychology, one needs an open but *critical* mind.
Hence, the wisdom of St. Augustine's advice that if one wants to
investigate the unknown, he had better be sure that he first has a
solid foundation in the known.

Occultism urges further detachment from the known world;
and while such inclinations may serve a useful balance to a rigid
or overly materialistic personality, they offer obvious dangers to
personalities already unstable or prone to reject the physical,
known world and its unpleasant realities. One of the most striking
examples I recall involved a young woman in her early twenties
who came into my office in the spring of 1967. She was slightly
above average height, pretty, with long black hair, and obviously
several months pregnant. The first sign that something was wrong
was when she signed the visitors' book with curlicued lines
vaguely reminiscent of Tibetan or Sanskrit script, but clearly a
meaningless jumble of lines. Her conversation, however, was completely coherent; she was intelligent and seemed quite rational.
We chatted about general things for a few moments and then
she told me why she had come. She wanted to know if an incubus
could make a woman pregnant. She claimed she had been visited
by a creature from the astral world who had seduced and forced
sex upon her.

In our age of quasi-sophistication about the occult most people
know that an incubus is some sort of demon or devil who sexually

assaults women during the night. The succubus, the incubus' female counterpart, attacks males. *Incubus* is a Latin word meaning nightmare. The incubus was recognized by law during the Middle Ages, and was believed in fervently by most people. Many silly theories developed to explain the phenomenon. In the sixteenth century a church authority stated that erotic encounters with demons in nightmares occurred most often in convents because they created their visible, physical matter from the menstrual substances available there. He didn't bother to explain the visitations of succubi to monasteries. But it was always thought to have its source in evil, and it was generally believed to be an evil spirit who descended upon women in their sleep, to overwhelm their senses and seek sexual intercourse. The person attacked succumbs because of the demon's knowledge and use of her own unconscious fantasies and repressed desires. In effect, one aspect of the psyche seems to be manipulating another, less dominant part for its own ends. In the classical description of incubi and succubi, however, full sexual arousal and pleasure was not always a part of the erotic encounters. Men and women both usually reported a sense of oppressive weight on their chests. Their arms and legs became leaden and they had no power to move or resist when the demon began its attack. The sexual dream is, of course, as ancient as sex. The relationship between sexual fantasy and sexual fact is often extremely thin, especially in the dream world. There are many records, from the time of witchcraft revival in the Middle Ages up to the nineteenth century, of women and men relating how they had been ravished in a dream and found evidence upon waking that some sexual activity had indeed taken place. It was not simply the subjective sense of something having occurred as in a dream, but the actual physical evidence that led many to believe that the dream was real and they had been visited by an erotic demon. From Sigmund Freud's viewpoint, erotic dreams were primary outlets for sexual repression or dissatisfaction. And in the case of nuns and monks who practiced celibacy, sometimes against their wills, the occurrence of erotic dreams is no surprise; especially considering that the nuns and monks who were members of various convents and monasteries were not there because of any deep religious conviction, but rather because it was considered a safe haven for a young girl, or a good steppingstone into church politics or government for an ambitious young man; or perhaps they were there simply as a convenience to the parents, who wanted their children out of their hair.

In this case the young woman was intensely anxious to find the answer to one question. It was not whether incubi existed or not. She had in fact found the experience erotically exciting and did not care whether he was real or not. She was convinced her pleasure was real and that seemed adequate. Nor was she interested in whether she might have hallucinated that evening when her demon lover had visited her. She believed completely and utterly in the reality of her experience. In her mind she had no doubts about having had intercourse with a spirit. Indeed, she even seemed pleased at the thought he might return. Her only true concern was to find out if a being from another plane—from an astral level—could impregnate a woman on the earth plane. Even though she appeared pregnant to me, I suspected it might be a false pregnancy considering her state of mind, so I asked her if she had been to a doctor to see if she was actually pregnant. She had not and adamantly rejected the idea. She wanted to know only one thing. Did I, as someone involved with parapsychology, believe an incubus could make a woman pregnant? I tried to explain that parapsychology did not include the study of astral-earth medicine or demonic love affairs. As the conversation progressed she became more and more agitated, and began arguing that she couldn't possibly be pregnant because in fact she didn't really believe astral beings could communicate sperm between the two worlds. At this point I felt the conversation was beginning to deteriorate, go in circles and repeat itself. Her agitation grew greater and I finally convinced her that while I did not know whether an astral being could make a woman pregnant (and I wasn't about to give her references to Aleister Crowley's theories that such transference was possible), perhaps she should see a doctor just to set her mind at ease. For then she would know once and for all whether she were pregnant—by an astral lover or not! I recommended she go see a specific medical doctor I had on file, who was also, I didn't mention, a psychiatrist.

I did not follow up this case except to discover that she did not go to this doctor. But oddly, I did see her once again. Almost a year later I was visiting a friend on the Lower East Side of Manhattan. Across the street from his building was a small store converted by a self-made guru who, I knew, taught as many young women as he could convince to join his group the refinements of Tantra Yoga and Tantric sex techniques. I had spoken to the man long enough to satisfy myself that he knew next to nothing about genuine Hindu and Tantric beliefs or practices. The whole thing was a setup, a con game to satisfy the old man's need for attention or lechery. I never bothered to find out which was the stronger motivation. I was surprised to see the young woman with long black hair, a beautiful blond infant in her arms, come walking down the street and turn into the old man's store. There was no doubt it was the same woman, so if it was an astral being who got her pregnant, Rosemary's Baby was born long before the book and movie were produced.

To my mind the girl clearly did not want to be pregnant and resisted the realization probably right down to the labor pains. That she was deeply involved in the occult and the outer fringes of parapsychology had become clear during our talk. It was not surprising that her unconscious resistance utilized in her moment of need a few outstanding and evocative facts from the occult lore she had read. What better source for a resisting psyche to call upon than such potent symbolic images; icons from the unconscious that had reverberated in mankind's primal mind since our time on earth began. What better method to avoid guilt than to put the responsibility and blame on an evil spirit who overpowers you in your sleep, on a demon lover who seduces you and, as she described it, with such powerful erotic stimulation as to make resistance impossible. All the responsibility for such sexual acts can conveniently be denied. One is simply an object being used by forces far stronger than one's power to resist.

This is danger number one: occultism offers ready and convenient means by which those already disturbed—or those on the border line—can justify or rationalize their neurotic needs. The deeper their involvement in occultism, the more likely it is that such people will utilize its teachings and symbolism in a psychotic way. This does not mean that a border-line psychotic will not suffer a breakdown without any occult material being available. But clearly when unstable personalities are attracted to occultism, it offers, when unwisely delved into, a haven for irrational impulses to manifest. It is a world where few stabilizing or discriminating personalities function as a counterexample. It provides fertile ground upon which neurotic and dangerously unstable personalities can flourish unquestioned.

Another example I recall did end sadly. Another young woman had a slightly different problem. At first I thought she was joking, but it was soon apparent that she was in deadly earnest and frightened to the point of hysteria.

She was a young Jewish woman, separated from her husband and having just lost the custody of her child as well. Her story began in a Horn & Hardart restaurant. She waited for a table with two strange young men and another woman in her late twenties. One of the young men was dressed in a skintight, gold lamé costume. She soon discovered that he was a rock 'n' roll singer and that his woman friend was a witch. The young woman told me that she felt immediate terror of this group but didn't know why. She felt a sudden chill and was about to leave when the singer grabbed her arm tightly and told her that not only was his friend a witch but that he was a vampire. Now I must admit that as I listened to this story it struck me as funny, for it sounded more like a Halloween hoax than anything to fear. But the disturbance of this young woman as she related her story was not laughable. I asked her gently if perhaps it had all been a joke, if they were not taking advantage of her. She replied that she had felt it was a joke herself at first, but as time passed she began to believe them. They were intense and deadly serious. The singer then added that not only did he love drinking blood, and had done so many times, but told her pointedly that he especially preferred young girls' blood. When she responded that she had rare blood and could not afford to lose any, it must have been clear to the pranksters that she was quite naïve and had taken them far too seriously. Terrified, she pulled away and ran from the restaurant.

During the next week she lived through very traumatic episodes, all involving blood. She related several examples. When

she came home one evening after work she opened the door to
find that everything in the apartment was in order except her infant son's picture, which had been hanging over the bed. It had
fallen off the wall and a large spot of blood stained the place
where the picture had been. She fled the apartment after grab-
bing her son's photograph from the floor. She was badly shaken
and to make herself feel better she thought some shopping would
help. In a boutique she began to try on an attractive bra and then
noticed that it was covered with spots of blood. She dropped the
bra, pulled her sweater back on and ran from the store. After
wandering the streets for hours, sipping innumerable cups of
coffee, she went home and after some hesitation went into her
apartment. Everything appeared normal and the spots of blood
had disappeared from the wall. She did not hang her son's picture
on the wall any more, however.

After this, she began going to the library and reading up on
vampires and witchcraft. She had already done a small amount of
reading and had always been interested in the subject, but now
she thought she had a compelling reason to study these books
more deeply. She went on like this for several weeks and had only
one other episode with blood. That occurred when she went into
her bathroom and found the toilet seat, the floor, the towels, everything covered with bright, fresh spots of blood. As I understood the sequence of events, she then began to hear voices
calling her filthy names, urging her to do self-destructive and violent things. It was because she recognized these as her own self-
destructive urges that she finally began seeking help outside of
occult books. She went to her rabbi, who was unfortunately very
unsophisticated psychologically, and simply tried to comfort her
and send her to a church social worker. He didn't recognize that
the episodes were becoming more frequent, of greater intensity
and expanding into a wider range of psychic attacks.

The voices continued cursing her and telling her to kill herself.
She tried a nearby Catholic church. The priest told her to pray.
She tried, but found the voices laughing in her head while she
prayed, and eventually they even grew louder. She then went to a
Protestant minister and was given similar metaphysical pabulum
as advice. She was nearing the end of her strength when I saw

her. She looked terrible; she was not unpretty, but her complexion was pale, her expression extremely tense and nervous.

She began our conversation by explaining that she thought someone in parapsychology might help her because she was being attacked telepathically by a vampire who was after her blood. His voice kept cursing her and telling her disgusting things to do. One didn't need to be a psychiatrist to see that she was deeply disturbed and on the verge of a breakdown. I talked with her for several hours, finally convincing her that she should go to a doctor to get help, or at least for some tranquilizers that would help her sleep. Fortunately, she took the advice and went to a doctor. I later discovered, however, that it was too late: she suffered a complete mental collapse. I do not know how long she spent in an institution, but I can't help feeling that however long it was, it was very unnecessary, for I believe her involvement with the occult had provoked an already dangerous situation into a mental breakdown.

I am not arguing here that *all* who are attracted to esoteric subjects are either better or worse than others. Many are good people in the sense that they are "seekers," they want to understand life and know who or what they are. Many are lonely and frightened people who in gravitating to the occult find surcease and comfort from the difficulties of a hostile world. But, by and large, they are gullible individuals ready to be manipulated by stronger or devious personalities. These gullible people may be honest in terms of behavior and the ethics of Western puritanism and Christian charity; but they are also clearly unsophisticated in the subtleties of intellectual honesty or discrimination. They are often incapable of handling the mysterious, evocative and dangerous powers of their own unconscious mind.

More than any other danger, the one of most concern is the possible piercing of the essential protective separation between the conscious and unconscious aspects of our personalities. Uncritical dabbling in the occult too often destroys that protective shield between the inner and outer world of the human personality asunder too precipitously, too quickly, leaving the individual's conscious mind flooded with powerful emotional material from the deeper recesses of the psyche—with no preparation, practice or even the vaguest idea of how to use such material or to defend oneself against it.

The result, in most cases, is a melancholy tale like those just related. The sad end of foolish and ill-prepared game-playing with powerful forces of the mind and with the very structure of one's own personality is wasted energy, wasted time—sometimes running into years—and wasted talents that the individual could be putting to better, more constructive use. It is this combination of playing with the complicated, powerful forces of the human mind and the lack of concern for critical analysis or disciplined growth that makes the occult world such a zone of danger.

10

ESP and Drugs

SUSY SMITH

Ms. Smith, the author of many books in the field of psychic research, warns here against mixing the development of extrasensory perception with drugs. Having experimented with hallucinogenic drugs herself, testing the hypothesis that these and other pharmacological compounds might increase psychic sensitivity, she writes, "I thanked God for my bad trip!" Susy Smith's writings include her autobiography, Confessions of a Psychic, *and her most recent work,* The Book of James.

Efforts to achieve instant ESP or mystical visions by the use of hallucinogenic drugs sometimes have spectacular results; but, as far as I have observed, the possibility of dependence on the drugs and the occasional traumatic experiences encountered are not worth the chance one takes. It is better to go the yogi and meditation routes to illumination for more security and permanence. And no matter what those mind-control courses that are springing up all over the country tell you, there is no really quick and easy way to attain ESP unless you have a natural proclivity for it to begin with. If you attempt to learn how to acquire it by attending meditation or development classes, the road is long and tiresome and you need a great deal of patience, but you are free from the problems presented by drugs.

It must be acknowledged, as Dr. Stanley Krippner says (*Pastoral Psychology*, 1970), that ". . . psychedelic drug usage typically gives an individual the subjective impression that he is extremely psychic; whether this impression is valid remains to be empirically demonstrated." Parapsychologists had long searched for any substance or condition which might induce ESP to occur more frequently or more consistently than it ordinarily does. Naturally they were glad to take advantage of the opportunity offered by drug trippers who thought they were producing ESP. Now that we suspect so much more about the possible dangers of taking such drugs, it is probably fortunate that they became illegal before parapsychologists acquired a name for encouraging the youth of America to get stoned so that they could become guinea pigs for ESP research. During the time they were doing the research, however, some interesting studies were reported. One done by Charles Tart (*On Being Stoned: A Psychological Study of Marijuana Intoxication*, Palo Alto, California, 1971) revealed that the proportion of marijuana users reporting paranormal experiences was much higher than in surveys of general populations. Dr. Tart said: "Either marijuana use affects judgment in such a way that a large number of ordinary experiences are judged to be paranormal, or there is a very high incidence of paranormal phenomena associated with marijuana, or both."

R. E. L. Masters and Jean Houston tell in *The Varieties of Psychedelic Experience* (Holt, Rinehart and Winston, 1966), about a patient—S-19, a housewife in her mid-thirties—who during an LSD session said she could see her little girl in the kitchen of her home, hunting for cookies and knocking over the glass sugar bowl from the shelf and spilling the sugar. She then forgot the episode; but when she returned home and could not find the sugar bowl, her husband told her that while she was away their daughter had made a mess while looking for cookies. She had knocked the sugar bowl from the shelf and smashed it, spilling the sugar all over.

This kind of telepathic rapport is fairly frequent between members of a family. It was possibly made stronger here because of the LSD. Situations of a somewhat similar nature also seem to be more frequent among trippers I have known.

A pretty Miami-Dade Junior College student named Gail told me of such an experience. She dated another Miami college student named Bill, she said, and they both practiced witchcraft and took *beaucoup* drugs. They had found that their ESP together became completely confusing when they discovered they had fantastic rapport when they were both stoned. The first time it occurred was when they had both had a large dose of acid; and it had continued after that for some time. They often spoke in the same language patterns to each other. People who were with them in a group, all tripping, could not tell them apart. They sat perfectly still, but sometimes people saw Gail on the right, when Bill was actually on the right. Or Bill on the left when it was Gail on the left. When one of them would say something, the other would finish the sentence. Gail would speak, and someone else across the room would respond, "What did you say, Bill?" They began to feel frightened about it because it was as if they had become one person.

"It was hard," Gail said, "to tell when you were you."

Charles Tart reports something similar. A twenty-two-year-old clerk told him: "Once on an acid trip in an apartment in San Francisco, a friend and I changed places. I was inside his head looking at my body and my face and hearing my voice when he talked. He was looking from my body into his face, and when I spoke it was with his voice."

Paulie, a hippie witch (or warlock, as he preferred to call himself) whom I knew in Toronto, had trouble of a similar nature with his friend and fellow warlock Cicero. He wrote me: "We seem to have a bad problem that I'm afraid will take a while to remedy. Cicero and I were sending such strong vibes to each other and were so locked in each other's brain waves that we can't help but give each other headaches. So we're wearing tons of jewelry to keep our own vibes in and others' out until we can calm our vibes down to where it won't be painful to us. Freaky things are happening, like: although he is staying at his home some twenty miles away, I feel the sensation of being wet when he takes a shower, and his legs ache because I do so much walking.

It's going to take some adjusting to get used to being so close together again. We're soulmates, but it seems to be going beyond that—it's as though our souls are finally merging before death and we're feeling what each other feels. We walk around reading each other's minds and using ESP as though it were going out of style. I hope we can get this super-ESP under control before our heads get to the point of unendurable aching."

Paulie wrote later: "Cicero and I aren't quite in such rapport as we were at first, but weird things still happen. Oliver, his wife, has hay fever, and just recently she has learned how to get rid of it temporarily. She wills it to Cicero and then both Cicero and I walk around sneezing until Oliver finally decides to relieve us and takes her hay fever pill. Wow!"

Wow! is right. How much of this sort of thing can one believe? And yet it is interesting that wherever you find drug use thriving you seem to discover people making statements of this nature. I do think it is a curious parallel that young people in Miami, Florida, Toronto, Canada, and Davis, California, where Dr. Tart teaches, during the same period of time described similar symptoms when they were turned on.

There are other rather disturbing occurrences reported, some regarding physical effects as well as mental.

In the late 1960s I was in Coral Gables, Florida, so close to the University of Miami that a number of college students lived in my apartment building. One group there told me that they were experiencing poltergeist phenomena in their rooms. They used grass, hash, or acid in their ceremonies to invoke the gods of witchcraft, and whoever they managed to contact had a tendency to rap on the wall . . . loudly and firmly. When I suggested this was more likely irate neighbors, they replied that it was the inside wall that rapped—the one between the two rooms of their apartment. Anyway, they insisted that most of their magic was rather quiet and subdued, because they took it very seriously, so they knew they weren't annoying the neighbors.

A coven of hippie witches settled down together on a Vermont farm in 1968, looking for peace and quiet and the opportunity to practice their magic without interruption. Soon a black warlock moved in with them, without an invitation, and stated that they had better conform to his desires because he had brought many evil spirits with him. Evidently he had, for soon poltergeists took over the house. Raps and knocks were heard, dishes flew about, windows were broken, and other wild activities occurred. The kids were quite naturally scared to death. Agitation built up, the peace farm disintegrated, and members went their separate ways.

As I said of this in my book *Today's Witches*, "Perhaps it was all in the minds of these young people, but minds clouded by hallucinogenic drugs and concentrating on the rituals of magic might be able to conjure up very formidable specters. When one is playing with the most mysterious force in the world—the mind —he is playing with something very potent indeed."

Witches have special ways to use the power of their minds, and who is to say it may not occasionally be successful in producing actual phenomena? I certainly wouldn't. I even believe what Gail told me about her date with Harry. I think. This young man, who practiced black magic, was pursuing her for dates. One night he called her when Bill, her steady, was sick, and so she decided to go out with him. When she explained to him that she was going with him only because Bill was ill, he said, "I know." He took full credit for having caused Bill's malaise. Later when Bill was out of town, she went out with Harry again. When Bill returned, he told her everything that had occurred when she was with Harry— where they went and what they did. It would hardly have been likely that he could have surmised what they were up to. It was, to say the least, unusual!

They had taken LSD and then gone out in a boat and concentrated on clouds. They made several clouds disintegrate by their thoughts and then decided to take on something really big. Could they make their magic work to the extent of raising a small tornado? They concentrated on forming a funnel-shaped cloud until they actually did make one appear. At least, they take credit for it. The next morning's newspaper reported that a small tornado had hit on the outskirts of town at the very time they were focusing their thoughts on producing it. I recall reading about it in the paper.

"I must admit," I wrote, "that it would be difficult to prove that two witches out in a boat had caused a tornado, but the coincidence is rather fascinating to think about. If it is ever shown scientifically that the power of the mind has actual physical effects, then we will know for sure what we now only suspect—that witches are playing with dynamite."

Another neighbor of mine was a lawyer who was in no way involved with witchcraft, but he loved to smoke pot. I presume he worked fairly competently during the day, but in the evenings he puffed for a while, then just sat and stared at the walls and watched the pretty pictures he saw inside his head. One night he concentrated on the rhinestone ball on a key chain of mine for a solid hour, completely entranced by the magnified effects of its reflections. His wife and I, unable to see what he did, found it all pretty tiresome.

Before I knew for sure about this lawyer's marijuana kick, I invited him to an ESP development meeting at my home. And there he sat—contributing nothing but his presence. There was none of the scintillating conversation usual when a group of my friends gets together. In fact, everyone else's enthusiasm was dampened by the uncommunicative lump who sat in our midst. Not realizing he was high, they just thought he was stupid. And he had nothing of interest to report after our meditation period, when most of the others had an ESP experience or two. Apparently his pictures had no psychical significance.

After this man's marriage broke up, I think he gave up smoking. At least, the last time I saw him he told me he had begun to realize what unproductive evenings he had been contributing to his wife's existence, and he declared he was breaking away from his peculiar pastime. As I write this, I can't help but wonder, however, if it is any worse to spend your evenings glued to your own inner visions than to a television box, or even a movie screen. Are we becoming a nation of picture watchers, of one kind or another?

I think it is this inner orientation of drug takers that bothers me more than anything else about them. Because it makes communication with them almost impossible. And this makes them hopelessly dull. The drugs have created in them a false illusion of profundity so that they think whatever they say is very wise, although it is seldom more than platitudes or repetitive phrases.

Drug users seem to become less involved in new ideas, or any of the exciting challenges of life. I am terribly glad it is not as popular a pastime now as it was for a while. The conversation level has risen, at least.

Prominent hallucinogenic drug researcher Dr. Reese Jones of the Langley Porter Neuropsychiatric Institute in San Francisco says regular users tell him they don't worry as much, but they don't think as well or as fast. If they get on hashish, which many marijuana users eventually do, it is considerably worse. Hash contains perhaps ten times as much tetrahydrocannabinol as pot, and that makes the problems with it more complicated.

"We tried hash out on fifteen subjects," said Dr. Jones. "They just sit there and stare. One subject had a paranoid delusion lasting three hours. In heavy dosage, marijuana has the same effect as hashish."

That is my main observation of habitual users—they are so apathetic. Because of my varied interests, I have a number of drug takers in my acquaintance, although most of my older friends and contemporaries are typical squares. But in 1968 I spent a most eventful three days with a group of hippie witches at the Yorkville Village in Toronto, which gave me an excellent opportunity to observe them in their native habitat.

Many in the hippie culture in those days were into witchcraft. It was even big in colleges then. Today I understand the college kids have passed it by and it is the high school students who have taken it up. I believe it is a transient fad with them and am not distressed about it, unless they become too involved with drugs because of it.

Witches are big on psychedelic drugs, and they are big on magic, and sometimes magic can get out of hand. Dr. Tart asked the marijuana-using students he polled to describe examples of magical operations. One answered: "I believe that magic is just 'doing' on a higher level of awareness. It is 'magic' to the spectator who does not expect or understand it. I have to be very stoned in order to be able to concentrate and flow at the same time to a sufficient degree to perform magic. 'Magic' tricks can be very beautiful, also astonishing. Maybe dangerous, too."

The dangers would involve black magic more than white, and,

fortunately, my friends were white witches, although some were changing over from black to white and regaled me with harrowing stories. I believe that in this change-over they were truly seeking an enlightening way of life. They were sweet kids, and apparently harmless—except to themselves. But if you mess around consistently with hash, grass, meth, and (if you are completely indifferent to your ultimate welfare) acid, you cannot be in any kind of really good shape. These young people were stoned most of the time. If nothing else, it robbed them of their youth. Youth should be a time of pep and vigor and enthusiasm. These people just sat around on the floor, leaning their backs against the walls or the furniture, and stared into space . . . hour after hour.

When they talked, if they talked, they expressed themselves as loving others—all mankind, to be exact—but they could not have loved themselves because they were all either mildly stoned or pretty well wiped out of their minds, and they lived that way. Vacant-minded and glassy-eyed, they wandered around Toronto's Yorkville Village during the day, hobnobbing with one another. Few of them had jobs. They admitted to begging whenever possible, stealing when necessary, and working only as a last resort. Living off welfare, whenever that could be finagled, was the height of achievement. One boy was pointed out to me as someone I should be delighted with because he had read one of my books—which he had stolen from a bookstore. Another admitted to being a professional panhandler. He and the girl with whom he lived cleared sometimes as much as $20 a day panhandling, and they were very proud of it.

The stories these young people told me about some of their ESP and out-of-body experiences while tripping intrigued me very much, however. Out-of-body travel is that curious phenomenon that occurs to so many people when they actually feel their consciousness leave their bodies and travel away somewhere else. An out-of-body experience (or OOBE) is not dreaming, daydreaming, or wishful thinking. One actually sees his body lying on his bed, while his consciousness is up at the ceiling, and then it may travel far afield. Then you are conscious, but at a different location from your body. There have been numerous cases where persons having astral projections (as this phenomenon is also called) have been seen somewhere else at the time. This is known as bilocation, or being two places at once, and Paulie seems definitely to have had this experience. Also, persons who have astral traveling abilities are sometimes able to bring back from their trips testimony about where they have been —knowledge they would have no normal way of gaining.

Charles Tart has an example of this sort of thing. A twenty-nine-year-old electronics technician said: "It occurred one noon hour where I work. I was meditating when I perceived that I was looking down on myself, then looking at the roof of the buildings. The ground passed under as if I was flying, it became a blur, then blue, then land again. I then found myself in a Lapp hut with an old shaman who was an old woman. She was brewing a tea of bird twigs and mumbling. The return was instantaneous. Someone at work shook my shoulder and I was back. At the time I did not know she was a Lapp. This came out after I described the kit and costume to my wife, who is Scandinavian. We later researched it in several picture books on the Lapp culture."

When my witch bunch told of their out-of-body travels I tried to get any evidence possible to verify their stories. I was successful, oddly enough, for those giving independent testimony backed each other up.

Cholly had a drug freakout a few weeks before I met her, and while she was in the hospital recovering J.D. came up to visit her.

"It was Friday," she told me, "and I'm usually down at the Village Fridays because that's when everybody goes there. I did so want to go with J.D. when he left, but of course I knew I couldn't leave the hospital. I turned on my radio after he went, but I didn't really listen to it. I leaned out the window and let my mind wander, following J.D. as he went toward the Village. Then, all of a sudden, I *was* behind him . . . my mind, my consciousness, was there. I followed him all down the Strip, knew when he ran into Paulie, and then saw the other people they met as they walked along. Even though my body was back there in the hospital, I was in Yorkville Village. Then the phone rang and I snapped out of it and was back in the hospital."

Cholly's story was confirmed by Paulie. "I was with J.D. at the time. Suddenly I told him there was an entity following us. I probed it."

I asked him what he meant by "probing it."

"Well, like I tried to get with it telepathically. I couldn't tell who it was, but I knew it wasn't an evil entity and that it was following J.D., not me. Then J.D. probed and he found out the same thing. He didn't know who it was, but it's a good thing he wasn't with another chick."

J.D. told me he also recalled the incident. "After Paulie said he thought someone was behind us, I probed it and felt its presence, too," he said. "When we later found out it was Cholly, she told us where we had been and who we had talked to and it was just like she said."

Paulie's first OOBE was not verifiable, but it conformed to the pattern. He said: "I was in my own place about a mile from Yorkville Village, completely wiped out of my mind. I was lying on my bed all alone, just lying there thinking. I really wanted to go down to the Village, but I couldn't quite move my body because I was so stoned. Yet somehow I got up, got my clothes on, turned out the lights, locked my door, and went downstairs. I locked the outside door and started walking to the Village. I didn't realize I was astrally projecting. I just thought I was walking normally. I couldn't hear anything but I thought it was because of the drug— I was really spaced. Cars went by, people passed me, talking, and I didn't hear a thing. Someone almost walked through me and didn't see me. When I got to the Village I started talking but nobody could see me or hear me. I began to think something was wrong, and then I had a sudden urge to go back. So I started walking home. I did it just as thoroughly as I had come out. When I got back to my place I unlocked the door, went up to my room, opened the door, then I got the shock of my life because I saw myself lying there on the bed. And then just like that! I ended back in my body."

Paulie had another story to tell me that was verified by several people whose testimony I got on my tape recorder. Michael was the one who told me the original story. He said, "About a month ago, Paulie and I went up to Ottawa together. I came into the place where we were staying one night about midnight and found him lying on the bed with something like a slight heart attack. He told me he had been thinking really hard about being in Toronto because he wished so to be back there. Then he had fallen asleep and waked up with this feeling like a heart attack. As soon as we got back to Toronto the next day, the guy we lived with said Paulie had been seen walking around the Village the night before. We thought maybe this was probably someone who looked like him [Paulie was a very distinctive-looking person in the hippie era because he was clean-shaven, wore his hair cut quite short, and always sported a ring in one ear]. But then we ran into others who knew him and they said they'd seen him too."

I asked Michael what time it was when they saw him.

"It was about midnight. The same time it happened up in Ottawa."

Incidentally, I think I should mention that there have been a few instances where one who had an out-of-body experience had such difficulty returning to his body that the symptoms have been described as similar to heart attacks. Maybe that is what happened to Paulie.

When I checked on Michael's story, a youth named Reb told me, "Paulie came up to my house, looking for Cicero and Oliver."

"Did you talk to him?" I asked. He nodded.

"What did he say?"

"He said he was looking for Cicero and Oliver. When I said they weren't there we exchanged a few pleasantries and he left."

"Do you remember when this was?" I asked Reb.

"No, I'm a bit stoned right now. I'm sorry. I couldn't say when it was. But I recall seeing him the next day or so and he mentioned he'd just gotten back from Ottawa. I said, 'Well, really. What were you doing at my house then?' "

I also talked to a fellow known as Teach because he had once been a teacher and to a man named Tom. They both confirmed this. It seems that it had become a bit of local folklore by that time because so many people had all said they saw Paulie on that night when he was in Ottawa.

Really, the more I saw of those young people of that era, the sorrier I was for them. I couldn't help but compare them with the youth of former days, when life was full of excitement. In olden times young men could rush out and slay dragons, or at least go off into the wilderness with gun and sword to find adventure. Today the most exciting thing they can do is to smoke a cigarette. It is like taking a dare or playing Russian roulette: if it is a straight cigarette, they are flouting the chance of eventually getting lung cancer; if they smoke grass they may be forming habit patterns of a destructive nature. I do not mean that marijuana is habit-forming—I mean that smokers of it form bad habits. They frequently begin to keep company with habitual trippers, users, and pushers, and there is nothing particularly choice about that. If they manage to keep from getting hooked on heroin, they still may become addicted to a drug-oriented way of life. If what I saw in Toronto was typical of that, I must say it was most uninspiring.

Even though I'm all for liberating women in many ways, I think it was nicer back in the days when a young man could swashbuckle a bit and girls were the object of romantic veneration. It's no wonder so many today are seeking their motivation in drugs and magic. What else exciting is left for them? In an unfortunately creepy way, they are trying to put some mystery and enchantment back into their lives.

Successful visionary experiences with psychedelics give some people the feeling they desire of high adventure. Yet the search for them can lead to bad trips, as I can attest personally. Once, long before it was illegal, and also before it was generally known how dangerous it was, I took LSD. I had come under the influence of several persons who were convinced from their own results that if one took the hallucinogen under proper conditions he could have a truly awareness-expanding experience that would make him understand God better. So with this as my stated goal, I accepted one of two capsules of acid a friend had gotten from a pusher in Los Angeles. He had such a mind-blowing experience with his that he insisted I share it, and I was willing. I left for Hawaii a short time later, and there I took it, under the guidance of a doctor who was experienced at handling psychedelic drugs.

My reaction to many things, unfortunately, is nausea. Although I love boating, and driving my car on curvy mountain roads, I often become seasick or carsick. So I also got acid-sick, almost from the moment I swallowed the capsule with hot tea. I remained that way the entire morning, nearly on the verge of throwing up every time I was conscious. The pusher's dose may have been right for the size of a man, but it was too strong for a woman. This, I now realize, is another of the main problems of drug taking. You don't know the proper dosage for your constitution, or for your brain either, for that matter.

Besides keeping me physically miserable, the LSD showed me colorful pictures, and helped me understand the mind of a snake, but nothing more. I had read Adelle Davis's *Exploring Inner Space,* written under the pseudonym "Jane Dunlap," and had been intrigued by the fact that she had experienced a whole evolutionary cycle during her LSD trip. Being interested in evolution, I now followed her route in a return to my origins; but nothing God-revealing occurred to me at all. I lived in a world of brilliant visual imagery for a time, consorting with brontosauruses and ichthyosaurs, and then I returned to the world of the present . . . and to nausea. It was as if there were different layers of consciousness, and when I was in the prehistoric world I was completely oblivious to anything else. Then I would fight my way up through the layers of consciousness back to reality and the horror of nausea. Each time I came back to myself and realized what was going on I'd implore my doctor, "Promise I won't stay this way. I'm completely insane. It's interesting to look at the pictures, but I'd rather die than have to live like this. Are you *sure* I'll come out of it?" He would reassure me, and then I'd submerge again, my mentality completely fusing into the pictures of prehistoric monsters appearing on my visual screen.

Once when I became conscious briefly and thought about what had been occurring, I said to myself, "All I'm doing is following Adelle Davis's route, exactly as she wrote about it. Bet I'll even meet that white cobra she saw." Never having been in the least enamored of snakes, I added, "Hope it doesn't take me over as it did her." But it did, immediately afterward. I identified with it in order to understand how it feels being a snake. It wasn't too bad, actually. It was a nice well-meaning white cobra who tried to convince me that snakes were good types after all.

The next time I surfaced, without the usual collywobbles I

might have had after an encounter with a snake, I began to be depressed because I wasn't having a God experience. All I was doing was traveling this evolutionary route I was familiar with, not showing any originality of my own and definitely not soaring to any ethereal heights.

"What's wrong with me?" I wondered. "Others reach out in spirit and have beautiful mystical experiences. What is going on here is nothing more than a bunch of pictures out of any movie." Was my soul too low-caliber to deserve the illumination I had expected? Obviously. I was a person of such negative spiritual values that I was not worthy of anything better. All that I was revealing about myself was trash, I reasoned. The next time I submerged, convinced by my soul searching of my innermost being that I had disclosed nothing of worth there, all the pictures became tinselly and tawdry, the colors neon-signish, fluorescent, and garish.

At the next surfacing, the picture show was over, having obviously—to me then, in my less rational state—performed its function of revealing me for what I truly was . . . nothing. The depression was complete, and it stayed with me much of the time for the next three months! During the afternoon the doctor and another couple took me to the beach. I talked constantly all the way there, trying to describe my experiences in as good a light as possible. Positive that my companions were judging me as shrewish and cheap, it seemed necessary to justify myself for having such a bad trip. Yet also, on a deeper level, I was perceptively aware that they were sorry for me because I hadn't been worthy of better.

It is true, as I said in *Confessions of a Psychic* (Macmillan, 1971) that those who have had illumination or any deeply spiritually enlightening experiences always and forever afterward tend to be a bit patronizing toward those who have not. I am sure that the more highly developed souls do not mean to, but most of them let their consciousness of superiority stick out all over them. Even though my spiritually enlightened doctor friend was trying to hide this now, I was definitely sensing it in him, for my acid trip made me able to see into the minds of those about me to an unusually perceptive degree all that day. I knew what the people

with me were thinking, and their actions always revealed that I
had been right.

At the beach I lay on the sand all afternoon, looking at pictures
of Chinese dragons in the wispy clouds, totally oblivious to the
effects of the sun, which caused an uncomfortable burn by evening. I was taken to dinner at a cafeteria, but I told the doctor
that people must think he had his moronic daughter out with him.
Indeed, that is exactly how it felt. Colorful pictures appeared in
my mind again at bedtime; but only a hangover was evident the
next morning, as if from some big alcoholic binge.

As I said, this depression stayed with me for months. I had
gone to Hawaii a well-adjusted individual, happy in my work,
loving the traveling and meeting people, completely at home in
my universe. It is to be wondered whether the despondency
would ever have been thrown off if I had been less harmonious at
the time of taking the drug. What if I had been a possibly neurotic teen-ager completely at odds with the world? Hospitals are
full of unfortunates who had just such bad trips and did not
readjust at all. Apparently for everyone who has a beautiful experience there is another who reacts negatively. I can only thank
God that I came out of it sane, for I now know the horrors of insanity.

Life was hardly worth living in that state of miserable depression, and I fought it all winter, mulling my situation over and
over. I had worked for many years to attain the state of well-
being I had when I went to Hawaii. I'd been practicing positive
thinking and had worked long and hard for spiritual enlightenment; surely I had deserved some kind of inspirational experience. Yet all that had resulted was this feeling of complete unwor-
thiness and inadequacy. So what if I had learned how it feels to
be a snake? That was hardly compensation for all the misery afterward. I was evidently not a person of character, after all, or
something better would have occurred when the opportunity
came to expand my awareness into illumination.

In March 1966 I was in Los Angeles, where I made a number of
personal appearances publicizing a new book; and on a radio program I finally achieved the insight that pulled me out of my
depression. On KABC Paul Condylis was discussing with me

what I had learned from personal experimentation with acid—
how dangerous to one's morale it might be—when suddenly it
dawned on me that having the bad trip was the right thing to
have happened to me, the only possible perspective for me to
have attained! What if mine had been the kind of rewarding experience Aldous Huxley had! I'd undoubtedly have written and
talked persuasively about it, and eventually might have had many
acid heads on my conscience. To think that it might have been
possible for even one or two young people to have started on the
dangerous path because of anything I might have said or written
was spine-chilling. I thanked God for my bad trip! And I went
away from there with my old personality reinstated, relinquishing
the mystical experiences to those who could acquire them legit-
imately without the use of drugs.

11

The Consolidated Athletic Commission

BOB BRIER

The tiny football players on the table top had become more real than reality, and some of them were obviously better performers than others. Could this be psychokinesis (PK), an example of mind over matter? More and more, the performances of these miniature players became the all-consuming passion of one man and his friends. Their "Consolidated Athletic Commission" took over where real life left off. Dr. Brier is professor of philosophy at C. W. Post College, Long Island, New York, and a former researcher of the Institute for Parapsychology, Foundation for Research on the Nature of Man, Durham, North Carolina. His most recent book, Precognition and the Philosophy of Science, *deals with the nature of reality.*

I own one of the only two complete sets of the *Sportrecord* in the world. (Richard Wyszynski owns the other.) It is far from my most prized possession, but I *have* kept them for over eight years and never considered throwing them out the various times I moved. In some way they are a reminder—a monument to what can happen when reason ends and the occult takes over.

Every parapsychologist has his collection of stories about the crazies—people who are in telepathic communication with Venus; ancient Egyptians who feel out of place living in Brooklyn; or widows and widowers who have to ask their deceased spouses for advice before making any important decisions. I am no different. When I joined the research staff of the Institute for Parapsychology in Durham, North Carolina, I began to meet people who upon later reflection seemed more fictional than real. I tried to reassure the engineer from Canada that his neighbors were not trying to control him telepathically; I attempted to convince the young high school student that since he believed in God it was unlikely that Satan would possess his body. Usually meetings with such people are brief and don't go beyond the initial contact. I have been in contact with Richard Wyszynski for the eight years since he first wrote for help. His story is not yet complete and by telling it now, I hope to make the ending somewhat happier than it might be otherwise.

When I first joined the Institute for Parapsychology I was completing my Ph.D. and had little experience in the field. Thus I was low man on the totem pole and frequently got the job of answering Dr. Rhine's crank mail. This is how I came to read Wyszynski's first letter, which was dated June 22, 1967. He wrote of his "activities of seventeen years past." They had begun when "in high school I found that I had neither physique nor skill to engage in the sports which attracted me." As a "compensation, perhaps," Wyszynski began "playing table-top games based on real-life sports; miniature football, miniature baseball, basketball and hockey." In the "four to five years that ensued after the inception of this games-playing cosmos," he and his friends developed a "near-fanatical zeal and fascination with the realistic transposition of 'real life' techniques, skills and emotions." Their "world of indulgent recreation took on startling structure." The letter continued: "Regulated play was established via league scheduling and rules, and each seasonal sport overlapped into another, so that a year-round basis was established. Things were generally run by me with the consultation of my friend/participants but a fictional governing body called the Consolidated Athletic Commission was given authority. A regular newspaper, which was to run fifty-four issues, diligently covered and reported (as if they were 'real') every single event.

"In order to heighten the statistical detail and interest, I decided to assign identities to each of the eleven (in football) figures which constituted my team on the table-top field. I chose real personages, usually older male friends whose skill or spirit I had admired. Then we began to keep statistical tab on every identity who participated on the teams, as if they were real: yards gained rushing, quarterback percentages, scoring averages . . . exactly as if you were reading the sports section of a real cosmopolitan newspaper. This carried over to all sports, and I noticed that putting together a batting order from a list of assigned identities involved taking into serious consideration the regular and past performances of each individual player as faithfully reported in previous statistics. It was as if each plastic or wooden figure had managed to really assume a set of performing characteristics compatible with the personality assigned to it, and began to DEVELOP as a full-fledged identity with appreciable idiosyncrasies, altho it was MY one hand (and mind) that batted for each person. I could not explain how one player (A) would hit .345 (with a predilection for left field and a mid-season batting slump) while another (B) would never top .280 but was a marvelous fielder. In order to cope with these problems of miniature discernment I assigned another personage to MANAGE the team, a non-player, to whose sageness I surrendered my whole body, as if it were a physical planchette on a ouija athletic board.

"The results were fascinating. The games we had eventually selected were extremely well made and true to life, so much so that they failed on the commercial market and are no longer available. In addition to all these psychic multi-identity exertions, I have reason to believe that we may have been on the verge of psychokinesis on many occasions . . .

"After a while we began voting for Most Valuable (Assigned Identity) Player of the Year, (Psychic) Coach of the Year . . . threw post-season banquets and awarded trophies. I wore my team's name on my (real life) jacket and found myself more in this fantasy world than in the real life one . . .

"This all ended sixteen years ago and I have lost personal contact with most of these cosmic charter members, tho I still cherish them as friends as an ace cherishes his old WW I buddy pilots . . . I couldn't help but envision how intensely life could again be if some foundation were to sponsor my old colleagues and I in a survey—experiment supervised, say, by your department for whatever benefit it may possibly have toward your own research and inquiry . . .

"In any case, I would welcome your comments and reactions to what I have outlined herein and assure you that I am always ready to present you with further data and whatever service it is in my power to provide."

I was intrigued by the letter. True, it did seem as if the writer had the reality of the miniature game world confused with life-sized reality; true, he did sign his name as Acting Director of the Consolidated Athletic Commission; and he did wear a real-life jacket with the name of his miniature team on the back, but he was coherent. The first step was to see if his miniature players really were behaving as if animated by some occult force, or whether Wyszynski were merely deluding himself.

I wrote and asked him to send the set of *Sportrecord* which chronicled the miniature league's activities. My intention was to see if the results reported were detailed enough for me to do a statistical analysis. Let's say a cardboard figure in a football game is named Jimmy Brown and whenever he is the ball carrier the number of yards he gains depends upon the throw of a pair of dice. It would be interesting if the records showed that game after game Jimmy Brown averaged more yards per carry than the other players. If it is "merely a game" and only the natural laws of our universe are operating, then there is no reason why over several years one cardboard figure named Jimmy Brown should do better than any other cardboard figure who has been assigned a different name.

After a month's wait, the fifty-four issues of *Sportrecord* arrived. Issue No. 1 was a small booklet made of four typed sheets and contained the results of the 1948 basketball season. All the participants' names were listed with the number of points their teams scored during the season. On top of the list was the entry: Wyszynski, Richard . . . 4602. The second-place finisher had 2155. A story "Richard W. Holds First Place with Amazing Count of Four Thousand Points!" told of the season's events.

The later issues were far more detailed and covered baseball, football, basketball, and hockey and had statistical summaries of all the games. I noticed that these later issues of *Sportrecord* more and more mixed life-sized with miniature reality. Right next to the exploits of the Zolons and Juggernauts, the real-life death of Babe Ruth was reported. There were even contests which imaginary readers could enter. The total commitment to these games by Richard Wyszynski was becoming evident.

I quickly scanned the records to see if there really was a player or team that was winning more than chance would allow. The headline of issue No. 47 caught my eye: OWLS FINISH 2ND UNBEATEN SEASON 110–104. For a miniature basketball team to go two seasons of play without losing was surprising. The success was attributed to Herb Savage, their coach, but this couldn't be the whole story. Something interesting was going on.

I did a detailed analysis of all the *Sportrecords*, looking for players who were more consistent than they should have been. They were there. There were baseball players who were consistent .300 hitters and quarterbacks who were great passers. Indeed, reading the five-year production of *Sportrecord*, I began to know the cardboard players' preferences—whether they hit to left or right field, whether with third down and five yards to go a given quarterback could be expected to complete a pass or have it intercepted. There was no question about it, the players were assuming the identities assigned to them by their life-sized manipulators.

It was possible that Wyszynski and his friends were using psychokinesis (PK for short)—mind over matter—to affect the fall of the dice in the games. Thus a passer who was expected to complete a pass might be successful because his manipulator used PK when throwing the dice to cause a high number so the pass would be complete and a considerable number of yards gained. This PK explanation was a parapsychological one, one which phrased an answer to what was going on in terms of the laboratory. I suggested to Wyszynski that he do some simple dice tests. He could throw the dice and wish for ones, twos, threes, etc. to come up and see just what his PK abilities, and those of his friends, were. I received a prompt reply. He wasn't interested in games! He had no desire to participate in activities that were divorced from reality. What he really wanted was for some foundation to support the reestablishment of league play, which had been interrupted for years because some of the participants had gotten married and moved away. This was not possible and we did not write to each other for a few years.

Then I received a note from him. He would be in Durham for a few days with a show in which he was playing. (He is a musician.) We set up a meeting.

Richard was pretty much as expected. He was in his thirties, slightly short, with horn-rimmed glasses. He looked like a man who as a child was a sports fanatic but never actually participated in sports. He was clearly hooked on his miniature games and the mysterious power that controlled the diminutive players. His music was merely a means of sustaining his body, so that all his energies could be channeled into the Consolidated Athletic Commission. It was only on the ball fields that he was in touch with reality; this was *his* world.

When I dropped him off at his hotel I felt sad, but not particularly for Richard, just sad. He wasn't the pathetic lunatic that I feared he might be. He was a warrior in the sense of Carlos Castaneda's Don Juan. Here was a man doing battle with reality itself, and we both knew that there was little help I could give him.

Again a few years lapsed, but I had not forgotten Richard Wyszynski and his miniature world. One Sunday morning I was reading the New York *Times Book Review* section when he was brought suddenly to mind. There was a review of a book entitled *The Universal Baseball Association: J. Henry Waugh, Prop.* The book was the story of a solitary participant in a miniature baseball game who became "too" involved. The author was Robert Coover and it immediately occurred to me that Coover might be Wyszynski and the Universal Baseball Association a cloak for the Consolidated Athletic Commission. I wrote to Richard. No, he wasn't the author but had read the book. It caused us both to wonder how many more like him there were out there; it was as if we were now sure that there was life on other planets and the question was, How much? With renewed vigor, Richard began making plans for the next season's play.

It was with great pleasure that I received No. 57 of the *Sport-*

record a few months ago. It has come a long way since issue No.
1. This issue is over one hundred pages and contains photographs
(One caption of a game photo reads: Record-breaking attend-
ance [3 including photographer] includes many well-known personages.) and biographical information on the participants. Like
the previous issues, it contains the details of the season's play—
and I was saddened to learn of the death of Herb Savage, the
Owls' great coach—but there was a definite change in the editor's
outlook. After devoting twenty years of one's life to miniature
sports it is difficult merely to report the results. It is time for
reflection and the latest *Sportrecord* contains much cosmic com-
mentary.

"The distraction of having to make a living separate from football is insidiously responsible for the lack of concentration necessary to field a winning team. The entire league suffers from it, and
there is no solution except to isolate yourself from the make-
believe world of fiscality into the real world of fantasy, at least for
short periods of time when you challenge an opponent to a six-
hour broadside. Think about your unemployment, your income
tax, your auto repairs, your doctor bills . . . and you're gone; the
enemy has crashed through your line and buried you. The only
thing to do is remember your TRUE identity—a capable and
dignified member of the existential elite—and never let the dung
of the socioeconomic perversion called civilization touch you. As
St. Paul said, They call us deceivers, and we tell the truth. . . ."—
Sportrecord Vol. 57, p. 115.

Wyszynski is a man whose everyday reality is what other people call fantasy. He has acknowledged and accepted the existence
of occult powers and they have consumed him. There are probably others who, like Richard Wyszynski, have participated in
miniature games and have found themselves drawn into a separate reality. I suggest they direct all inquiries to:

> Richard C. Wyszynski, Director
> Consolidated Athletic Commission
> 851 North Leavitt Street
> Chicago, Illinois 60622

12

Reincarnation as Alibi

CAROLEE COLLINS

*Is reincarnation good for you? The author expresses doubts about
this Eastern concept that is currently finding increasing numbers
of believers in the West, notably the United States. Ms. Collins
cites several cases that suggest reincarnation to be a convenient
way to avoid action and responsibility, and even a means of ra-
tionalizing adultery by references to marriages in many previous
incarnations.*

*Experienced and sophisticated reincarnationists will agree with
this. New enthusiasts may not.*

Karen, a pretty young blonde, was quite the most glamorous
woman in the congregation of a Spiritualist church in a northwest-
ern city. She also had the biggest smile on her face. Some of the
other young wives in the rather compact group were much less
happy. One or two, in fact, looked desperately sad. There was a
reason. In the closed sessions with the medium, available only to
the inner circle of members, a rather curious philosophy was
taught. Reincarnation, naturally, because that's the in thing; but
reincarnation with an interesting twist. The "great master teachers" who supposedly spoke through the allegedly entranced medium maintained that members of this entire inner group were
over the centuries constantly reincarnating into different rela-

tionships with each other. Why they might not have felt it more
stimulating to interrelate with new people occasionally was not
explained. Indeed, it was probably not even questioned, since the
word of these "great masters" was taken as law in that circle. And
so each of them in turn had been mother, father, sister, brother,
aunt or uncle, wife or husband, to all the others. And because
Karen had at one time or another been legally wed to each of the
men in the congregation, no one would dare to castigate her if she
now slept with most of the good-looking ones. The wives, and
Karen's husband, were told that it was their karma to endure
whatever life handed them, and if the prettiest girl in the crowd
got most of the goodies, that was their tough luck.

As times changed and new members joined the group and old
ones managed to tear themselves away, this mode of conduct was
somewhat altered. Or maybe it was just that the injured spouses
finally became aware of what they had been suckered into; but
anyway, the last time I saw Karen she was not as closely involved
with the church as she had been in the past.

This is just one example of how an uncritical belief in reincarnation may mess up lives. My purpose here is to mention a few
such instances as warning to those who newly accept this doctrine
without thinking about some of its possible pitfalls.

Reincarnation, of course, is the philosophy of rebirth. It is of
ancient Oriental origin, but has in recent years become exceedingly popular among occultists in the West as well. It forms an
important principle in the oldest surviving religion in the world—
Hinduism—whose origins can be traced back to 4000 B.C., and it is
a central part of the doctrines of Buddhism. Reincarnation was
well known in ancient Egypt and was taught by several Greek
philosophers such as Empedocles and Pythagoras. This philosophy presents the idea of a long succession of lives on earth for
every soul. Each life is thus like a day in the school of experience,
presenting new lessons through which the individual may develop his capacities, grow in wisdom, and eventually reach spiritual maturity. After that, depending on which concept of rebirth
he accepts, he may unite with Brahman, the World Spirit, and
thereby win salvation from the necessity of further rebirth, or, as
a Buddhist, culminate his long chain of lives at the moment when

he realizes the nirvana state—the extinction of his own ego. It is quite possible for the Westerner to combine several of the Oriental concepts in his philosophy. Rarely in America is the Hindu "Wheel of Life" accepted, where the individual believes he must live thousands of lifetimes almost interminably until he learns the secret of getting off the spinning wheel. Western minds prefer the thought that within five or six lifetimes at the most we may learn the secret of stopping the rebirth pattern.

As described by Eugene S. Rawls in *Yoga Philosophy for Americans*, an unpublished manuscript, the nirvana state is one of enlightenment and liberation. It is not a state of personal unawareness, as some, thinking "with a limited frightened finite mind," profess. He says that instead there is the flooding of the mind and being with supreme eternal consciousness. "The old, logic-bound man is dead. In his place is a supreme man, enlightened and complete. The river has reached the ocean and become one with it. The dewdrop has merged into the shining sea."

"Doesn't this sound great?" asks Susy Smith in *Reincarnation for the Millions*. "And poetic?" But too many others have indicated that the nirvana state is one of a melding into the universal unconsciousness, which rather tends to give her pause. ". . . it worries this logic-bound wretch that without my frightened finite little old mind to accompany me I might not know it when my dewdrop merges with the shining sea. I, Susy Smith (in a highly perfected state, of course), want to be there when it happens and know what is going on!!! Am I an egomaniac or something?"

Allan Kardec, the Frenchman whose concepts of Spiritism, with an attending philosophy of reincarnation, are popular in Brazil, says in *The Spirits' Book* that no matter whether or not one wants to be reborn, he will have to anyway. In vain you may rebel against the necessity to be reborn again, like a child refusing to go to school, or a condemned criminal resisting prison. You will have to submit to your fate, no matter how unwilling you are. Kardec adds that this pattern might not be so bad, after all, for conditions in your next incarnation depend upon yourselves now; and by your actions in your present life you might make your next one almost endurable.

Commenting on this, Susy Smith presents a rather startling picture of herself: "Even with Kardec's reassurances, I can see myself hanging onto the edge of the etheric, kicking and fighting like a petulant child, and absolutely refusing to come back into another body. I'll set up such a fuss as Heaven never heard, before I'll come back again and go through all the hell on earth I've had to endure this time. Oh, dear, probably just by having such naughty thoughts I'm ruining my chances for a better life experience next time round."

Advanced reincarnationists know that the whole point is so to live your life now that you won't have to hang on and cry to keep from coming back. You should become so enlightened in this lifetime that there is no question of your having to return to earth ever again.

A few pointers here may help to guard against extremes and errors:

Don't become smug about your philosophy. The seekers for improvement of their lives are usually wonderful people, but those who are new at reincarnation may easily become proselytizers. They are so "gung ho" on it they attempt to convert everyone they meet, and they also, unfortunately, sometimes look down on those who are not so wise as they.

A standard reply heard by countless people who have admitted that they do not like the idea of rebirth is, "Well, when you are ready . . ." This implies that you will accept reincarnation as the correct answer to life's mysteries when you have advanced to the stage they are in. It also obviously says something unflattering about the persons who make the statement, and it is something they really should not want revealed. It says that they believe themselves to *be* ready, having advanced spiritually more than you have. Wasn't it Gilbert K. Chesterton who suggested that pride in the fact that you are not proud is self-defeating?

Also revealing their spiritual pride are those who believe they are at the top of the heap. They know from some source—personal revelation, readings from a psychic, or whatever—that they have achieved a point in their own development where they will not have to live any more lives on earth after this one. Just to believe that about yourself shows an arrogance that could not exist in any person who had actually reached such a highly developed state.

Yet there are many who are completely convinced they have achieved this height of advancement who are actually so boastful of it that they must really be on a lower rung of the ladder instead.

Gina Cerminara, in *Many Lives, Many Loves,* mentions a woman who claims to be so spiritually advanced that she will never have to live another life on earth, and yet she will take a kitten out and leave it along a highway to be killed just because she doesn't want to bother raising it. You can imagine what Dr. Cerminara, an ardent cat lover and reincarnationist, thinks of such cruelty!

We all know the woman who has been Cleopatra. This has become an inside joke even among reincarnationists. A friend of mine overheard two men talking, one of whom said he had been George Washington. The other replied indignantly, "That is impossible, because *I* was George Washington!"

And yet one cannot help but be sorry for people who take seriously their past lives as important people. It is not funny when a girl is put into New York's Bellevue Hospital because of losing touch with reality over such a belief. A young woman in New York got up at a meeting and announced, "It has been revealed to me psychically that I was Mary Magdalene." She was quite humble about it, but began to live her role so intensely that she had to spend several months in the mental institution. Finally a friend visited her and told her a true story. Once, years before, during Edgar Cayce's lifetime, she had visited the Cayce Foundation at Virginia Beach and met a woman who was glowing with joy because she had just been told by Cayce that *she* had been Mary Magdalene. Somehow, learning that the role of Mary was already taken cleared the girl's befuddled mind, and she was soon released from the hospital. If she hadn't been so gullible, she would not have had to undergo the experience in the first place.

Reincarnationist-psychic Marshall Lever says in his *Newsletter* of September 1974: "We have had many people tell us that they have been Julius Caesar . . . St. Francis . . . Mary, mother of Jesus . . . Alexander the Great and a myriad of other famous people of the past. Reincarnation is to help you step above weaknesses of the past, not to glorify them. There are many that

we want to identify with because of their inspiring life . . . The
St. Francises and the Marys probably did not need to return. It is
not who you were, but what you are now. A spirit contact that
dwells on who you were of importance should be viewed as a
name dropper, not a reliable contact. If a spirit contact tells you,
by name, who you were, and you are impressed, ask yourself,
'Why am I what I am now?' " And, we could add, also ask yourself, "Why am I impressed? How much ego need do I have?"

If you have been in the psychic field any length of time you
have probably learned not to be dogmatic about anything, and
most particularly not to take anything anyone tells you as gospel.
Those who are strongly opinionated are not to be trusted, because
they seldom know what they are talking about. And, although
much that is wise and evidential has come from the Ouija board
and automatic writing and mediums and sensitives and psychics,
it is certainly not wise to follow their advice uncritically.

Olga Worrall, the Baltimore healer-sensitive, tells of a couple
who ruined the lives of two families because of their easy acceptance of what they were told by a famous psychic. A heretofore
reasonably happily married man, father of several children, was
informed that he had been married in another life to an attractive
woman whom he met in the psychic's "clinic," and that they were
"soulmates" destined always to be together. The woman was
married and had a family; but the two left their spouses and
promptly set up housekeeping together—because it had been
legal in a previous existence and was their destiny! They might
have done this anyway, had they chanced to meet under other
circumstances, but perhaps not as blatantly and self-righteously.

Obviously, some people structure their lives around a belief in
reincarnation in ways that are self-destructive. A case in point is a
lower-caste native of India who lives in squalor and poverty
without rebelling, because he believes his present state is a kar-
mic penalty he must accept to expiate the sins of past lives. It
seems to me that the whole idea of reincarnation should, more
sensibly, be to better your life and make a serious attempt to
improve character so you won't have to come back again and do it
all over. Yet, some allow themselves to be dishonest, rude, and
promiscuous just because of their belief. They think, "Why not

have as much fun as I can now, for I have all eternity to keep doing it until I learn to do it right."

While some people actually find strength through the vicissitudes of their lives, by belief in reincarnation, others are kept from having proper compassion for those who are ill or handicapped or poor. They believe the state one is in is his karma and he obviously deserves it, or he wouldn't be in that fix.

I know a woman, a former Christian Scientist, who turned toward "advanced metaphysics" and became strong on reincarnation. Neither of her beliefs taught her any particular charity toward the handicapped. First she ascribed illness to "wrong thinking," and later to "karma." I have seen her avoid the sick, so she wouldn't be "contaminated" by them. Once she attended a dinner party with a woman on crutches in advanced stages of multiple sclerosis. She did nothing to help her in and out of the car, either coming or going to the party; and she almost totally ignored her during the meal.

Of course, this is an extreme case. And I am happy to relate that further spiritual growth has mellowed this woman quite a bit. But consider how it is done in much of India, even to this day: the poor and ill are supposed to have chosen their lot to learn from it, and so it is not up to you to thwart their karma by helping them. Charity is unnecessary, for the poor need to be poor in order to learn, and you would be circumventing their eternal design if you aided them. This may even extend to not rescuing someone from drowning, or not feeding one who is starving.

Reincarnation is such a popular belief today among New Age people in the West that one is hardly allowed to make a statement unfavorable to it. But no matter how good a concept it is, it is bound to have drawbacks for some people, and it can be misused if not understood properly. This is what is increasingly occurring as "just everybody" grabs at reincarnation as a philosophy that will explain life to them. It requires intelligent appraisal if one is to use its precepts wisely.

13

The Death
of the Teen-age "Witch"

PAUL LANGDON

In the midst of her twentieth-century life, the young girl confessed defiantly that she had been wedded to the devil. Her confessors became her torturers and killers, a man and a woman whom faith had led to delusions of their own role as a "Holy Family" that had been chosen to prepare the world for Armageddon.

The year was 1969, not 1596. The town was a citadel of modern civilization, not a medieval village. But a group had banded together to beat, and beat again, and to torture a bewildered, brainwashed young woman accused of witchcraft—until she died; and they now stood trial for the killing.

It took almost three years for the trial preparations at Zurich, Switzerland. She had died on May 14, 1966. Her name was Bernadette Hasler; she was 17 years old. The Hasler parents had turned their little girl over to the practitioners of a "Holy Family." This weird cult was directed by a defrocked and excommunicated South German priest, 61-year-old Josef Stocker, and his mistress, 54-year-old Magdalena Kohler.

The fate of Bernadette was merely the most extreme example of the religious fanaticism that held the cult together in a boiling cauldron of emotion. Their original "inspiration" had come from an obscure Carmelite nun, one Sister Stella, who claimed a "direct telephone to heaven." However, the Stocker-Kohler team found not only an outlet for its religiously-oriented sexual sadism within the cult, but also a means for demanding money and luxuries from its followers. The cult, with headquarters outside Zurich, had begun with the visions of the nun Stella in about 1959 in the German town of Singen in the Black Forest.

The nun, known as "Little Star" to her followers, had told Stocker and Kohler that they had been chosen to lead the survivors through a future Apocalypse. The couple later convinced their followers to stock the headquarters of the "Holy Family" with sacks of flour, sugar, hundreds of cans of food, and even a cow boarded with a nearby farmer.

Forced to flee Germany, Stocker and Kohler spent seven years on the Hasler farm, in hiding. Little Bernadette Hasler then lived a slave's existence, while being mentally and physically persecuted, largely by Magdalena Kohler. Over and over again, for months on end, the young girl was bullied into "confessing" her alleged dealings with the devil, her impure thoughts, her wicked desires. (The Haslers, over the years, spent 200,000 Swiss Francs —U.S. $46,000.00—on the two cult leaders.)

The type of religio-sexual confessions Stocker and Kohler forced from their followers is illustrated by the statistics in one written account: "I have taken communion improperly, 6,000 times; I have prayed wrongly 450 times; I have given 750 tongue kisses; 1,000 times have I undertaken the sexual act in my imagination."

Bernadette was forced by Mrs. Kohler to write detailed confessions covering 330 pages. The pathetic statements of the young girl reflected the sexual suggestions of her "Mother Confessor," rather than her own naïve imagination. She wrote, for instance, "I love the Devil. He is beautiful. He visits me nearly every night. He is much better than God. I would like to belong only to the Devil."

Such "confessions" then prompted Stocker, Kohler, and four members of their cult to beat the young girl with horsewhips and canes, "to drive the Devil out of her." According to one psychiatric authority during the Zurich trial, Professor Hans Binder, Bernadette had been driven into a veritable "sin mania," perhaps unable to differentiate between reality and the hallucinatory existence created by Stocker and Kohler. The psychiatrist noted that the cheerful child, given to fun and laughter, had turned into "a depressed creature," who saw her life as "a chain of sins."

As punishment for her "sinful life," the girl was not permitted to go for walks, had to give up her violin lessons and was not allowed to talk with other children. Her "Holy Parents" abused her with such epithets as "Satan's Mate" and "Devil's Whore." The Kohler woman (whose relationship with Stocker was supposed to be merely "spiritual," but who had given birth to a child) called Bernadette a "perverted piece" and a "lying swine."

But when Magdalena Kohler was asked, during the trial, whether she disliked Bernadette, she answered, "No." And when the president of the court asked why, then, she had cursed the girl, the answer was, "I merely loved the girl. I only cursed her because she had a pact with the Devil."

According to Dr. Binder's psychiatric findings, Magdalena had created such a world of delusion that she was "sincerely convinced she was only doing what God demanded. She had no idea that it was, in reality, her own unconscious, primitive self that prompted her gruesome actions against Bernadette." The emotional breaking point for the girl came, apparently, when Kohler refused Easter confession for her, one month before she was beaten to death. It was at this point, according to the psychiatric analysis, that Bernadette crossed the border into a hysteria of being possessed by the devil. It was then, in defiance of Stocker and Kohler and the God they allegedly represented, that Bernadette insisted on having a "pact with Satan." Having been refused the support of God, she turned to the devil for a Satanic counterpower. This, Professor Binder said, while obviously irrational, was the "logic of a defiant heart."

The charismatic power of Magdalena Kohler over members of the cult was illustrated, during the court hearings, by the case of one of her followers, 37-year-old Paul Barmettler. She had forbidden him to have sexual intercourse with his wife, and he complied. Together with his brothers, 46-year-old Hans and 41-year-old Heinrich, Barmettler participated in the maltreatment of

Bernadette that led to her death. A fourth cultist and torture participant was Emilio Bettio.

Barmettler paid the "Holy Family" 10 per cent of his income, took over the mortgage payments on the chalet in Ringwil, near Zurich, and—because of a "holy message"—abandoned his hunting hobby. His brother Hans, a railroad official with a modest income and the father of five, also made monthly payments to Stocker-Kohler and contributed to the purchase of a handsome car, a Mercedes 300. The third brother, Heinrich, also a railroad worker, broke an engagement at the behest of Magdalena. He remains a bachelor.

The sexual control which Magdalena exercised over these men was counterbalanced in Bernadette's confessions. Her statements contained a description of her "marriage to Lucifer," head devil: "I wore a white dress and he had his black, shiny fur. It was a beautiful picture." The confessions also contained the passage that after the death of her "Holy Parents," she planned to marry 10 additional men, with whom she would have one son and one daughter each, so she could become the mother of a whole new tribe.

Stocker and Kohler beat the girl once or twice daily. The other men, called upon to help, at times were summoned by telephone to participate in the torture and degradation of the young girl.

The final scene followed a dinner on May 14, 1966, in which the six cultists participated. Once again, Bernadette's alleged "Devil's Pact" was discussed in detail, together with her "desire to cause the death" of Stocker and Kohler. The girl was sent to her room and ordered to crouch on her bed, kneeling, resting on her elbows and hands, exposing her backside to the torturers.

According to the court testimony, as summarized in the Swiss newspaper *Blick* (January 8, 1969), "an orgy of brutality began, in order to drive out the Devil—as the sadistic cultist put it—and to make her feel the rightful anger of the Lord." This account states that "the quietly whimpering girl was beaten by all six 'devil exorcists' in succession, whereby whips, canes and a plastic pipe were used to beat her on the buttocks, back and extremities." More than 100 strokes fell on her.

When, in her pain, the child lost control over her bowels, she was forced to place excrement in her mouth and told to "eat it." This resulted in a vomiting attack, and Kohler pushed Bernadette into the bathtub. Finally, the young girl had to wash her soiled clothing in the water near the house and was permitted to go to bed. She died the next morning; according to the Judicial-Medical Institute at Basel, her death was due to an embolism of the lungs. Her body showed numerous bruises, abrasions, and broken skin. She died a virgin.

The hold which Stocker-Kohler had over the Hasler family is further dramatized by the fact that Bernadette's parents agreed to a scheme whereby Bernadette's body would be taken to the Barmettler home, in the village of Wangen, in order to avoid police attention.

The Haslers originally became enmeshed in the sexually sadistic delusions of Stocker and Kohler after they met in 1956. The Haslers believed the latter's messianic claims, which led to the establishment of an "International Family Society for the Advancement of Peace," supposedly designed to prepare for an "end of the world." The Hasler home was known as "Noah's Ark" among the schoolmates of the Hasler girls.

Bernadette's father, Josef Hasler, said at the trial, "I could not know, then, that this was the beginning of a road of suffering for our daughter." Hasler maintained that Stocker and Kohler estranged them from their daughter and persuaded them to turn over their second daughter, Madeleine, as well. The girls were not permitted to speak to their parents, but restricted to the "godly" education offered by their "Holy Parents." After Bernadette's death, the father went to rescue Madeleine from Stocker-Kohler. He said that he had literally to "tear her away from there," and that "she no longer regarded us as her parents; she had only eyes and ears for her 'Holy Parents,' Stocker and Kohler. After we told her of the torture death of Bernadette, her eyes opened. She told us that even the smallest children in that home were beaten to a pulp."

The shockingly successful brainwashing techniques applied by the "Holy Family" enslaved the Haslers as well as others. The team censored all mail. They took control of all monetary transactions and doled out food to the family. They used their Mercedes

300 for "missionary trips." Hasler recalled: "Hour-long prayers became brainwashing sessions. Until the early morning hours, satanic words were poured out and then we were ordered to be silent. I could no longer speak to my wife, as I would otherwise lose God's forgiveness. When my wife had to go to the hospital, because of a premature birth, I was forbidden to visit her."

Bernadette's father, slowly emerging from the grip of the "Holy Family" that caused the tragic death of his daughter, noted that he had "lost practically everything" and that "only debts remained." Asked about the trial, he said later, "If I had to judge those two today, I would beat them to a pulp and feed them to the pigs."

When the details of Bernadette's death were made known during the trial, her father cried out, "You have killed my child!" Paul Barmettler muttered, "Not killed, only beaten."

Mrs. Hasler, after lifting the nightgown from Bernadette's body and seeing the torture marks, had cried out and collapsed. But Magdalena Kohler blamed the Hasler parents: "You are guilty that Bernadette was possessed by the Devil. You did not bring her up right!" She tried to force Josef Hasler to take the guilt for his daughter's death upon himself: "If you refuse, you become a traitor to our Holy Work. Anyway, you will only have to serve one year, at worst."

Magdalena Kohler's fanaticism emerged in a statement she wrote one month before the trial, which took place in Zurich in January 1969. She said, "I have, in everything I did, acted under orders from God. All force, and all that has happened, was done on divine instructions. To avoid discipline, or faith, to withhold oneself from divine orders, leads the soul to punishment in hell and eternal damnation."

Speaking for the defense, Dr. Hans Meisser cited this statement to show that Magdalena was "a simpleminded woman, who grew up in an environment of narrow superstition and fear of eternal damnation. She is convinced that, one day, she will have to fight a duel with the Devil." He added that, while living secretly at the Hasler farm, the Kohler woman was "psychologically destroyed" and "believed more and more in her delusion, in her own supernatural powers and divine mission." The defense attorney added that the cultists had not meant to kill the young girl.

Another defense attorney, speaking of Emilio Bettio, said that his client was fully convinced that he was not beating Bernadette, but Lucifer. The lawyer pointed to the strong religious upbringing of the defendants and described Bettio as an "infantile, dependent" personality, that of one "who lived in constant fear of the eternal damnation that Stocker and Kohler preached with devastating effectiveness."

State Attorney John Lohner demanded penalties that would "serve as a warning to all those still enmeshed in superstitions and in abusing religious faith." He urged Catholic Church authorities to aid in "cleansing the soil that nurtures belief in and fear of the Devil, so that such crimes as that against Bernadette Hasler may never be repeated."

Speaking for the Roman Catholic Church, the Bishop of Chur, Dr. Johannes Vonderach, reaffirmed traditional concepts concerning the existence of the Devil, but said that the torturers and killers of Bernadette had violated Church principles in three ways: they had accepted totally imaginary "messages from beyond," had falsely accepted demonic "possession," and had acted against this mistaken condition on their own, with primitive and destructive means. Bishop Vonderach added: "Just as the Church separates itself from superstitious belief in miracles, it rejects a false belief in the Devil. However, as it regards the Devil seriously, on the basis of Holy Writ, it places itself doubly under the protection of the crucified Lord." The Bishop noted that the Church only very rarely, and when all scientific explanations have been exhausted, accepts the reality of demonic influence: in such cases, and only through a qualified priest, may a prayer of exorcism be uttered, whose wording has been fixed by the *Rituale Romanum*; "the bodily use of force is excluded."

Public opinion in Switzerland, and particularly in Zurich, was aroused by the "witch trial in reverse." Letters and telephone calls urged severe punishment of the accused, and extreme threats were directed against Magdalena Kohler. Threats stating that the court house would be blown up, unless "the most severe punishment were fixed," were made in anonymous telephone calls. On February 4, 1969, the court sentenced Josef Stocker and Magdalena Kohler to 10 years in prison, while Bettio was sentenced to four years and the Barmettler brothers to three-and-a-half.

The trial did not explore the background of this unique twentieth-century witchcraft trial in detail, because prosecution and defense were largely concerned with the intent and actual crime of the defendants. However, in terms of religious pathology and the impact of psychological delusion on criminal behavior, a look at the development of the Stocker-Kohler cult reveals some interesting successive steps: early and increasing fanaticism, messianic delusions, the creation of a self-centered cult that set its members apart from reality, and the acting-out of sexual sadism.

The initial role of the Carmelite nun Stella, known as "Little Star," remains oddly obscure; this is partly due to the fact that she was removed early on to a cloistered existence in Augsburg, Germany. Her original name had been Olga Endres; she met Stocker and Kohler while the two were visiting Jerusalem in 1956 during a "pilgrimage." Stella had, for a number of years, claimed that she was receiving messages of instruction directly from Jesus Christ. It had become her practice to transcribe these "Messages from the Savior" to typewritten form. Her superiors either failed to recognize her apparent mediumist psychosis or regarded these messages, in some manner, as genuine or at least uplifting.

Stocker and Kohler were only too willing to accept her "revelations." Josef Stocker had joined the Palottine Order in 1929. (By the time of trial, he was severely ill with diabetes: his left leg had to be amputated below the knee, as had the toes of his right foot.) The joint "pilgrimage" of Stocker and Kohler included a visit to the Shrine of Fatima in Portugal, where they claimed that a vision had prompted them to visit the Near East. In Jerusalem, Stella belonged to the Congregation of Borromaes. Her mediumistic or pseudomediumistic messages were regarded by her superiors, at least temporarily, as "an extraordinary mystical phenomenon," rather than as an expression of psychopathology. (At the time of the trial, Stella said she regarded this period of her activities as "total nonsense" and doubted the validity of the "Messages from the Savior." However, one church historian, Professor Dr. Walter

Nigg, described her role as being, "if not in a judicial sense, at least in a religious sense that of a key person, who bears a heavy moral guilt that cannot simply be eradicated by calculated disregard of the past.")

Stella, Stocker, and Kohler returned together from the Near East to Europe. Their development into a pseudofamily, with Stella as the "child" of Josef and Magdalena had odd psychological overtones; Stella was even ordered by Magdalena to play with dolls. Magdalena Kohler testified that "Herr Stocker was the Father, I was the Mother, and Stella the Child." She added that "God" had ordered her to buy Stella a red teddy bear.

This *ménage à trois* continued to exist in Singen, Germany, where the newly formed apocalyptic cult prepared for the end of the world. One room remained empty, reserved for the Pope. Magdalena said: "It was supposed to be his place of refuge, once the final catastrophe crashed down on mankind."

The Palottine Order instructed Stocker to cease these activities, but he refused and was excommunicated. Stella was ordered to return to a nunnery. Stocker twice succeeded in taking her away from the cloister, and she was twice returned to it. By then, Stella had been reduced to infantilism. Magdalena Kohler had taken the reins for the "Holy Family's" ride to disaster. Stella recalled that the cult headquarters agreed with her less than the cloistered existence: "Times were not as good as here in the Cloister. I no longer had a will of my own, and I was in constant inner fear. I was spoken to as if I were a child." She added: "Today I no longer play with dolls. I no longer write Messages from the Savior. I was suffering from a malignant delusion."

But, back in 1957 and 1958, Stella prophesied the end of the world, complete with a rain of brimstone. According to Professor Nigg, the road from the cult's "Holy Work" of saving souls to the death of Bernadette was "not a straight path, which by some intrinsic force had to lead to this immensely tragic end." The church historian, formerly at the University of Zurich, defines the fate of Bernadette as follows:

"Like a witch in the Middle Ages, Bernadette began to play the game that had been forced upon her, so that, defiantly, she accused herself of the most repulsive sexual misdeeds with the

Devil . . . Abandoned by all human sentiment, without the slightest support, she died alone in the night, without any hope of divine aid, an expectation that had long before been destroyed within her very soul."

III

Possession and Exorcism

14

"Phantoms Stalked the Room . . ."

ALAN VAUGHAN

The author of Patterns of Prophecy, *articles editor of* Psychic *magazine, describes his horrifying experience with possession by an unknown, destructive entity. Mr. Vaughan, in this unusual and courageous autobiographical account, describes how a thoroughly modern researcher-investigator can stumble into a pit of horror because—despite twentieth-century sophistication—he is dealing from ignorance. He suffered, as he puts it, "the awful consequences" of his experiment, "possession"—one of the oldest and most fear-inspiring experiences of man. Mr. Vaughan is co-author of* Dream Telepathy (1973) *and* Psychics (1972). *He has written more than forty articles and book chapters on parapsychology, including a chapter on psychic sensitives for Edgar D. Mitchell's definitive book,* Psychic Exploration (1974).*

Vaughan is a practicing psychic as well as researcher. He developed his psychic abilities in Europe during a Parapsychology Foundation research grant project investigating mediumship and prophecy in 1967–68. He has been teaching psychic development classes for six years, currently at the Institute for the Study of Consciousness in Berkeley.

Nearly a decade has passed since I had my first—and last—encounter with a horror conjured up by a Ouija board. For a long time afterward I could not bear even to talk about it; reliving that experience in my mind would rekindle a sense of terror; my voice would tremble; and anxieties would flutter in my stomach. Somewhere in the back of my mind was the apprehension that if I so much as thought of *her*, she might return to possess me once again.

It all began in late 1965. I was a science editor for a college textbook publisher on lower Fifth Avenue. Physics and chemistry were my usual fare at the office, which I shared with an imaginative editor named Delores. In between bouts of reading galleys and blue-penciling manuscripts, Delores and I would talk about mostly strange things. She was fascinated by, yet skeptical about, psychic phenomena, a frequent topic of our conversations. I was even more skeptical. I had long ago made up my mind that psychic phenomena and the supernatural simply did not exist. I had read a couple of J. B. Rhine's books on his ESP card experiments but found myself easily persuaded by critics that "something was wrong with his statistics." That masterful classic, *Illusions and Delusions of the Supernatural and the Occult*, by D. H. Rawcliffe, had quite convinced me that ESP, spirits, werewolves, vampires and assorted monsters were nothing but the product of primitive thinking and misinterpretation of natural phenomena. Further, I had never had a psychic experience nor did I know anybody who had ever had one. It was a classic case of profound ignorance.

Ouija boards were one of the strange things that Delores told me about. She had once experimented with the Ouija at a friend's home and the board spelled out mysterious messages. I assured Delores that there was nothing supernatural about that. Minute muscular movements of the fingers drive the planchette to the letters to spell out a message from the person's own subconscious. I had once played with a Ouija when I was a child but (now I would say fortunately) nothing happened. Yet Delores piqued my curiosity and I thought of a good excuse to purchase a Ouija board: a friend was convalescing from an operation and perhaps the board would entertain us. So, visiting Annalene at the hospital, we tried out the Ouija while her husband, Walter, looked on with a good-natured but skeptical smile. Nothing happened.

Later, Annalene and I tried the Ouija once again when she was out of the hospital. This time, a Sunday evening—November 7, 1965, to be precise—the board did work. The planchette fairly flew in answer to our questions. I had noticed in the New York Public Library a curious pamphlet entitled "The Coming Destruction of New York City," so I asked the Ouija when New York might experience disaster. "1973," was the reply. "How?" we asked. It spelled out W-A (we were certain the next letter would be R) -T-E-R. "Do you mean a flood?" we asked. "Yes," it said. (Incidentally, the worst flooding in New York City's history happened in 1973.)

We wanted to get information that we could verify immediately. A radio news announcement stated that the columnist Dorothy Kilgallen had died of a heart attack. We asked the Ouija if this were true. "No," it said; "poison." Ten days later it was revealed that Dorothy Kilgallen had died of poisoning as a result of taking barbiturates and alcohol. (There was some speculation that this news was withheld until after her Catholic funeral, lest it be thought that suicide was involved.)

I was fascinated by this revelation. How could the subconscious give information I didn't know myself? Somehow the Ouija was "psychic." I didn't, at this stage, consider the possibility of any outside influence being at work. Or that I myself might be psychic.

For the next few weeks the Ouija and I were constant companions. I took it to work. Delores and I were able to get oddly spelled messages. They mostly seemed to make fun of us.

I invited three friends to my Lower East Side apartment to have a go with the Ouija. One of the girls, from Ireland, knew that spirits were supposed to appear. So we asked, "Who is there?" "Z," came the reply. "What is your name?" "Z," came the reply from our anonymous visitor. "Are you a spirit?" "Yes." "Are you a man or a woman?" "Male." Further attempts at getting biographical information from our presumptive spirit visitor were unsuccessful. He stuck to his code name of Z and would reveal nothing else about himself.

But when we asked other questions, Z was most eloquent in his replies. He had a peculiar, old-fashioned vocabulary that made

me suspect a nineteenth-century origin. Whereas most of the
"spirits" Delores and I had conjured up took a lot of linguistic
short cuts, Z insisted on spelling out every single letter in his
flowery replies to our questions. The planchette, powered by four
of us, whizzed about the board in a dazzling display of speed and
accuracy. Z really did seem to be a spirit entity. And this conviction sprang more from an actual feeling I had of his presence than
his words. In some way I couldn't then explain, his essence of personality was more palpable to me than the personalities of the
living people in the room. I sensed a great rapport with him and
felt comfortable in his presence. Z seemed very wise.

The next morning, a Saturday, my enthusiasm for the Ouija
prompted me to try it alone. I wasn't alone for long. A spirit appeared on the board who called herself "Nada." She said she
came from Nantucket, an island I had no connection with, and
that she had died in 1919. Her husband had died in 1912, she said,
though she had a daughter living named Caxton. I assumed that
was a married surname. Other details about her life were sparse.
When I asked her where her husband was buried, she replied,
"Churchyard." And she kept repeating the phrase, "You are living, I am a spirit." She seemed to be jealous of my living body.

Marveling at the strong force she exerted on the planchette, I
telephoned to a friend's house to ask him to come over and observe this amazing phenomenon. There was no answer. And then
I did the stupidest thing in my life. I asked Nada to come into my
body and guide me to where the friend was.

No sooner were the words out of my mouth than I felt a strange
sensation in my brain. A force of some sort now was uttering
words I could hear in my mind. "You are living, I am a spirit," she
repeated.

Guided by Nada I left the house in search of the friend. My
body became a puppet for her whimsey. I would be walking
along when suddenly she would turn my direction, whirling me
around. The sensation in my brain I can only liken to the odd
feeling one gets when holding magnets together of opposite
polarity. Like a mechanical man I tromped erratically through the
neighborhood, walking into strange buildings and out again,
searching for the friend. It finally dawned on me that Nada didn't

know any more than I did where he was. Her being a spirit did not make her all-knowing. Yet I was still fascinated with the strangeness of such beings.

That evening I took the Ouija with me to visit a girl friend. Riding on the bus uptown, I became relaxed and was startled when I began to hear Nada in my head again, "You are living, I am a spirit." She seemed very neurotic.

When I arrived at Glenna's apartment, I told her of the day's events and asked her to join me in working the Ouija. We tried it together for a few minutes but there seemed to be interference. So then I tried it alone. "Who is there?" I asked. "Pocahontas," came the surprising reply. "When did you die?" "1919" came the ridiculous answer. I knew it was Nada playing games. "No, when did Pocahontas die?" "1621," replied the board. I had not the foggiest idea when Pocahontas died, but looking it up later I found the date 1617. I supposed a girl could forget the exact date after four centuries. Nada explained that she had been Pocahontas in a previous incarnation, and that Pocahontas had died in England. That checked out, but it was possible I might have read it somewhere. Pocahontas did not seem any more enlightened than did Nada.

Tiring of Nada's neurotic answers, I suggested to Glenna that she try to work the board alone since Nada was obviously not going to leave me alone. I told her about Z, who had been so remarkable the evening before. Glenna sat patiently with the board and waited for the planchette to move. She had not tried it before. I concentrated on Z and in a few minutes I felt his presence in the room as I had the night before. "It's moving," shouted Glenna. "It's going to Z." Rapidly the board spelled out a message which she called out to me, letter by letter, as I wrote it down: "AWFUL CONSEQUENCES—POSSESSION."

It struck me with a chill that possession was what I had let Nada do to me. That voice in my head was no longer a curiosity— it was a frightening invasion.

I stood at the window looking down Second Avenue from Seventy-third Street and thinking I wanted to run all the way downtown. I wanted to get away from Nada. I ran out of the building and wandered feverishly around for a while, and then I returned. "It's no use," I told Glenna, "she's still in my head." I fell asleep on the couch in an instant.

The next morning I asked Glenna to come with me and the Ouija to visit another friend, Harold, who had invited me to lunch. Over lunch I told Harold the story of the events of the last few days. "I want to find out how to get dispossessed. Perhaps Z could tell me." Once again we tried to get Z on the Ouija for his advice. Harold, however, was completely puzzled by the whole thing. He had never tried a Ouija before and with the three of us only gibberish resulted. I became increasingly frustrated. Suddenly I had the impulse to pick up a pencil and paper. I would try to do it alone. Now I could feel Z in my head as well as Nada. Z dictated a message that I wrote out:

"Each of us has a spirit while living. Do not meddle with the spirits of the dead. It can lead to awful consequences."

As I wrote out those words, the realization hit me for the first time that *I* had a spirit. It was not an intellectual abstraction but a powerful gut feeling. Instantly I felt a strange, powerful sensation of energy rising up within my body. I was like a container being filled with spiritual energy, working its way up until it filled my mind and even extended beyond the confines of my skin. Instantly both Nada and Z were pushed out by my own spirit. A feeling of relief flooded over me. But it was more than relief: I felt an exuberance of health and well-being I had never before experienced. The spiritual energy waxed and grew stronger. I could somehow sense that it extended not only beyond my physical body but into some other dimension—another dimension where I could feel the future and become telepathically aware.

Harold and Glenna looked at me with amazement. "Your face was white and pinched a moment ago," said Harold, "but now your color is ruddy and you look relaxed." It was exactly the way I felt.

Then I looked down again at the Ouija. I was flooded with revulsion for it. "Destroy this thing," I commanded. Harold obligingly threw the Ouija down an incinerator chute. And that was the end of my experimentation with the Ouija.

For the next couple of hours I marveled at my newfound spiritual essence that was making me psychic. I began reading the minds of Glenna and Harold and predicting events that seemed so obvious in the extended awareness I was experiencing. It would seem to be what W. G. Roll has called field-consciousness and perhaps related to the effects of the Kundalini, as it is called in India. At that time, however, I had never heard of any such thing and so was completely taken by surprise.

That night, however, the real terror began. When I lay down to sleep, the gates of hell seemed to open. Everything that I had been taught as a child to think of as superstitious nonsense—ghosts, vampires, werewolves, monsters, devils—suddenly became possible. If spirits existed, how about them? I had long been a fan of horror movies and fiction. The fun had been that such things were beyond the realm of reality—but now they took on a threatening possibility of existence. The most palpable threat of all was: what if Nada should return? I trembled through three sleepless nights in the most abject terror I had ever experienced. Nightmares I had had as a child seemed pale by comparison. Now there were no nightmares, for now there was no sleep.

Phantoms stalked the room. Menacing, grotesque heads of monsters leered at me. The hot breath of demons issued from behind every door. Hell was peopled—if that's the word—with clawed, fanged entities who were hungry for human souls. I recalled how as an imaginative child I would see skeletons fashioned from the darkness of the room, and how my mother would comfort me by telling me it was impossible. Ghosts didn't exist. But now the comfort of that protective thought had been ripped out of my mind. I was in a state of perpetual alarm, my glands reacting to panic signals that continually sent adrenaline into my already confused brain. If I drifted off to sleep, I would awake with a start—threatened by still another creature of the mind clawing at my soul's substance. The pit of my stomach again signaled "Panic, panic—run, run." But there was no place to run to.

Again and again, the thought of Nada returned. What if she should get inside my head again? What if I should become possessed forever? What if . . . what if . . . but now there were no limits to "if." The worst seemed continually about to happen.

It got so bad one night that I went to stay in the apartment of friends. I was terrified of being alone. As I lay on the couch that night, reflecting that people being nearby didn't really help, I was scared out of my wits by an ominous thrashing noise that emanated from the kitchen. It was a mouse in a bag of garbage. It should have been funny, but it wasn't.

Exhausted and sleepless, I telephoned to the office the next day to say that I couldn't come in. The reason, I truthfully reported, was that "I had been possessed by a spirit." I rather expected my boss to think that I had flipped out, but he was sympathetic. He said that it reminded him of the dybbuk, a spirit in Jewish lore that is taken to possessing people. His remarks were not exactly comforting.

I wondered if perhaps I had gone crazy. Had anybody else ever been possessed? I knew it happened in novels, but I wondered about reality. I browsed through a small bookshop to see if any book might explain what was happening. There I found what I now realize is a fairly rare two-volume set of books that are the cornerstone of parapsychology: *Human Personality and Its Survival of Bodily Death* by Frederick W. H. Myers. People not only experienced possession but many other strange psychic manifestations as well. Myers's work, published posthumously in 1903, was the result of many years of research produced by the Society for Psychical Research in London. Later I was to go there to make a complete study of parapsychological phenomena.

If the possession by Nada and my consequent self-exorcism had been terrifying, they had the net good result of propelling me full time into parapsychology. The question I had set out to answer—Was I really possessed or was it some kind of temporary insanity?—took on subtle shades of interpretation. The paradox of parapsychology seemed to be that the more one learned, the less one could be certain about anything.

Schizophrenics often hear voices and complain that they are possessed. Yet, as far as I could determine from such cases, the "possessing spirit," as the victim termed it, usually had some sort of link with the main personality and memory of the victim. With Nada I had no common interests nor even much of a curiosity beyond the fact that she said she was a spirit. What had struck me most about her was her apparent severe neuroticism—characteristic of what Spiritualists term "earth-bound entities." These seem to be especially prevalent, I learned, when people were working Ouija boards.

An obvious line of investigation would be to find out if there had been such a living entity as Nada. She furnished me a last name once or twice, but the spelling kept changing: Banaman, Bannaman. I wrote to the appropriate records division of Massachusetts—which I was informed kept the records for Nantucket —but they could not trace such a person with the information I had given them. If the presumed living daughter named Caxton should step forth and identify her mother, then that would, to me, constitute fairly reasonable evidence.

Another line of reasoning is taken up by J. B. and Louisa Rhine, who suggest that no matter what evidence one can come up with to identify a discarnate entity, it could all be explained away as ESP. With a magic formula like that, one can readily see why Rhine has abandoned survival research. Mrs. Rhine, incidentally, has written about the dangers of the Ouija board, maintaining that subconscious material can surface to cause a great deal of trouble. With that diagnosis I cannot quarrel; however, I would add that it is only *one* of the dangers. People who are highly mediumistic, as I now realize myself to be, can get into far more interesting trouble than the average person.

Now that Ouija boards are outselling Monopoly as America's most popular "game," more and more people are encountering the dangers of the unconscious. Whether or not one agrees with Mrs. Rhine's anti-survivalist stand, it is well to heed her warning about the use of automatic writing and Ouijas or psychic automatisms (*Newsletter* of the American Society for Psychical Research, Winter 1970):

". . . the use of automatisms can be considered as a method of tapping the unconscious. It involves a sufficient degree of mental dissociation that muscular movements can be made without direct conscious intention or awareness. Consequently, in spite of the differences, the material so produced can be considered as about on a par with that of dreams. It is of interest in parapsychology only if it brings information not traceable to sense perception but which is objectively verifiable. In other words, it is of interest only if it gives evidence of ESP. The automatic method as such has no parapsychological value of its own.

"In several ways the very nature of these two automatisms makes them particularly open to misunderstanding. For one thing, because they are unconscious, the person does not get the feeling of his own involvement. Instead, it seems to him that some personality outside of himself is responsible. In addition, and possibly because of this, the material is usually cast in a form as if originating from another intelligence. In this feature it is in contrast with dream material which the person usually feels he is himself experiencing.

"Another characteristic of many automatic responses that tends to be misleading is the fact that it is 'unlearned.' While in some cases automatic writing must be cultivated, in others it occurs spontaneously just as does the ability to move the Ouija pointer. With that, certain individuals can and others cannot produce the movement. Thus, it can look to the naïve as if the 'gifted' person is somehow being influenced by an extraneous personality, when, as a matter of fact, the ability to dissociate is instead the magic characteristic that separates those who can perform from those who cannot.

"The general verdict is that these automatic responses have no parapsychological significance per se; have only a slight likelihood of conveying psi information; may be intriguing to the uninformed and possibly have unhealthy effects on naïve, suggestible persons. As entertainment, they are scarcely to be recommended."

It is significant, however, that the greatest outcry against the use of Ouijas has come from the Spiritualists—not the parapsychologists. In England Spiritualist groups are petitioning to ban the sale of Ouijas as toys for children—not because of vague dangers of "unhealthy effects on naïve, suggestible persons"—but because they fear that the children will become possessed.

The mechanics of mediumistic dissociation are subtle and scarcely understood even after nearly a century of scrutiny. There is no doubt that some individuals can dissociate to bring forth a fragment of their own unconscious personality. Or they might, like the psychologist Carl G. Jung, identify this aspect of the unconscious as an "archetype." Jung had several encounters with his archetypical guide, whom he called Philemon. The presence of Philemon, though benevolent, is scarcely distinguishable from a Spiritualistic "spirit guide." Strange feelings and noises accompanied the writing of a book guided by Philemon. "The atmosphere was tense, and the rooms seemed to be filled with invisible presences." Both Jung and his sons had strange dreams, and "they all felt that something like a personified Destiny had entered their daily lives to spy on them. All these experiences ceased the moment the book was finished." (M. Serrano, *C. G. Jung and Hermann Hesse*, Schocken, 1966, p. 94.)

Would the psychiatrist-parapsychologist Jan Ehrenwald extend his definition of mediumistic trance to cover the experiences of Jung? Here is Ehrenwald's psychiatric interpretation of trance:

"It is a state of mental dissociation hysteric in origin, induced by suggestion or auto-suggestion in persons with a particular tendency to give way to such influences. The trance state, once established as an habitual pattern of reaction, gives the person concerned an outlet for unconscious or repressed tendencies which are prevented from being expressed in ordinary life. The productions of the mediumistic trance are in this way largely comparable with the familiar symptoms of hysteria and especially of hysteric multiple personality." (J. Ehrenwald, *Telepathy and Medical Psychology*, Allen & Unwin, 1947, p. 402.)

I have never heard any psychiatrist accuse Jung of being a hysteric, yet he did seem to experience the same dissociation of which Ehrenwald speaks. I would suggest that the outward forms of dissociation—running the gamut from psychiatric multiple personality cases to mediumistic spirit guides to Jungian archetypes and even to angelic beings or diabolic entities—represent a wide variety of phenomena, all of which can and do happen, but which are not the same in psychological content. Only their appearances are similar.

Yet, playing with the unconscious can be a dangerous game. Possession, whether "real" or "subconscious," can be a terrifying experience. It can have, in the words of Z, "awful consequences."

15

The Ouija Board Temptation

Kent Jordan

The "talking board," for all its popularity and apparent innocence, is not a toy. It can lead the lonely, the vain, the ignorant, the psychically ambitious down into uncontrolled automatic writing and various degrees of possession. Mr. Jordan traces the history of similar devices and cites cases that testify to the dangerous ease with which the human subconscious may be conjured up—as if it actually were the ghost or demon it sometimes pretends to be.

Divide the word into its two syllables, "oui" and "ja," and you have the French and German words for "yes." A "Ouija" board is, literally, a "yes-yes" board, and in more than name. People turn to it the way men in high position turn to a yes man, for reassurance, for an echo, to hear what they want to hear. But using the Ouija is even more risky than listening to someone who is only there to please you, to tell you how wonderful you are; it can also enslave you, turn against you, and even destroy you.

Stay away from Ouija boards! And if you do get involved with one, then keep it on the play level, as a thing of make-believe. It may be a means of communicating with discarnate spirits; but if so, it can open the road to an unappetizing bunch of low-minded entities, what Spiritualists call "earth-bound" spirits. Chances are that you are not in contact with anything but your own subconscious, serving up, from the dream world of nightmares and wish fulfillment, a dangerous brew of seductive hopes and fears.

The Ouija board emerged from a variety of similar devices in the late nineteenth century.

In 1891 OUIJA was registered as a trademark in the United States Patent Office. In the original trademark registration certificate, and also in the certificate currently in effect, the description of the goods on which the trademark is used includes the term "talking board," and this has continued to be the descriptive name in common use.

In 1973, Parker Brothers reported that sales of Ouija boards had increased by 10 per cent over the previous year and reached a total in the United States of more than 400,000. The box in which a Ouija board is sold contains the statement "How or why it works is a mystery." Russel Chandler, the Los Angeles *Times* writer on religion, reported on February 17, 1974, that not one of three physicists working at the California Institute of Technology could "offer a scientific explanation for Ouija power."

Similar devices permit an unknown force to operate through the human hand in selecting a letter of the alphabet from a board —by moving a glass, a sliding device, or a pendulum. Mediums or medium-like oracles, even in prehistoric times, used such devices, just as other seers have used everything from sheep's intestines to tea leaves, from sand, mirrors, and water surfaces to crystal balls as points of concentration to envisage the future.

The Greek philosopher-mathematician Pythagoras, who lived in the sixth century B.C., described such a device. A more direct forerunner was described by Ammianus Marcellinus, the fourth-century historian: it was a round metal dish, the letters of the alphabet engraved on its rim. A pendulum was used that moved first in the direction of one letter, then another, and so on. Anyone can make a primitive device of this sort by simply writing the letters from A to Z on a piece of paper and fashioning a pendulum out of a string and anything with a little weight to it, even a paper clip.

How can anything so simple be dangerous? Or how, for that matter, can it be regarded as the opening door for a conversation with unseen forces, be they good, evil, or neutral?

The answer is within ourselves. As with just about everything else, when it is done with discretion, it can be perfectly all right. If it is done carelessly or with too great an emotional investment, it can become a dangerous addiction. We are not the first to investigate the unseen world, nor are we the first to find ourselves entrapped, now and then. Biblical caution against divination may well have been directed against excesses. In Roman times, a device using a code was said to have become a widespread obsession among large sections of the populace. In this case, it was a ring tied to a thin thread and held into a glass. Depending how many times it struck the glass walls, the unseen force gave its answers.

"Talking board" devices used to be very popular, and still are in some countries. One, the planchette, popular in the nineteenth century, is a small heart-shaped board that rests on three legs. One of the legs was a lead pencil that could be replaced. If one put the fingers or fingertips on the planchette, it often moved on a piece of paper and wrote messages allegedly from the spirit world. The planchette bridges the practice of talking board communication with that of "automatic writing," which may be regarded as one step beyond the board devices.

A Baltimore customs inspector, William Fuld, adopted "Ouija" as his trademark and used it on a talking board which he had invented. The Baltimore *Sun* reported in an obituary on Fuld in 1927 that he had made more than $1 million with his patented invention. In 1966 Parker Brothers acquired the trademark and the business associated with it, namely, the business of manufacturing and selling talking board sets. Parker Brothers also acquired a patent issued to Fuld in 1892. In this way, the name Ouija® on a talking board came to mean that Parker Brothers is its source.

Chandler gives this graphic description of the Ouija board: "Basically, the Ouija board itself is a rectangular piece of pressed cardboard or wood about eighteen inches by twelve inches. The words 'yes,' 'no' and 'good-bye' are printed on it, together with numbers from 0 to 9 and the alphabet. The message platform, which is free to glide over the surface of the board, is about six inches long and has three felt-tipped legs and a short pointer.

Usually, two persons, seated facing each other, put the board on their laps or upon a table and then place their fingertips lightly on the platform. The platform moves in response to questions, apparently propelled by imperceptible muscular movements of the operators."

Rosalind Heywood, a British authority on psychic research, also noted, in *Fate and Fortune* magazine (Vol. 1, No. 2), that "involuntary muscular movement" is involved. Here we come to the crux of the Ouija problem: Where do the messages come from? If their source is independent from the Ouija operator, why can't it move the writing mechanism independently? So far, no mechanism, regardless of how delicate, has been developed that would exclude a human operator—literally, a "medium," in that he or she is the intermediary between the unseen force and the physical act of writing.

Mrs. Heywood notes that, "as the people involved are not consciously pushing the pointer, it is natural for them to accept the claim" that the messages are from an unknown entity, "especially as the board becomes more fluent when treated as if it were a person." Technically, the Ouija board is only a game, and is marketed as such. But, Mrs. Heywood asks, "If it is only a game, why do some people have such an absorbed and sometimes overemotional interest in it?" She attributes this emotionalism to what "goes on below the threshold of surface consciousness." She adds: "Because the wishes of the conscious and the subconscious levels of personality do not always tally—subconscious material may want to become manifest which the conscious self wants to repress—a sort of psychological censorship seems to operate. The conscious self has so much to cope with in everyday life that additional, unwanted material from the subconscious may be suppressed. Not only does this keep it out of sight, but it also prevents the conscious self from being overloaded with too many impressions."

The board functions as an alibi for the emotions. By seeming to communicate ideas, as it were, "from the outside," the persons operating it feel they have no responsibility for the content of the messages. Moreover, when two people operate a board, responsibility is diffused or neutralized. A message can be attributed to the spirit entity, which supposedly has more wisdom than the earthlings operating the board, and given much more weight than anything said by a mere incarnate human.

The subconscious may also act as a transmitter for ESP impulses. One interesting case was related by Dr. Gardner Murphy, former Director of Research at the Menninger Clinic in Topeka, Kansas, in *The Challenge of Psychical Research* (New York, 1961). He described a group of Spiritualists, meeting regularly in Flushing, Holland, who used a talking board device. One evening, to their surprise, it told them that an Englishman would write a song for them. Four spoke only Dutch, and the other two had learned some English but had not kept it up. What came through the homemade "talking board" turned out to be a poem supposedly written by the anonymous British spirit.

They were puzzled by this communication, but one of the Spiritualists found at least a partial solution. He was told, a day or so later, that a fifteen-year-old boy who lived across the street from the weekly meeting place had become intrigued and hoped to participate in their meeting. Not allowed to go to the mysterious get-together, he was much frustrated about the whole thing. So, on this July evening, he sat in his room, as the participants entered the building on the other side of the street, still wishing to join them. Instead, he picked up a schoolbook and began reading an English poem; but it was rather boring, and he was in a drowsy state while the meeting was going on.

Several psychological elements enter into this case. The most evident is the boy's desire to enter into the meeting, which he obviously did by some extrasensory means in the telepathy category. When the Spiritualists heard what the boy had done, they asked him to write out the poem from memory. They discovered that it was virtually identical to the one the board had spelled out. Had the boy's drowsy state, a form of dissociation—or altered state of consciousness—turned him into a telepathic transmitter? Had one participant acted as a receiver-transcriber of the poem? Or had several, or all six, of the spiritualists acted as a collective receiver-transcriber? One thing was sure: this was no spirit of an Englishman communicating, unless one is to assume that a discarnate entity had, of all things, gone to the trouble of reading a poem across the street and communicating it to the sitters.

Distinctly frightening was the experience of a young Pennsylvania housewife, whom we shall call Frances Mathews. She had experimented with a Ouija board with other young married women. Intrigued, she got one of her own and began to try it out herself. As her husband traveled a lot, and her eight-months-old baby slept most of the day, she found the board, as she later put it, "first a welcome companion and later my dearest and most understanding friend." She became very fluent in working the board, and quickly went on to automatic writing. She stopped watching daytime television shows, and became eager to feed the baby and put her to bed, just so she could converse with her "understanding friend."

All went well for a while, and the board was what psychologists call "supportive" in its communications. Now and then there were supposed entities who identified themselves briefly as deceased relatives, but mostly the board talked as if it were a single person and began to sign off as "Your Dearest Friend," or simply as "YDF." Successive messages, over a period of several weeks, made it clear that the "communicator" was a man. Soon his messages became intimate. Frances became uneasy when he wrote, "I can see you at all times, and there is no way in which you can hide."

As a result, the woman began to feel that there was a disembodied Peeping Tom in her life. The first thing that suffered was her sexual relationship with her husband. Before, she used to welcome him ardently from his sales trips. Now, self-conscious about being observed, she used all kinds of excuses to avoid sexual contact or even fairly routine intimacies with him. After that, the communications became lecherous and sneering, suggestive and obscene. And yet, she could not abandon the contact with the personality who, as she saw it then, had caused her to cut off all her other social contacts. She lived for the automatic communications, although she feared them.

The case of Frances Mathews eventually became a psychiatric one, and its details fill over one hundred typewritten pages in the files of a psychiatrist who is also a student of parapsychology. It was when the "dearest friend" sought to break up not only Frances's marriage but cruelly suggested that she "get rid of the kid," the little baby, "so we aren't constantly interrupted," that the woman first visited her clergyman and then was lucky enough to see the particularly knowledgeable psychiatrist. It took her nearly a year to become not only intellectually but emotionally convinced that she had talked herself, by way of the board, into a dangerous delusion—combining loneliness, curiosity, sexual frustrations, and a long-standing fascination with the supernatural—or what the psychiatrist called "a unique form of narcissistic hallucination."

Mrs. Heywood cites a case that occurred in the United States in the 1930s. A jealous woman had developed the notion that her husband, a man then seventy-two years old, was having an affair with his secretary. Her jealousy led her first to a talking board and then to a professional detective. The board told her that her suspicions were correct, although the detective found no evidence whatever. The end result was murder. Her husband killed her. He related at the trial that his wife had hit him over the head with a pistol while he was sleeping. While he was unconscious from the blow, she tied him to the bed, and then burned him with a red-hot iron until he "confessed" his affair and promised to pay her $15,000 in compensation. Afterward, freed from the bonds, he killed her.

These are extremes of talking board addiction, but they are not isolated. These are simply more violent than cases that happen virtually every day, and which cause disorientation, withdrawal from reality, domestic strife, and mental breakdowns. They may involve people who, if there were no talking boards or similar devices, might go off the deep end in some other way. True. But it is necessary that the negative potential of these automatisms be recognized.

Both the boards and automatic writing also have positive potentials in the area of mental health. If they actually reveal elements of the subconscious, they might offer short cuts or hints in psychotherapy. A unique approach to this idea was made by Anita D. Mühl, M.D., onetime staff member of St. Elizabeth's Hospital in Washington, D.C. Her book *Automatic Writing: An*

Approach to the Unconscious (1930/1963) shows that Dr. Mühl originally regarded automatic writing as indicating "a disordered mental state." But after she studied 150 cases, she found that it need not be, but simply "script which the writer produces involuntarily and in some instances without being aware of the process, although he may be (and generally is) in an alert waking state." She noted that such writing may be "antagonistic to the ordinary characteristics of the individual" and express "asocial tendencies."

Dr. Mühl found dangers in automatic writing identical to talking board addiction and other psychic risks. She observed a tendency toward "splitting the personality to the point where it endangers the individual's healthy mental adjustment," an "increasing tendency to withdraw from reality," as well as tendencies "to become afraid of the process" and "to neglect other routine tasks for the novelty of the writing experience." By incorporating automatic writing and its special censorship-releasing features into psychotherapy, Dr. Mühl found she could use it to "obtain many repressed conflicts easily," to recapture early childhood impressions, and to get "at unconscious processes quickly."

The board, automatic writing, and similar psychic or pseudo-psychic automatisms thus have their positive as well as negative side; still, they are obviously psychological dynamite and to be treated with care. That the board, for one, can be used in the most flagrant frauds was illustrated in the case of Miss Clara Hoover, heiress to a tanning industry fortune. Miss Hoover had been introduced to a talking board by her sometime friend and masseuse, Mrs. Margaret Faulkner, owner of a health food store in New York City. As reported in the New York *Times* (March 6, 1970), the board operated by Mrs. Faulkner spoke of serving "the good angel" and directed Miss Hoover to give her, over a period of time, a total of $59,285.

In his directions to the jury hearing the case, N.Y. State Supreme Court Justice Jacob Markowitz said, "I've never seen a case of more palpable fraud." Mrs. Faulkner said in her own defense that she had taken various amounts of money in sealed envelopes, which she had never opened, to a gypsy named Yuma in an unidentified church for transmission to "the good angel."

The gypsy did not appear in court, and Miss Hoover moved to San Francisco.

The board, in this instance, was just another con gimmick, although the case suggested that Miss Hoover did, at least for a while, believe that a discarnate entity communicated through it. The history of Spiritualism is, unfortunately, cluttered with similar cases: spirit voices urging the often bereaved, elderly, and lonely sitters to give or will their money to the medium, the "blessed instrument of this communication," to buy them houses, finance vacation trips, or be otherwise lavish with gifts.

The proper attitude in all of this—even if one fully believes in life after death or extrasensory perception—is to have a normal, healthy, ongoing life in which nothing supernatural or seemingly supernatural becomes the center of existence. The best place for a talking board is in the back of a little-used closet.

16

Letter to a Student

John D. Pearce-Higgins

*Canon J. D. Pearce-Higgins, vice-chairman of the Churches'
Fellowship for Psychical and Spiritual Studies in Great Britain,
wrote this letter to an English student who had asked about the
use of various automatisms, such as the Ouija board, automatic
writing, the glass-and-alphabet method and other techniques of
apparent communication with spirit entities. The author, who has
extensive experience in "exorcism" and has encountered many
cases of emotional conflict caused by the thoughtless use of automatisms, gives his reasons for cautioning against the use of such
techniques.*

Thank you for your letter. I am interested to hear about what you
have been doing, and if the letter I am writing is a bit discourag-
ing, please do not think that it is because I do not believe in survival, or that it is possible to obtain evidence for it, but that I am
concerned that investigation should be done safely and in the
right way. I take it you have been using the glass-and-alphabet
method. What I have to say applies equally to similar methods, of
which the simplest is table tipping, and then there is the Ouija
board, with letters and a pointer, and there is also the planchette
board, which is really a pencil on wheels, and produces results
similar to "automatic writing"; that is when you sit down with a

blank sheet of paper and a pencil in your hand and hope that the
hand and pencil will write something that at least makes sense! In
all these cases it is expected that the glass or board or pencil or
even table will produce something *of their own accord,* without
your own conscious control. That is why this sort of activity is
known as "automatism" because it is done, apparently without
the conscious mind of the person interfering. Of course, when you
are using a glass or a table someone in the party may very well
cheat and push the glass or tip the table, but I am assuming for
the moment that this is not done.

Most young people seem to assume that if they try one of these
methods they are going to get immediately into touch with spirits
of the dead. *Nothing could be further from the truth.* Assuming
that the glass does start to move, it is probably in the first place
being pushed unconsciously, by the nervous movement of someone's finger or arm. Of course, the only way in which to make sure
that no-one is consciously cheating is for everyone to be blind-
folded, and to have an observer there to note down what the glass
indicates. Communications appear to take place through the subconscious mind. When you use the glass, the movements initially
appear to be made unconsciously through the arm of someone
using the glass—and maybe later the glass takes on an independ-
ence of its own through some sort of physical force supplied or
drawn from the bodies of those present, but still in a way not
known to or controllable by your conscious mind . . . and away
you go!

At this stage, it is highly probable that all you are getting in the
way of messages, if any, is the product of the subconscious minds
of some of those present. In your subconscious mind many things
are stored up. First of all, of course, your memory of information.
Then there is the memory of your personal life, much tinged with
emotion, painful or pleasurable. In fact, it seems quite clear from
what we have learned through hypnosis, that everything that has
ever happened during your life is stored up in this subconscious,
or unconscious, part of your mind. The further away we get in
time from an event, or the more painful it was, the more difficult
it is to bring it up to consciousness. You probably don't remember
what happened on your fifth birthday, but under hypnosis (as-

suming that you are one of those people who can be hypnotized) you may recall details vividly.

There is an interesting case of a girl born in Germany who came to England at about five. When "regressed" as it is called, to ten, she spoke perfect English; when regressed to four and one half, she could neither speak nor understand any English at all. Under hypnosis we seem actually to relive a specific situation. Now, in our memories are often very painful incidents, times we made fools of ourselves, times we were afraid, times when people did unpleasant things to us, so that we hated them. These we tend to forget, because they are painful to our self-esteem, or embarrassing, or not very respectable, and we don't want to admit to ourselves that they ever happened or that we felt like that. Today we are all taught to be kind and helpful and honest—and not to cherish hate or jealousy against people. Yet, in fact we often do hate or are jealous of people, and don't want to admit it to ourselves. And there is a sort of censorship in the mind which prevents these feelings from surfacing—it only comes out in unguarded moments; when you use a glass, etc., this is precisely the sort of unguarded moment when the little demon of jealousy or hate can slip out, particularly because you think that what you are getting comes from outside, from the spirits. In other words, this may be a method of bringing the repressed contents of someone's subconscious mind into consciousness. Pleasant things often surface easily of their own accord, especially when we are daydreaming, but unpleasant things tend to surface by accident, as it were.

I'll give you an example. Late one night, not long ago, the phone rang. An almost frenzied young man at the other end shouted at me, "We've got an evil spirit in the house, can you help me to get rid of it?" When asked, he told me that he and his young wife, and a friend, Bill, had been doing the glass-and-alphabet business together. They seemed to be getting along fine, and had received some nice, encouraging messages. "Then suddenly last night," he said, "the glass went berserk [always a sign of danger] and spelled out that Bill would strangle his girl friend with his bare hands." Bill fortunately was not much worried, but the young wife was terrified, and said they had a devil in the house—hence the phone call.

My reply to him was that it was almost certainly someone's subconscious hate-wish coming out—or it might even be that Bill really wanted to break with his girl friend but would not admit it to himself, and that in any case there was no truth in it. My advice was to put it away and never do it again, and I don't think he and his wife ever will. This sort of experience is very common—all goes well for a bit, you get what seems good evidence, and then suddenly, bang, comes some horrible prophecy of death—such as one of you is told that he has only three years to live (these death prophecies are common) or something equally unpleasant. If you really believe that this message is coming from the spirits, and even more important, if you really believe all spirits to be able to see into the future or to be infallible, then you are going to be in real trouble. Many people have this sort of experience, get terrified and fortunately give it up.

Here's another case. I was asked to address a Youth Club which had been doing this, and especially to speak to two girls who were seriously affected: one, a first year university student, the other a high school girl. Both girls had lost their fathers—an interesting psychological point. They had been doing automatic writing. At first it went fine; the student appeared to contact her dead father, who seemed to know all about her, and gave good evidence. Then a friend of her father came through and claimed to have been her "guardian angel" for many years. Presently, having got her hooked by what appeared to be good evidence, the messages came: "Life does not hold much for you really, dear, it is such a lovely world over here, you had better come over and join us." So the girl threw herself under a bus. Mercifully, she wasn't killed; she was taken to a hospital and after a year, although she was well enough to come home, she was not free of the compulsion to write of obsessive ideas. The other girl got roughly the same advice from her "father"—but she took fright and consulted the curate, who brought me in.

Now, there are two possible explanations of this. Remember that both girls were fatherless, obviously needing a father figure, possibly finding life without a father's support difficult. There are times when life gets on top of even the bravest of us; most people have suicidal impulses at some time or other, but we fight them down because we know it is wrong for us to give way to them. Here, the "death wish" surfaced as a piece of good advice from an apparently loving father; I feel it was almost certainly a death wish from each girl's subconscious mind. This was part of the explanation I gave them. I added that if, by any chance, it was a genuine spirit communication, then the spirit was certainly not Father in either case, but some low-grade mischievous or malicious entity who had jumped in to control the writing, masquerading as Father, getting the information from the girl's own memories of Father, and trying to wreck her life. My explanations seemed greatly to relieve both of them, and as far as I know both girls are now back on an even keel.

To those who do not believe in the possibility of communication with the dead through any form of automatism, or indeed in any other claimed method, clearly such phenomena must be products of the person's own subconscious mind. I am a little surprised to find that some parapsychologists tend to take a rather optimistic view of possible dangers. But those who write in this way have had little experience of the disastrous psychological effects that can be produced; it is precisely unstable individuals who resort to this form of experiment. Inevitably, the personalities of young people who try this method are still in a formative and therefore unstable period. Such disturbances are difficult to cure, and there seems little reference to them in the literature of psychiatry.

Again, unfortunately, young people taking to some form of automatism almost always believe that this is a method of contacting the dead. This is the thrill—and the danger. Again, assuming that what emerges is only of subconscious origin, it would be advisable for anyone, even on this showing, to have some elementary knowledge at least of what "depth psychology" is about, which few students have. A book like Sigmund Freud's *Psychopathology of Everyday Life*, which is very readable, will alert most youngsters to some of the tricks which our unconscious mind can play on us in order to circumvent the censorship imposed on antisocial behaviour or emotional attitudes which are disapproved of by the conscious mind.

I know of an interesting instance where a Ouija board was being used. There was a psychoanalyst present, and she finally decided to put her hand on the pointer: it started to spell out pious, uplift, mildly religious sort of material. She was disgusted at what was coming out—soppy stuff—and presently gave it up. Next day, after reflection, she admitted that the religious aspect of life was one that she had resolutely suppressed from her conscious thinking, and that it was highly probable that the material had represented subconscious emotional and religious attitudes in herself. Much of what people appear to think is of "spirit" origin is almost certainly of subconscious nature—maybe harmless, but certainly not indicative of survival. And if you were to start automatic writing in order to find out the content of your own subconscious mind, you require an independent psychologist to help you interpret yourself to yourself, and to elucidate the material whose true meaning (as in a dream) is often presented in highly symbolical form in order to get past the conscious censorship.

Modern psychology does not like to accept the possibility of "possession" by evil spirits. There is no doubt that in cases of schizophrenia, or multiple personalities, or "autonomous (i.e. independently functioning) complexes" the repressed part, if it succeeds in surfacing, disturbs the normal consciousness as if it were "possession" or control by some outside force. An automatism might easily allow such a complex or suppressed personality to surface and take control, and the cure of this would need expert psychological help. So it is a dangerous practice even from the orthodox psychiatric point of view. It means delving into the mind's cellar, where you are likely to find rubbish rather than pearls of great price!

Assuming however that it is possible to contact spirits in this way, they will be using the same mechanisms as those which bring subconscious material to the surface: the reflexive nervous system which we unconsciously use to write, to lift an arm, without really knowing how we do it. We must then next ask, "What sort of spirits are likely to try and come through, and with what motive?" Here the answer is rather a complicated one.

Assuming that we survive death, where do we go after death? I believe that the evidence confirms, more or less, what St. Paul said in I Corinthians Ch. xv, when he speaks of the "spiritual body." At death, we shed the physical body which is then cremated or buried or otherwise disposed of. We emerge from the physical body clothed in a "spiritual" (or "astral" or "etheric") body, which apparently looks and feels like the physical body we have had during lifetime, except that it does not suffer from any of our earthly physical disabilities.

Now, people who die normally in old age, normally decent people, on leaving the body are met by friends and helpers (the Bible calls them angels—a word which really means "messengers" and does not necessarily imply wings!). Under the care of these spirit beings they are conducted up into the realms of Light—Paradise, in biblical language—which appears to be the first of the many "mansions" or "stages" of which Jesus spoke in St. John Ch. xiv. Here, after a period of readjustment, or as the Bible calls it "judgment," they are assigned to suitable tasks, which enable them to continue their spiritual development. If they are ever allowed to communicate with their loved ones on earth, it is in order to help them, or to comfort and reassure them that they have survived death. Or, maybe, if they have left something undone, wish to right a wrong, or ask forgiveness, they come back to do this. The great majority of such "returns" happen spontaneously, in dreams, visions, or through a medium.

These are normally decent people who have given some thought to the problems of the after-life, and who have done their duty to the best of their ability while on earth. If we die as reasonably good people, we shall find ourselves in a good state after death. Unfortunately, there are lots of horrible people in this life, who die very far from being in a "state of grace." Some think of nothing but looking after Number One, of gratifying their physical appetites for drink and sex and all that money can buy. Such people, especially if they happen to die violent deaths—either by suicide or murder, or are hanged or go to the electric chair, wake up on the other side resentful, angry, vicious. These people apparently do not go up into Paradise at once—they aren't fit for it—although I believe that eventually they, too, are rescued and brought up into the Light. But immediately after death they may hang around the earth for a long time. This is especially true of many of the people we find in haunted houses causing Poltergeist disturbances. They are puzzled, because no one takes any notice of them (we can't usually see them), they don't realize they are dead, because no one ever told them that they would survive perhaps, or because they find their spirit body so like their old one that they don't realize what happened. But it is mostly their lack of moral and spiritual development, that keeps them tied down.

Now, these are the spirits nearest to earth. These are the easiest to contact, and when a group of people sit round a table and invite all comers, which is what you are in fact doing with Ouija boards and such, it seems that they are delighted to jump in, and try to create as much mischief as they can. Many of them are clever impersonators. Fishing out of the minds of those present, by telepathy, details from their past lives, they can easily masquerade as a father or mother by drawing on the memories of your life which mother or father shared with you when they were alive. Then, having got you hooked, they suggest suicide, or threaten you with the fear of death, or advise some foolish action.

Not long ago, we had to deal with an unhappy woman who thought she was a great medium. She did automatic writing and seemed to be getting all sorts of goody-goody advice. She was in love with someone else's husband, but he acted rightly and cut off his contact with her and she lost touch with him. Presently her messages told her that the man's wife had died (she was indeed a sick woman) and that he had gone to England (they all lived in the Far East). She was told to go to England and find him. She sold up and did so. Nowhere could she find him, even though various mediums whom she consulted sent her off on false trails. Eventually she came to us, and we told her that all her messages were fraudulent. She was reduced to poverty, and eventually had to be repatriated by the consul in London. When she got back home she found that the man had never left the country and the wife was still alive. This experience may have been due either to her own subconscious wishes, or to fraudulent spirits. In either case, it was disastrous.

Why could this happen? The answer is that she was trying to develop her own mediumship alone and without help. If you use a glass or Ouija board or planchette or automatic writing, what are you doing? You sit down and invite some external forces to make use of you. You do not know who is going to come. Your own motives also have much bearing on this. If you are going to do it for kicks, or out of idle curiosity, you will get jokers and pretenders answering your call, because there seems in the spirit world to be a law that "Like attracts like." Even if your motives are really serious, it is not necessarily a protection because it is so much easier for earthbound spirits to jump into control, than it is for those who have already made some progress and who apparently find it difficult to "gear themselves down"—to get down to our level of consciousness which they have now left behind.

So that is why these apparently simple methods of attempting contact with the dead are extremely dangerous. All the experienced mediums I know say the same—don't do it!—and they know, because they so often have people brought to them who are obsessed or possessed by some mischievous or damaging spirit who has got control of them and won't let go. They find they are compelled to go on with automatic writing—at all hours of the day and night, they may begin to hear hallucinatory voices telling them to do stupid and filthy things; they are no longer masters in the house of their own minds and souls. It is often a difficult matter to cure them, and there aren't many mediums who can do it. Sometimes the Church can do it: a sincere priest, by the laying on of hands with prayer in the name of Jesus Christ, and relying on the power of God through the ministry of His angels, can do it—it is one of the powers given to the clergy by Ordination; but all too often they either do not realize this, or are unwilling to use it.

Recently I was told of a boarding school where a number of boys were experimenting. After one group had been going for a while, a communicator who said he was the "dead" grandfather of one of the boys came through and ordered them to stop at once as it was most dangerous (I feel this was a genuine communication) and they did so. But one of the other groups apparently got hold of an evil spirit whom they were unable to shake off until the chaplain held a service of prayer and laying on of hands in the school chapel. Whether this was a genuine "exorcism" or simply a cleansing of feelings of guilt I do not know—it does not matter; clergy often have to do things of whose exact nature they are not sure—the important thing is that it succeeds.

Nearly every time that I am asked to go and talk to a school Sixth form it is because someone has gotten into trouble, either in or out of school. I was once called to go to a house in the suburbs where a group of some highly intelligent young people had got into bad trouble. One boy seemed to have contacted a spirit-girl who appeared to mesmerise him. Eventually things got so bad that he was found in a semi-trance condition, walking down to the railway station with the intention of throwing himself on the line. Fortunately, a friend spotted that he was "not himself" and brought him back. In another case, five friends, very nice young people started off fine with the glass—they had an apparently spiritual Inca priest, who said he had been sacrificed on the wheel of torture because he had worshipped the God of life, and not the Inca God of death. Well, he may have been genuine, for he does not seem to have been responsible for what happened later. One night they went to see friends in North London and had a sitting for kicks. A murderer and his victim communicated, and also a suicide who said he had been buried on Hampstead Heath with a stake through his heart. They had no idea how to deal with the situation, and were scared stiff. Eventually the murderer and his victim (whose identity they told me they had later verified from local records from the names and details given) said that as they had been decent to them, they would not harm them and they were thankful to end a situation which they were quite incapable of dealing with.

In the United States, I met a charming young married woman, with two children and a good husband, who got obsessed through automatic writing—she was hearing voices, and suffering compulsions. I prayed with her and performed a service of "exorcism," but it took another six months, with the aid of a powerful prayer group and friends, before she was clear. Last week a middle-aged man came for help—he had taken part, against his better judgment, in a glass circle at a party and had "picked up" something. Not being deeply involved, a couple of treatments put him right, but he was lucky, for an experienced spiritualist friend recently told me that some people he had tried to help had taken three years to clear, and we have also found this a slow business in some cases.

My associates and I have found that it is not merely the unstable who should avoid this sort of practice; we can guarantee no protection to ordinary balanced people, and the only safe procedure is to stop all automatism, once and for all.

17

How to Guard
Against Obsession

PAUL BEARD

Mr. Beard, president of the College of Psychic Studies, Ltd., London, has studied numerous cases of "obsession" by spirit entities or other influences on men and women who have permitted themselves to be carried away in experimenting with Ouija boards and automatic writing. The pattern he describes is virtually universal and has been observed by the victims of such influences, as well as by psychic researchers and Spiritualists, in many parts of the world. Paul Beard is the author of Survival of Death, *a book that weighs the evidence for and against the survival of the human personality after bodily death.*

In order to free a victim of obsession from a controlling influence, two questions have to be considered: difficulties due to the obsessive influence, and those due to the person who has become "invaded." Obsessing influences can be either intentional or accidental. If the influence has become entangled with the aura of the sensitive man or woman, without meaning to and without knowing how to help himself, this can best be dealt with by a medium used to psychic "rescue work," and is not likely to present much difficulty. If, however, the influence is purposive and mischievous or evil, its hold is likely to be tenacious and subtle.

Such an evil and obsessive influence seeks to break down the protective aura of the person attacked, hoping to obtain contact within the aura at any time and achieve its true purposes: to break down the personality it is obsessing in order to reduce it to neurosis or even possible suicide.

The power to obsess largely depends upon the "host"—however involuntary the "host"—being willing to give it house room. Quite a number of people who are well aware in theory of the dangers of automatic writing nevertheless allow themselves to become obsessed, because they are insufficiently alert to see through and resist the types of argument which the influence uses in order to retain contact with them. Some of these will be mentioned below.

The first line of defense is for the host to adhere strictly to the rule not to consent to write for more than one hour a week. A great number of obsessions commence through neglect to observe the rule. If the influence suggests or requires the sensitive host to write more and more often, upon whatever pretext, this should be considered as the strongest possible warning signal. The purpose is then nearly always malevolent. If he does not resist, the host is likely to find himself or herself writing in the end almost continuously, even while traveling, etc., in fact at all hours of the day or night.

In order to persuade the victim to continue writing, the influence will usually seek to intrigue the writer and gain confidence by imparting facts, very likely about discarnate relatives, which are true, or alternatively it may give facts about things in ordinary life which the host is invited to check to "show that there can be confidence in the writer." Warnings are likely to be given about the health of relatives in distant places. Frequently the host is told to go on journeys, which later prove to be useless; someone may be falsely declared to have been taken ill; the host is instructed to go to a railway station to wait for someone, or to visit an unknown address in a distant town, or even embark upon an air journey. Messages of an alarming type are frequently given. The purpose is to get the host agitated, for this makes the influence harder to resist. It may suggest actions which violate health precautions, such as going without food, or undertaking night-long vigils; this is an attempt to bring about some degree of physical and nervous exhaustion.

Further moves may be more subtle. The influence may tell a story of its own dire need for help, and play upon the sympathy of the host. It may claim to be an outcast of some kind, or beg the host to pray for forgiveness for him. Or it may invent other misfortunes for which it demands intervention. The most common claim is that the influence will help the host to carry out some great work which he or she is declared to be destined to achieve, and in which the influence offers assistance. The purpose of all this is to play upon the host's sympathy or vanity, so as to be able to retain contact.

This is the moment when the host should consider why it is that the influence has drawn near, why, in short, he or she has been chosen as the victim, for that is the intention. Likely circumstances are that the person attacked may live alone, is in poor health, or harassed in some way; perhaps uses the hands in daily work such as typing; is emotionally lonely, or not resistant to glamour. In short, there are likely to be reasons which make it particularly appealing for the host to establish a relationship on an emotional basis with someone in the next world. The obsessor will not stop until it has obtained a complete and very unhealthy domination over the victim's whole being, even when it falsely represents that its intervention is benevolent and helpful.

How is all this best dealt with? While help is at times needed and can be given by sensitives and helpers especially trained in psychic "rescue work," the victim must clearly recognize that it is up to him or her to do the part of the work appropriate to themselves. One important feature of the difficulty is always that the victim has, and has shown, a certain fault or weakness in the character by which the obsessing influence has gained its hold. If the victim is willing to take this weakness in hand and gradually correct it, the help of a rescue medium will not always be needed. But if there is an unwillingness to do anything to correct it, the medium may not succeed, as the victim is still leaving the gate open, and thus undoing the sensitive's work. Frequently, something in the victim's character, vanity or obstinacy, for instance, unconsciously prefers the drama to continue, however uncomfortable and dangerous it is. This weakness is often hard for him to recognize, and harder still to acknowledge.

What the victim should do, in practical terms, is very simple: it is to deny any and all access to the influence, to "starve it out." To achieve this, however, needs perseverance and alertness. All attempts whatsoever by the influence to induce more writing must absolutely be forbidden, even though the most compulsive and urgent reasons be suggested, including that the victim is being "tested" in his faithfulness to the obsessor by those "misguided" people who advise him to stop. No credence must be given to any suggestions of the obsessor, whether these flatter, praise, or promise great things; all reasons in the end will be found to be false. The influence may also say that it is now "too late" for the victim to escape.

By this time the obsession will probably have made a sufficient split in the victim's aura to "talk" by word or thought within the victim's head. These words and thoughts must also be resisted completely, although at first it will not be easy.

The best remedy, then, but one which may take a little time to apply completely, is a complete focus of attention upon other things. Reading, music, television, the cinema can all be helpful, as can visits to friends, sharing in others' family life, etc. Attempts are likely to be made by the obsessor to draw attention to itself through "significant" thoughts in books or through words which seem to have prominence in a television program. The victim must avoid being drawn back to the obsessor in this way, and must simply turn back to what was occupying him before. Fresh air and regular food and sleep should especially be sought.

It is essential that all attempts to "argue" with the obsessor are avoided. As long as the obsessor can talk to or think with the victim, it will result in the strengthening of his hold. He must, at every attempt, be cut dead. If the obsessor pleads that he himself needs help, the plea must fall on equally deaf ears, for this will be false. If the victim thinks in any way at all about the obsessor, and how to defeat him, this, too, is an indirect link with him, which, even if not avoided at first, must be eliminated later, as the victim feels more free. The victim must be clear that he or she must seek never to think in any way about the obsessor, even to oppose him, but constantly focus attention on something as far apart from the obsessor's interests as possible. To put attention on him—even in opposition—is to maintain the link that must remain forever broken.

Once even a few minutes' complete attention on something else is secured, the victim can feel that a good stride forward has been made. The aim will then be to secure more of these complete acts of attention, to lengthen them, and thus lessen the hold. When in particular trouble the victim may mentally visualize being completely encircled in a cocoon of light. This visualization needs to be carried out both with attention and intention. The victim might envisage being enfolded by wings of protection, made of brilliant white light. Help may also usefully be sought from a prayer group. This, however, does not lessen the need for the starving-out process described above, which must be kept up without any let-up whatever.

Once the victim begins to feel free, which should be within one or two weeks, great vigilance should continue to be exercised, for even if the obsessor leaves, or has to leave, it is likely that a further attempt will be made and this must be resisted equally strongly. No automatic writing should be attempted again when the victim is cured.

18

The Exorcism Fad

MARTIN EBON

*Claiming to be "possessed" can be a way of avoiding respon-
sibility for one's actions, or it may truly be a state where the
human and demonic meet. But current fascination with possession and exorcism has largely been the result of exaggeration and
commercial exploitation. Martin Ebon, who edited* Exorcism:
Fact not Fiction *and is the author of* The Devil's Bride: Exorcism,
Past and Present, *deals specifically with the fictional treatment of
exorcism in novels and motion pictures. He warns against the encouragement of popular delusions, be it by religion, commercial
enterprises or ill-informed commentators.*

A Dutch Reformed pastor, Willem C. van Dam, decided that the
kleptomania—a seemingly irresistible urge to steal—of one of his
parishioners was due to demonic influence. Van Dam's patient-
parishioner, a young woman, had not responded to other forms
of ecclesiastical treatment, such as prayer. The clergyman
concluded that this was no psychological aberration, but "something outside" her person, which would respond only to "the
weapon of exorcism." Van Dam said that he "took all the faith I
had into my two hands, looked at her and said something like
this: 'You evil spirit, who forces this girl, this child of God, to
steal, I command you in Jesus's name to go hence, go away, where

Jesus commands you to go, and never to return.'" As Pastor van Dam recalls, "The whole thing was over and done with in twenty seconds."

This sort of thing works now and then, but it is hardly the only and final answer to psychological or psychosomatic illnesses. There is no danger in the faith and action of Van Dam, but in widespread acceptance of the idea that men and women are not responsible for their actions, that satanic forces are exercising irresistible influence all around us, and that exorcism is the ultimate and inevitably effective cure. If this were so, a multitude of antisocial behavior, from mythomania (compulsive lying) to homicide, could be cured by exorcists. And while modern psychotherapy may be regarded as a contemporary extension of traditional forms of exorcism, we are certainly nowhere near definitive knowledge of the human mind and of the influences and actions related to it.

Van Dam, in an interview in the German weekly magazine *Der Spiegel* (September 23, 1974), acknowledged that many symptoms shown by people allegedly possessed by demons are in the category of parapsychological phenomena, such as prophetic ability and a knowledge of languages outside the person's normal ability. But the range of parapsychological studies today is wide enough to cover most, if not all, the symptoms traditionally ascribed to possession. It is therefore necessary to guard against all too easy acceptance of claims for possession and its cure by exorcism. What cannot be attributed to mental disturbance, to psychosomatic illness, very nearly always falls into one or another parapsychological category. This includes telepathy, clairvoyance, precognition (prophecy) and psychokinesis (abbreviated by experimenters as PK), the influence of mind over matter.

The motion picture *The Exorcist*, which was a worldwide sensation beginning in 1974, had a strong impact on public thinking in this field. In the United States, England, and on the European Continent, clergymen of all faiths, as well as psychotherapists, reported on new waves of people who attributed their urges and compulsions to devils, demons, or evil spirits.

In the United States, the public was exposed to contradictory views expressed by religious spokesmen, including priests, as well as to smooth reassurances by William Blatty, author of *The Exorcist*, and by the director and cast of the film. One Paulist priest, the Reverend Ellwood Kieser, praised the movie, because it "shows the divine in man and the demonic in man really fighting it out," while Father Juan Cortes, S.J., of Georgetown University, suggested that the film "encourages the very illness we want to take away." Blatty, interviewed in *People,* called Cortes "a very dear, kind, well-meaning man" and then accused him of sour grapes, because "he wanted to be in the film." Although exorcism is part of Anglican-Episcopal as well as Roman Catholic, Greek Orthodox, and some Protestant Fundamentalist concepts, caution has been expressed by Anglican-Episcopal spokesmen. The Archbishop of Canterbury, the Most Reverend Michael Ramsey, while in New York early in 1974, said, "I believe there is genuine demonic possession and a genuine exorcism, but the genuine element is probably in the minority. If there is an immense craze on the subject, it is a sign of spiritual immaturity." Canon William V. Rauscher of Woodbury, New Jersey, former president of Spiritual Frontiers Fellowship, described the film as "posing a pastoral problem," because "it puts us back into the medieval concept" and triggers "psychological problems—people who think they are possessed, but aren't."

The religious and the parapsychological approaches to possession and exorcism can benefit from an informed review of the various factors. Blatty admitted that true possession, and therefore true exorcism, are very rare; however, he also maintained that the case of a fourteen-year-old Washington boy, after which he modeled the movie, was authentic and authenticated. As the Washington case has been kept secret, it is worth inquiring into this authenticity. After all, with all the dramatic license the motion picture took, it did claim the legitimate ancestry of the Washington exorcism. Let us sort out the known facts about this case and see whether it was, in fact, what Blatty claims it was: that ultra-rare occurrence, a genuine case of demon possession.

The facts that emerged from newspaper accounts in 1949 were scant but relatively precise. The name of the boy around whom the phenomena were centered has been given as Douglass Deen,

which is presumably a pseudonym. The family lived at that time
in a suburb of the nation's capital, probably Mount Rainier,
Maryland. The phenomena began with typical poltergeist elements, notably untraceable scratching sounds (by now, parapsychology no longer identifies such phenomena with the traditional "noisy ghost" element, which is a literal translation of the
German word *Poltergeist*, but tends to attribute them to possible
physical expressions of emotional turbulence, notably during the
pre-puberty period). The Deen family was Lutheran, and the pastor of their church took young Douglass into his home on February 17, 1949. During the night, the phenomena included a vibrat-
ing of the boy's bed, the movement of a chair across the floor by
several inches and up against the wall. This happened while the
boy sat on the chair; he said, "It's going over with me, Pastor,"
and then the chair fell over and the boy fell to the floor.

This sort of anticipation of physical events can be found in
recent poltergeist cases. One is cited by W. G. Roll in *The Poltergeist* (1972). Roll, who witnessed a series of such phenomena in
December 1968 in a house in Olive Hill, Kentucky, recalls that
twelve-year-old Roger Callihan said at one point, "The table will
flip over," and it did. In Washington, or rather Mount Rainier, the
lights stayed on while Reverend Winston saw that the cot on
which Douglass was sleeping was moving, as was the bedding.
The clergyman was impressed by the fact that all items "moved
as a unit." He decided that Douglass needed either medical or
psychiatric treatment, and the boy was taken to Georgetown University's Medical Center. As these approaches did not succeed in
quieting the boy, he was moved to St. Louis, where a Jesuit, Father William Bowdern, pastor of the Collegiate Church of St.
Louis University, was appointed by Archbishop Ritter to under-
take an exorcism. It was presumably Reverend Bowdern, now in
his seventies and retired, who was tracked down by *Newsweek*
(February 11, 1974), which quoted him as saying, "I have never
talked with Blatty and never will." This was in reply to the author's claim that he had seen a copy of the exorcist's diary of the
case and that the priest had confirmed that it was "the real thing."
The Jesuit, who had made a vow to his superiors never to discuss
the exorcism, said, "I have lived in dread of calls from people like

you. It started with the book and then the movie, and if it keeps up some fine lives are going to be ruined. The boy in the case has grown into a fine man with a lovely wife and children."

Additional indirect testimony comes from Dr. Henry Ansgard Kelley, professor of English at the University of California in Los Angeles and author of *The Devil, Demonology and Witchcraft* (1970). Kelley wrote in *Commonweal* (November 6, 1970) that "diabolical possession is caused by belief in diabolical possession; possession without the devil remains simply an autosuggestive trance or a hysterical fit. The performances of mediums and the displays of convulsive revivalism come under the category of non-diabolical possession." Concerning the Washington case, Dr. Kelley had this to say:

"The Catholic Church still preserves all the forms for exorcising the diabolically possessed, and therefore there is always the danger that ordinary pathological or nervous conditions will be complicated by the introduction of the devil. The suggestive power of the rituals of exorcism can be illustrated by an episode that took place in 1949. A young teen-age boy in Washington, D.C., became the center of poltergeist phenomena, those mysterious events that sometimes occur especially around persons entering puberty. The boy's Lutheran pastor had no advice on the subject, but a Jesuit friend of the family in St. Louis described the incidents to his local chancery, and without further investigation word came from Archbishop Ritter to the rector of the Collegiate Church at St. Louis University that he was to begin exorcism at once. As soon as the exorcism began, the boy began to suffer convulsions and other symptoms of the possession syndrome. The exorcist was convinced that diabolic obsession had changed into diabolic possession, and after a harrowing thirty-five days of anti-demonic prayer and ritual, he was able to restore the boy to normality. Which seems to demonstrate that what is induced by suggestion can be cured by suggestion."

Kelley elaborated on these observations in press interviews. The Washington-St. Louis case was one of the last such cases he studied during his thirteen years as a Jesuit seminarian. During this research Kelley talked to Bowdern and recalls that "the exorcist himself sensed that material changed in his mind. If he didn't write down the evidence immediately, it would change; there was a terrible tendency to exaggerate." One publicized claim was that the Sacred Host presented to the boy at Holy Communion would "fly around the room and then come to rest on the plate." This, according to the exorcist, was "nonsense." When given the Host, the boy would "pass out" and "spit it out on the plate." He calls this story "typical of the exaggeration" that is characteristic of the myth-making surrounding possession and exorcism.

Several of the reports on the Washington-St. Louis case claimed that, while "possessed," the boy could speak and understand Latin. Such seemingly supernatural knowledge of a language not known to a person is regarded in the *Rituale Romanum,* which contains the official Roman Catholic exorcism rite, as one of the possible proofs of genuine possession. But according to Dr. Kelley's informant, "the boy could speak only one word in Latin, *Dominus,* which he could have picked up from the Mass." The only unusual manifestation Father Bowdern recalled was vertical, clawlike lines on the boy's chest, which could be read to spell "hell." These red welts would appear and disappear and might have been "caused by hysteria."

One psychologist-parapsychologist, Dr. Lawrence LeShan, attributes such "stigmata" as the lines on the chest to "conversion hysteria, a psychological disease imitating a real one." He observes that stigmata-type swellings can appear on the body of mental patients, just as a hypnotist can cause blisters on the hand of a hypnotized person whom he tells that he is being touched by glowing coals, although he is only being touched with a pencil. LeShan, author of *The Medium, the Mystic and the Physicist* (1974), believes that possession phenomena may be "physical symptoms arising from psychic disorders" and that exorcism may merely "delay other treatments and attack symptoms rather than causes." According to Dr. Kelley, another exorcist involved in the Washington-St. Louis case, and one whose testimony he regards as highly reliable, was the Reverend William Van Roo of the Gregorian University in Rome. This priest concluded that the boy was simply ill, probably in a psychosomatic manner, and that there were no signs of diabolic possession until the exorcism began.

This is about as close as we can get, right now, to the unadorned facts of the 1949 case on which *The Exorcist* is said to be based. Until such time as the St. Louis archdiocese releases a factual account of the exorcism procedure, one can only conclude that the case for genuine possession was a good deal less convincing than Blatty and others have led us to believe. Actually, the evidence points to poltergeist phenomena indicating family tensions and considerable inner turmoil on the part of the young boy, as well as psychosomatic symptoms which, chameleon-like, took on the colorations of possession diagnosis and exorcism procedure.

Parapsychologists recognize the pitfalls on the roads of the Washington and St. Louis priests. The first rule of a poltergeist investigation, and of other claimed psychic phenomena, is to doubt the testimony of witnesses. Just as the exorcist in the Washington-St. Louis case realized that he could not trust his own selective memory of what he had done, seen, and heard, psychic investigators are alert to dramatization, exaggeration, and faulty memory on the part of the participants and observers of emotion-laden phenomena. Roll describes how he told the Callihan family in Kentucky that the things going on in their house need not be the result of "evil influences" or "demons." Instead, he said, some people seem to "function rather like batteries, giving energy to such occurrences," and that there was "nothing bad or evil about this energy." It is difficult enough to pin down the psycho-physical elements of poltergeist phenomena, without having demonic concepts superimposed on them.

The Daly City, California, case of exorcism is even more reminiscent of poltergeist phenomena than the Washington-St. Louis case. The Reverend Karl Patzelt undertook the exorcism of a home in which he had found "obsession," rather than "possession." This means that odd and frightening phenomena took place all over the home, affecting the family only indirectly. As I understand it, the *Rituale Romanum*'s exorcism segment applies only to direct possession of an individual by a demonic power. Traditionally, and at least in biblical language, there is overlapping between the terms "devil," "demon," and "unclean spirit." At any rate, no entity appears to have controlled a member of the Daly City household. Father Patzelt, writing in the Jesuit periodical *Provincial News*, described the forces at work as showing "exterior signs of the devil."

The New York *Times*, in a dispatch from San Francisco (January 27, 1974), reported that local priests and theologians did not doubt the phenomena reported, but raised these questions: "Whether what happened was caused by demonic forces, as Father Patzelt contends, or instead does it have a physical, psychological or even parapsychological explanation; and whether exorcism was needed or perhaps long-term psychotherapy." The psychological makings of the psychokinetic (PK) phenomena existed, as did the religious coloration they displayed. The phenomena apparently began after the birth of a child to a couple where the husband, a twenty-eight-year-old man, was an Orthodox British-born Jew, and his twenty-six-year-old wife was an Irish Catholic. With the baby on the scene, conscious or unconscious tensions within this mixed marriage might well have provided the energies of which Roll writes. Whatever was involved—from unconscious psycho-physical force to a personified demon—it would seem to have acted with a purpose. The exorcism was successful, and simultaneously the husband-father converted to Roman Catholicism. Considering the fact that a number of outsiders observed the Daly City phenomena and apparently the exorcism rites themselves, it would be extremely useful if the local archdiocese were to release the factual details of this case, rather than permit sensationalized reports about it to contribute to the exorcism chaos in the public mind.

In fact, lack of guidelines in the area of possession and exorcism is regrettable. Confusion is not dispelled by the presence of priests before television cameras who, in many cases, seem concerned with projecting an image of charming worldliness. Saying that it is helpful that baptism rites are said in Latin, because their exorcistic passages might upset a baby's parents—as was said in one television interview—glosses over a fundamental element in Christian belief: that man must guard against demonic influences from birth and that a diabolic influence, related to original sin, has to be eradicated during baptism. Altogether, traditional ideas about the diabolical and demonic can't simply be laughed off or shoved back under the carpet. Either they are valid, or they are not; either possession exists, or it does not.

From the parapsychological point of view, this question can be answered with a good deal of precision. The *Rituale Romanum*, dating back to 1614, says that knowledge of unknown languages, unusual powers and knowledge were among the phenomena that pointed toward genuine possession. The phrasing of the ritual was fairly recently changed specifically to include mental illness among the factors that rule out genuine possession. If we now keep in mind that recent thinking at the Vatican has made allowances for the parapsychological elements as well, the area of genuine exorcism is narrowed down to virtual oblivion. Knowledge of an "unknown" language can be ascribed to telepathy, to clairvoyance, or to some kind of xenoglossy as it is known in mediumship. Physical phenomena of the poltergeist type, including any kind of "obsession," such as Patzelt encountered, might fall into the category of psychokinesis. Unusual powers might either be in the nature of physical strength, which could be a side effect of mental instability, or mental power—knowledge of events in faraway places or in the future—in the telepathy, clairvoyance, or precognition categories.

Just about any phenomenon of possession can now be explained away, either as the result of mental illness or as one or another of the parapsychological phenomena. The *Rituale Romanum*, specifically designed to counteract the uncontrolled sixteenth-century wave of exorcisms, said that an exorcist "must have a critical approach that does not quickly yield to a belief in possession." The late Father Gebhard Frei of Switzerland has noted in *Probleme der Parapsychologie* (1971) that modern findings in medicine, psychology, and parapsychology make it difficult to "conclude indisputably" that possession does, in fact, exist. He added that this placed a heavy burden on the bishop or priest who may have to decide whether a possession case is genuine or not, because, "at least theoretically, certain doubts may nearly always exist."

I cannot see, from a parapsychological point of view, that these doubts were allayed, or even sufficiently dealt with, in either the

Washington-St. Louis or the Daly City cases. And yet, within a specific religio-cultural framework the use of exorcism may have distinct psychotherapeutic uses. It should not, of course, distract from more effective ways of therapy; but the number of psychotherapists who will tolerantly consider a bewildered would-be patient's reports of his psychic experiences, including the poltergeist type, is severely limited. A priest who practices pastoral psychology might do so in an exorcistic manner, and be quite effective. His "treatment" is likely to differ from non-directive methods of psychotherapy; if nothing else, exorcism assumes the deep personal involvement of the exorcist. The areas of faith healing, pastoral psychology, and other "unorthodox" methods of therapy would seem to have specific functions in unique situations. Much, as usual, depends on the human qualities and professional competence of the pastoral psychologist.

Students of the recent history of psychical research are familiar with the extraordinary technique developed by Dr. Walter Franklin Prince, onetime research director of the American and Boston Societies for Psychical Research. His paper "Two Cures of 'Paranoia' by Experimental Appeals to Purported Obsessing Spirits" has been reprinted in *The Psychoanalytic Review* (Vol. 5, No. 6, 1969) and is therefore easily available in libraries. Dr. Prince combined some of the most sophisticated elements of exorcism and psychotherapy. He felt that he was practicing a form of suggestion and explained: "That my acknowledgment that the imagined obsession might be actual ones, my agreement that the patient might be right in his (or her) opinion, put him (or her) into a favorable state of mind, a state of satisfaction with the admission, in which my exhortation to the imagined spirits to cease their mischief could act as suggestions operating in the patient." Prince acted *as if* there were a possessing spirit (he used "obsession" interchangeably with "possession"), just as an exorcist traditionally assumes that there is a demon, a diabolical entity, or an "unclean spirit." Others who have dealt with such problems, notably Canon J. D. Pearce-Higgins in England, have avoided the "exorcism" label and, assuming that not "unclean" but rather misguided spirits might be controlling a man or woman, emphasized spiritual cleansing and positive prayer.

What can we salvage out of this rather distressing exorcism chaos? Public fascination, bordering on mass hysteria, concerning possession and exorcism has brought the issue of this traditional therapy to the surface. It should get everyone down to learning what it is all about; parapsychology has traversed this road toward caution and critical appraisal for several decades. Parapsychology can bring a solid body of data to bear on the exorcism craze, particularly from its poltergeist and related PK studies; it has the history, the body of knowledge, the tools, and the attitude ready-made. It has developed its own appraisal of the psychology of testimony. Above all, it knows a good deal about the manner in which the experimenter can influence his experiment, by conscious and unconscious and even telepathic means.

The role of the parapsychological experimenter is akin to that of the exorcist, at least in a specific psychological area. The experimenter must guard against unconscious collusion with the subject of a test, just as the exorcist must guard against such a relation to the possessed. An all too dramatic exorcism case may do little more than give the exorcist the ego satisfaction of a successful battle with Satan, while the possessed acts as the battlefield in this glorious contest. Similarly, an immature ESP experimenter may see himself as a modern alchemist, while his subject glories in apparently exceptional qualities.

Parapsychology, throughout its existence, had to be on guard against being transformed into a vehicle for delusion. Certainly, much of the public fascination with ESP has been an outgrowth of the drug culture, involvement with witchcraft, astrology, and other fads. But valid parapsychological evidence has no kinship with crowd delusions. Against a strong current of fiction and mass thrills, channeled by the mass media, the line between the imaginary and the real must be maintained. Where motion-picture magic can turn delusion into a convincing image of reality, the actualities of religion, of psychology, and of parapsychology are all under attack. They must not yield, they must not retreat in confusion.

IV

The Scientific Diagnosis

19

Emotional Reactions to Psychic Experiences

FREDA MORRIS, Ph.D.

Dr. Morris, a psychologist in private practice in Berkeley, California, spent four years as assistant professor of medical psychology in the Neuropsychiatric Institute of the University of California, Los Angeles. The findings she reports in this paper are largely based on firsthand information gathered during this period. Dr. Morris is particularly interested in the use of hypnosis in learning and is a member of the American Society of Clinical Hypnosis and the Society for Clinical and Experimental Hypnosis.

Fear and superstition are the quintessence of the emotional disturbances often observed in persons who have had psychic experiences. There is controversy about which comes first—the emotional disturbance or the psychic phenomena. Contending that all parapsychological phenomena are in fact delusions of mentally disturbed persons recalls the defensive positions taken by entrenched scientists of the past in the face of challenging new scientific theories, e. g., the germ theory of disease, the heliocentric conception of the universe.

Equally, the fear and superstition which haunted early man with regard to the elements and disease held no greater sway than that which haunts modern man with regard to his own nature, especially with respect to any experiences suggestive of psychic phenomena. People who have psychic experiences are living in a world that does not explain experiences they have, and they understandably react to these experiences with fear and emotional disturbance at times.

Paradoxically, primitive societies of the past and present have seen to it that their members were emotionally and intellectually supported when they experienced psychic phenomena, but for many years civilized man has been limited in help available to him when he found himself troubled by such experiences.

Historically, religious counselors fulfilled the need to some extent until philosophic rationalism in the church reduced the acceptability of psychic experiences. And early hypnotists in the tradition of Mesmer used his techniques to help people with psychic problems—the hypnotic trance facilitating clairvoyance, telepathy, out-of-the-body experiences and similar occurrences often was used to gain control of undesirable psychic events. Yet while conservative elements in medicine and science were able to prevent the development and widespread use of Mesmer's techniques, they resurfaced in America in the 19th century in the work of the spiritual healers, clairvoyants, medical doctors, as well as some churches.

Sigmund Freud, the father of psychoanalysis, in his late life indirectly revealed an interest in psychic matters in a letter to a friend in 1920. Within the psychoanalytic situation, Freud once concluded that telepathy is most apt to occur as emotionally charged ideas move from the unconscious into pre-conscious areas of the mind. Several of his students made use of his discoveries of the nature of the unconscious to explore the psychic world and found his theories of value in helping persons who were troubled by psychic experiences.

Other notable men who held a special interest in psychic phenomena within the psychoanalytic tradition included the late Carl Jung, Sandor Ferenczi, and Nandor Fodor. Jung had a life-long interest in the psychic field, wrote extensively about it and his own psychic experiences, investigated these phenomena, and introduced theories about them, which are becoming more and more popular. Fodor, also a distinguished psychoanalyst who investigated and wrote extensively on *psi*, is credited with pioneering psychoanalytic techniques with psychic phenomena. Current prominent psychiatrists who are exploring the psychodynamics of psychic experiences include Jan Ehrenwald, Jule Eisenbud, and Ian Stevenson.

In the group of humanist psychologists, one is apt to find therapists sympathetic to psychic problems, particularly since the current interest in Zen and Yoga has introduced a broader view of man, which is more open to encompassing psychic experiences.

The emotional reactions of people to their psychic experiences vary, depending upon personality type, attitude, and the emotional content of their experiences. Given the fact that the ordinary complications of living, such as an accident or divorce, can seriously disturb some people, it is easy to envision a person unable to manage anxiety associated with psychic experiences.

When a psychically naïve person begins to experience psychic phenomena, he also may begin to limit his social relationships, see his friends less often, and fail to share with them the things that are really bothering him for fear they will lose respect for him or think him strange. Thus, he may begin to feel alone and isolated just at the time when he is becoming more fearful of the psychic experiences. Without the support and reality contact provided by friends, he may begin to fear for his sanity as the psychic experiences become more frequent and strange.

For instance, if the nature of the phenomena involves movement of objects (such as flying vases, etc.), he may fear for his physical safety or that of his family. Or if the phenomena involve "communication" with the spirits of the deceased, his fear of death may take a myriad of forms: psychosis, neurosis, nervousness, obsessions, and compulsions, or psychophysiological reactions such as tiredness, stomach distress, headaches, and general aches and pains. Frequently there may be nightmares or insomnia.

Why do people sometimes need psychotherapy as a result of having had a psychic experience? To understand this need, one should try to understand how he would react if the following events were to happen. Imagine a happy and successful family man contentedly dozing in his chair dreaming:

His father, dressed in a plaid sport coat, is driving down a freeway. A truck pulls alongside, a tire blows out, and the truck swerves into him. His father's car door flies open and he falls to the pavement into the path of a blue Volkswagen. The dreamer awakens in horror and fear, his layman's knowledge of psychoanalysis (It must mean I hate my father) not quite resolving the apprehension. Then, before his open eyes, there appears an apparition of his father. His father smiles and the sound of his voice says "Son, don't grieve for me." The apparition then disappears. Obviously shaken, he doesn't want to answer his wife's solicitous questions for fear she might think he is going crazy. He begins worrying about himself, wondering if he has been working too hard. The phone rings and startles him. It's his brother saying that their father was just killed. A truck hit his car. He fell out and another car ran over him. "Yes," he answers, "it was a blue Volkswagen. Yes, Dad was wearing a plaid coat. How did you know?"

How *did* he know? And how would anyone feel at this confirmation of the premonition? Would he fear for his sanity? Would he assume that his father was still alive in spirit and could communicate with him? Would that idea upset him? Would he say that the dreamed prediction was a chance happening? Or would he search for some understandable explanation?

The three most common reactions vary in their psychological sequellae:

1. Fear of insanity leads to such gross psychological defenses as attempting to forget the experience ever happened, and is the least adaptive reaction.
2. Admission of the experience ("of course, my father came to me in spirit") without expecting to understand, prevents anxiety but perpetuates ignorance.
3. Seeking further knowledge and an explanation of the phenomenon combats anxiety and seems to have the most salutary effect. However, explanations will be characterized as superstitions to the extent that they do not stand up against scientific investigations.

Many people who have psychic or psychic-like experiences become obsessed with determining whether the phenomena actually exist outside their minds (forgetting that philosophers have pondered for centuries whether the rock is "real" or an illusion of the mind).

Psychic phenomena seem to be a function of the unconscious mind, as well as the overt personality and conscious concerns of the individual. In fact, it seems that psychic phenomena can be used psychoanalytically like dreams, to understand concerns or conflicts of the individual. But whether any one experience is psychic or not is not critical. It may be helpful to assume that there are a combination of factors (including the mind) involved in producing psychic phenomena, and to take the experience at face value, while keeping careful records of the occurrences so they can later be evaluated.

Gertrude Schmeidler, a distinguished parapsychologist and psychologist, has suggested that psychic experiences can be expected in two distinct groups of individuals: those whose "normal controls and inhibitions have never fully developed" and those who are "so well-adjusted, so stable, that they can relax their controls without undue anxiety." This hypothesis was arrived at by noting that some studies suggest psychics are not well adjusted while others find them to be exceptionally productive, creative, and healthy. Furthermore, Dr. Schmeidler postulated that psychic phenomena are in some sense functions of the unconscious mind. It is known that the archaic, unconscious processes observed in psychosis are also very important in creative thinking, in dreams and fantasy, which may explain the aforementioned paradoxical finding.

It appears that pathological responses to psychic phenomena are more often psychoneurotic, with anxiety, physical symptoms, and depression, than they are psychotic with reality distortions.

The case which follows illustrates several problems and reactions. A young couple, who will be called Ted and Karen, began to experience what is commonly known as a poltergeist disturbance (now technically called *recurrent spontaneous psychokinesis*). They carefully guarded the fact of their experience from their parents and friends for they believed they would not get a sympathetic hearing. Naturally their relationships with close friends deteriorated because they could not share their feelings in any meaningful way without mentioning what was foremost on their minds. They feared they would lose respect or be considered weird. As the activities of the poltergeist increased,

Karen in particular developed fears and both physical and psychological complaints.

When they finally contacted the Southern California Society for Psychical Research asking for help, they were referred to the author. I found them to be rational, pleasant, and appropriate in their feelings and behavior, showing no signs of mental disturbance in a standard psychological interview. It seemed extremely unlikely that they were delusional or hallucinating. I used hypnosis with both Ted and Karen to reduce their anxieties, to get additional information, and to check the accuracy of their reports.

Ted and Karen had shown little interest in the psychic until their current experiences, which varied from disappearing objects to confirmed premonitions and ultimately led to investigations by several researchers and psychics.

The most frightening incident was related by Ted as follows: "I looked down at the inside of my arms and found them streaked, marked, criss-crossed all over with ballpoint ink, as if someone had taken a ballpoint pen and just marked back and forth on both my arms. This was very startling and I ran to show Karen. When I got there, I found her all marked up the same way. Neither of us had a ballpoint pen anywhere near. This experience really made the hair on the back of my neck stand up. Karen was quite shaken by it, too."

Ted went on to tell how he had tried to reproduce the phenomenon artificially, e. g. transferring ink from a paper by pressing it against his skin. He tried every way he could think of to establish similar lines on his arms without actually marking them and found no way that this could be done.

After a series of experiences such as this and after several psychics independently told them of a death in the house long ago, Karen became quite frightened. She described herself as being hysterical for a month or so during a period of great poltergeist activity. That is, she was very upset, nervous, unable to sleep, and occasionally had headaches and feelings of tiredness and weakness.

On one occasion Karen walked into her bedroom feeling fine, but upon entering the room she blacked out and fell. There was no warning, no dizziness or weakness, she just suddenly became unconscious. Ted came upon her lying on the floor and lifted her onto the bed, where she soon regained consciousness. He then called a psychic, who came to see Karen and explained that a spirit was trying to possess her. The psychic went through an exorcism procedure, immediately after which Karen said she felt like a new person.

Karen commented later, "Of course, it might have been psychological. I feel really strange because I don't know if I believe in exorcism and these protective measures or not. What scares me about the whole thing is, why are they always trying to possess me, and is it really that easy? Having our spirit here doesn't frighten me. I feel that it's a friendly spirit but I think there have been others that can really cause trouble."

At present, Karen is feeling quite comfortable psychologically. She feels she has a "relationship" with the spirit and can talk to it if necessary, but she prefers to ignore it if possible. She does not like to talk about the spirit because she says this makes it get more active. Ted is concerned about Karen's health and, though curious about the nature of the phenomena, he does not try to bring them about. He has seen enough to know the phenomenon is a reality and awaits a scientific breakthrough for an explanation.

The effect of the psychic experiences on Karen was physical disability. In the next case there was primarily an emotional reaction which was long term and quite incapacitating.

Patricia, a woman in her forties, had made her living for several years as a bookkeeper in a grocery store when her trouble began. She had a reputation among her friends of being able to go into a trance and to become aware of information not ordinarily available. However, she had had limited experience with the trance state and knew little about psychic phenomena.

One day about four years ago, three girl friends called on her, bringing a young Mexican girl about whom they were concerned. The girl was in trouble emotionally and needed some kind of assistance. The friends asked Patricia if she would go into a trance to see if she could get information that would be of help to the girl. Nothing else was said to Patricia that would have given her any clues as to what to expect. Patricia's description of the trance experience follows:

"It is very hot and dry. The air is filled with tension. Two men push a boy about 16 out of an old dusty car. They get out and roughly shove him toward an old shanty. The boy's hands are tied behind him. My mind's eye follows them into the shanty. The boy is terrified, and I feel his fear as if it were my own. The men are filled with hate and revenge, and I feel their hate as if it were my own. They throw a rope over a rafter and put the noose around the boy's neck. They make him stand on a crate. Then one of them kicks the crate out from under him. The boy soon dies and the men leave."

Patricia went on to explain to them that the murder had been for revenge over the kidnapping of a baby girl many years earlier. She had a very difficult time coming out of the trance and brought all the emotions she had experienced into the waking state. The friends then told Patricia that the girl's 16-year-old brother had been found hanged in a shanty on the desert and the police declared it suicide. The sister could not accept this. The Mexican girl also confided that she was not her parents' own child and now suspected she had been kidnapped.

Patricia was miserable, not only because of the experience in the trance state but also because she was frightened to have her report confirmed so clearly. She swore that she would never again let herself go into a trance or have a psychic experience if she could prevent it. With this decision, Patricia's life closed off. She became increasingly depressed and disinterested in anything. Finally she was no longer able to work. After about four years, she came to me for treatment and by then was experiencing deep feelings of guilt when she heard about anything wrong that had been done. She was fully aware of the irrationality of her reaction, yet was helpless in overcoming her feelings. She had decided she was unwilling to live unless she found a way to overcome them.

In her treatment, hypnosis was used to help Patricia explore her own emotions. She spent several sessions reliving her unhappy childhood, but to no avail. Then, on the supposition that a creative, constructive effort involving psychical research would help rebuild her defaulted self-concept, she was asked to prepare and deliver a lecture on psychic phenomena to a large group of high school seniors. She was taken aback by the request, but diligently fell to the task and succeeded admirably. This seemed to be the turning point for Patricia. She began to read psychic literature avidly and was delighted that scientists would seriously consider these phenomena. She asked the author to help her gain more control of her trance states through the use of hypnosis. In the hypnotically induced trance state she was able to have psychic experiences without becoming overwhelmed as she had in the past. Within a few weeks she had secured a job as executive assistant for a psychical research society in Los Angeles and was enjoying herself immensely. She became happy and outgoing and is doing an excellent job in the Society.

In the case of Patricia, severely maladaptive emotional turmoil followed efforts to suppress psychic experiences and a happy outcome followed development of an active interest in psychical research.

The next case demonstrates essentially a healthy, adaptive reaction to psychic experiences from the beginning. Nancy's reaction is most likely a function of the matter-of-fact way psychic phenomena were accepted in her childhood home. There, she was encouraged to be aware of her psychic experiences and to share them with her family. Nancy called with the following story:

"There's something going on in my apartment that has been going on for about a year. I'm not particularly upset by it but I'd like to get it under control if there is a way. I know I'm not going crazy, but I'm afraid it may scare hell out of my ten-year-old son some time. There seems to be a very active poltergeist that moves things around the house, throws things, and makes noises. I have a room divider made of beads. Several friends have seen these move about in strange ways and even fall off the strands. A friend who didn't believe in anything like that saw the beads moving and then felt his coat tugged as he walked by the beads. Once a bead even flew off and hit me on the head.

"In trying to explain to myself how this works, I just can't say whether I believe in spirits or ghosts or not. I know ESP is real because I've had so many experiences with it. The first ESP experience I remember was when I was six years old. I had a dream in which I saw my grandfather's foot stepping on my goldfish. I woke up and told my cousin. When I went into the kitchen, there was my fish crushed on the floor. I asked my grandfather about it and he said he had stepped on it. This poltergeist experience, though, is something I don't comprehend. I don't know what to think about it, but I wish I understood it."

One of Nancy's friends who had seen the room divider beads move was interviewed. He said that there were no air currents in the apartment and that the beads moved in about a twelve inch arc for no reason he could imagine. Once he watched them for about fifteen minutes. When asked what his reaction was, he said he wasn't particularly upset or dismayed since he had some knowledge of psychic phenomena. He said that Nancy also seemed to accept things that happened without being upset.

When I called several months later, Nancy reported that she is continuing to develop her psychic ability and is reading psychically for her friends. The poltergeist is active at times but by now her son seems able to accept it as a matter of course.

The cases presented here give a glimpse of the range of emotional reactions to a few types of psychic experiences. The magnitude of the problem in terms of individuals affected cannot be estimated with any degree of accuracy. But aside from the human suffering which results from the ignorance surrounding the subject, it is clear that a large part of our world awaits exploration.

If we accept orderliness as a characteristic of our universe, how do we account for psychic experiences? Attributing such phenomena to chance or to the vagaries of the universe precludes integration with the body of scientific theory and knowledge. However, the prediction and control which scientific explanation facilitates would be possible with discovery of energy forms compatible with what is known of parapsychological experiences. Currently, a group of physicists is theorizing about a new particle basic to all other particles, groups of which behave like a wave form which can be modulated and ejected from complex molecules such as those in the brain.

There is a great need for further research that would integrate the findings of psychical research into basic particle physics. As of now, there is no known particle or energy form which has the characteristics necessary to explain the phenomena reported. Perhaps a new theory of physics which supersedes Einstein's theory is needed. This is a very big order, but it seems one that must be filled before we can begin to understand what is happening in the psychic world.

The acceptance of parapsychology as a science by the American Association for the Advancement of Science was a great step forward. This recognition by a major representative of the scientific community is matched by an increasing acceptance on the part of the general public.

In the meantime, while science gradually develops knowledge in this area, people who feel they have psychic experiences should approach them with an open mind and also follow the common rules of mental health. Equally important, it sometimes may be necessary to hold in abeyance the interest and activity in psychic matters if emotional health is lacking, and it is not advisable to persist in developing psychically, while neglecting physical or emotional health. For instance, if there are ongoing feuds or other strained relationships—envy, jealousy, hate, fear, and so on—they should be ameliorated before delving into or continuing to develop the psychic.

In general it appears that for most people it is not healthy to try to cut one's self off from the psychic world when it manifests itself, nor does it further the advancement of scientific understanding.

I personally encourage people suited to handling the psychic part of life to enhance psychic experiences in a common-sense fashion. This must be done in the context of balance in work and play, rest and good nutrition, and close, warm, open relationships with friends and family. Moreover, reading responsible books, magazines, and journals on psychical research and keeping notes on the psychic experiences are beneficial.

Though psychic phenomena seem to be a function of the unconscious mind, they also seem related to the personality and conscious concerns of the individual. In my opinion, the combination of psychoanalytic understanding and hypnotic techniques seems to be the most effective approach in dealing with emotional responses to psychic experiences.

In learning to live with this part of man's makeup, perhaps it is equally important that we encourage the use of funds in the advancement of the study of basic particle physics and psychical research. It is to be assumed that all human experiences follow natural laws that will some day be understood.

20

The Experimenter's Responsibility

J. FRASER NICOL

Mr. Fraser Nicol has had many years of experience as a psychical researcher, in the course of which he has investigated almost all categories of phenomena, including apparitions, prophetic dreams, haunted houses, poltergeists and other spontaneous occurrences, as well as numerous mental and physical mediums, genuine and fraudulent. For about two decades of his career he directed his activities and published reports upon the so-called statistical types of research in psychokinetic dice throwing and ESP card guessing, sometimes in collaboration with his wife, née Betty Humphrey. Those experiments involved nearly a quarter of a million tests. At various times he has conducted investigations for the (London) Society for Psychical Research, of which he was a member of the governing council and chairman of the research committee; the American Society for Psychical Research (New York); the parapsychology laboratory at Duke University; and the Parapsychology Foundation (New York), with which he served as research and editorial consultant.

Psychical experiments in card guessing and the like have been going on now for a period passing ninety years. Why is it, then, that among fair-minded students there is so much uncertainty about the whole subject?

The basic reason for skepticism is easily stated. In all experimental sciences belief in the existence of a phenomenon is founded on what scientists call *"repeatability of the effect."* If a scientist reports a certain significant discovery in a new experiment his claim will be believed when and only when other scientists trying the experiment report the same result. If they fail to get that result they will be forced to conclude that there was an *undetected flaw* in the original experiment.

In the established sciences there are probably tens of thousands of repeatable experiments. In psychical research after nearly a century of almost continuous investigation there is no repeatable experiment. Not one. That is the Achilles' heel of our subject.

A consequence of this history of unrelieved failure is that some critics hold that believers in paranormal phenomena must be self-deluded. This, however, is going a little too far. Taking the psychical research field as a whole, including brilliant evidence from telepathic mediums, spontaneous cases and other sources, the evidence for the paranormal is too strong to be so scornfully dismissed. Nevertheless there is an uncomfortable element of truth in the delusion theory. For many ESP and other experiments have been done that will not survive close examination. Yet, though the experiments are riddled with flaws they will be naïvely quoted by professional parapsychologists as if they were perfectly genuine.

It is the purpose of this chapter to present the reader with specimens of bad experimentation and baseless claims.

Before displaying those exhibits, however, we must first ask: In what way do investigations in the accepted sciences differ from those in psychical research? In the established sciences the experimenter is looking for natural or normal causes of the phenomena he is investigating, whereas in psychical experiments the researcher's task is to make "normal causes" *impossible*. If under such conditions "something happens" then a paranormal phenomenon has been uncovered. Such occurrences fall into four main categories: telepathy (transmission of information from one mind to another), clairvoyance (discovery of facts not known to any person), precognition (prediction), psychokinesis (influence of mind over matter). Telepathy, clairvoyance and precognition are all described as "extrasensory perception" (ESP for short).

In all those departments of research the opportunities for error are almost beyond counting. In this regard most researchers can tell wry stories about themselves, especially of their early adventures. It will be chastening to begin with a story against myself.

Many years ago I conducted a series of experiments to test the belief that the mind can influence the fall of dice. If there were such a thing as an unbiased die, honestly and fairly thrown, the probability of a particular face turning up would be 1 in 6, since there are six faces. If such a die were thrown say six hundred times the final result would be approximately one hundred of each face. In my experiments, in which a number of people acted as subjects on different occasions, it became evident that one die which we occasionally used was biased *against* face 3. Instead of one sixth of the throws turning up face 3, there were only about one seventh.

Late one evening, being in the right mood to exercise psychokinetic power (supposing I possessed such an extraordinary gift), I resolved to concentrate my will to improve on the past performances of the recalcitrant face 3. During several hours I made 2,640 casts of the die. After an indifferent start the number of 3's increased remarkably and at the end of the night's work the score was 493. This was 77 above the number expected by chance for that particular face, giving odds against the result being merely a whim of chance of 20,000 to 1.

Inspired by this apparent evidence for psychokinesis I tried on two subsequent occasions, when in the same confident mood, to "will" faces 5 and 1. Disappointingly and mysteriously the results were close to chance.

Many years elapsed before I was completely disillusioned. One of the several dice used in the prolonged researches had survived, carefully preserved and identified. I now carried out a large number of throws without willing any particular face to turn up. In the original psychokinesis experiments none of the subjects had shown any evidence of psychokinesis. All that we got was the chance frequencies for each face. But now in this new experiment the face frequencies were utterly different. *The die had changed its bias.* It followed therefore that there was a perfectly natural reason for my amazing success on that one memorable evening. I had chosen face 3 when it happened that there was a small percentage change in the frequency for that face. There was nothing "psychic" about it.

My experience with the mischievous playfulness of dice was not unique, for there was the case of a Dutch scientist, H. C. Hamaker, who for purely mathematical purposes threw a ten-sided die hundreds of times on a table whose top was almost but not quite horizontal. If the die was thrown "downhill" it produced certain face frequencies; thrown "uphill" the frequencies were utterly changed.

Dice thrown on tables are not to be trusted, and I regret to say that this is particularly true of the millions of die throws performed by Dr. J. B. Rhine and his colleagues in the parapsychology laboratory at Duke University. Many of those experiments are flawed by more errors and misconceptions than it is possible to describe here. But the most famous "discovery" was that a dice thrower's success ratio varied during the course of an experiment. This was christened a "position effect." It is, however, no more than a first cousin to my own hopes of long ago. And the published reports on pyschokinesis are in most cases rife with errors and misconceptions, which become plain to anyone who cares to examine those reports with an unbiased mind.

The case for telepathy and other forms of extrasensory perception is much better than it is for psychokinesis. A hundred years of researches have produced evidence of such strength as to put the reality of the phenomena beyond rational dispute. Nevertheless reports are sometimes published, usually by novices, but occasionally by experienced researchers, that are an embarrassment to read.

The material to be transmitted between agent ("sender") and percipient ("receiver") is usually the well-known ESP cards which show one of five suits: circle, cross, square, star, wavy lines. In some experiments, a percipient is seated at a table. Opposite him the agent-experimenter shuffles a pack of cards, lays them face down on the table, picks up the top card and fixes his gaze on it until the percipient announces his guess. And so on, through the remaining twenty-four cards in the deck.

The risks run in such an experiment are numerous. To take an actual happening, a scientist, having a friend of mine as his subject, carefully shuffled the pack but as he laid it down he thoughtlessly tilted the pack with the result that the subject easily saw the bottom card.

A greater danger is reflection of the card face on a polished surface. This may be the table top presenting the image of the card as it is removed from the deck. Or, when the agent is looking at the card face the percipient may notice its reflection on a mirror hanging on a wall, or a picture, or a window, or any shiny surface. A fascinating example of the reflection fraud was reported by two famous British researchers, the Honorable Everard Feilding and Wortley Baggally. A father had reported that his fourteen-year-old daughter could guess playing cards with a high degree of success when he was acting as the sender. Observing some of the card guessing, Feilding and Baggally suspected that the girl was detecting reflections of the cards in Daddy's eyeglasses. So it was, and the astute young girl confessed. I may add as a personal experience that the late Edward Osborn and I investigated a similar case in which an adolescent boy could guess cards with high success when his bespectacled father was the agent, but not at all when his parent's face was out of his line of sight.

It naturally happens that the same deck of cards is used over and over again. In such circumstances a subject may have the opportunity to put secret markings on the cards. But with some ESP decks the marking has been unintentionally made in the course of printing. Apparently, when the symbols are printed on the face, a slight shrinkage is produced on the card. When such a card is held face down at a suitable angle to the light the impression on the face becomes visible on the back.

An agent, if he is not on his guard, may give away cues without being aware of doing so. A charming example was narrated by a very candid experimenter, Mrs. M. de G. Verrall, lecturer in classics at Newnham College, Cambridge, England. She recalled how, testing her little girl Helen, aged about eight: "I was looking at 8 of hearts, and H. guessed 7 of hearts, adding, 'That must not

count, for I heard you say hearts.' On further inquiry, she said
that she heard —t, —t, —t, —t, and then 'art, 'art, 'art. My attention
had, as I knew, wandered on this occasion, and it is possible I did
say the word unconsciously."

Even when an experimenter-agent remains perfectly silent he
may unwittingly provide cues by unconscious movements of his
lips, which an observant percipient may interpret, not always correctly but sufficient to win a score of hits well above chance.

The greatest of all dangers arises when agent and percipient
are personal friends, for unless the researcher's experimental conditions are so tight as to make fraud totally impossible, the two
other participants may plan out a scheme whereby they will obtain huge but bogus scores in ESP card guessing. Young people
are particularly clever at devising schemes to deceive solemn scientists. Such frauds have a very long history. In the early days of
organized psychical research in Britain the physicist Professor
(later Sir) William Barrett heard the extraordinary news that no
less than four of the youthful daughters of the Reverend A. M.
Creery, and also the family's maidservant, possessed the gift of
"thought reading." In their subsequent investigation Barrett and
other leaders of the Society for Psychical Research in Britain
found that the girls were highly successful in guessing playing
cards, personal names and names of places. One of the girls
would be sent out of the room while the researchers in the
presence of the other members of the family would decide on a
card or name or object. When the girl was brought back into the
room, she would give her impression of the target after a short in-
terval. The ratio of success was extraordinarily high. On a few occasions the target was known only to one experimenter, yet there
was still some success. Nevertheless the general picture must have
raised some doubts.

Eventually two of the girls were invited to Cambridge, and
there, in the presence of Professor Henry and Mrs. Eleanor Sidg-
wick and Mr. and Mrs. Edmund Gurney, the girls were detected
using code. Gurney afterward reported:

"The code was as follows:—When the two sisters were in sight
of one another, the signals used were a slight upward look for
hearts, downwards for diamonds, to the right for spades, and to

the left for clubs. Further, the right hand put up to the face meant king, the left hand to the face meant queen, and knave was indicated by crossing the arms. It is doubtful whether there were any signs for other cards. We failed to make any out clearly. A table showing the degree of success in guessing each card suggests that there were signs for 10 and ace, but that they were either only used occasionally or used with poor success.

"In experiments in which a screen was placed between the two sisters, so that they could not see each other, auditory signs were used to indicate suits. A scraping with the feet on the carpet meant hearts, and sighing, coughing, sneezing or yawning meant diamonds. If there were signs to distinguish between the black suits they were—like the signs for 10 and ace in the visual code—sparingly used or often unsuccessful."

When the girls were put in separate rooms they completely failed.

In Wales, two adolescent cousins named Jones were investigated for card guessing by Dr. S. G. Soal of London University, and others. At one point they were detected using an auditory code of a method very similar to that of the Creery girls. Their audacity was such that they even changed their code in the presence of an investigator who did not know what they were talking about because they spoke in the Welsh language.

A recurring problem in psychical investigation is that persons hitherto unknown in the subject will venture into difficult research without prior training or even a careful reading of the literature. A famous researcher, the late Whately Carington, used to say: "Will practitioners in other fields please note that the methods of orthodox science are not necessarily good enough for psychical research."

One scientist who has apparently never heard of Carington's warning, and certainly has only the slightest understanding of the tough techniques of this subject, is Dr. Warner R. Wilson, Psychology Department, University of Hawaii. Dr. Wilson carried out ESP tests with 621 students in groups of about 40 at a time; hence there must have been 15 or 16 separate sessions. The subjects sat at tables in groups of three or four; and so there would be an average of about a dozen such groups in the room at each session.

The ESP targets consisted of "a column of ten plusses and zeros" in random order. These, we are told in the printed report, were enclosed in "opaque envelopes," and two identical sets were available to each small group. The different groups, however, had different sets of targets.

The flaw is the envelopes. So-called "sealed envelopes" were a source of endless controversy in the primitive period of psychical research long ago. Experienced investigators have long recognized their use (except under very exceptional circumstances) as being an open invitation to cynical tricksters to exercise their ingenuity. An envelope can be judged opaque if it has survived the necessary tests. Dr. Wilson does not say that he made any tests, so one must assume that he made none.

Let us apply tests to a supposedly opaque envelope. I write ten plusses and zeros on a cardboard file card, which is then placed in a thick manila envelope on the table. In that position it is "opaque." Raising it toward the light I can read the plusses and zeros with very little difficulty. Next, holding it under the table and switching on a small flashlight underneath, I read all the symbols as clearly as if there were no envelope enclosing them.

Other methods are available for discovering the secrets of sealed envelopes. One is by means of two thin knitting needles placed together and tied tightly at one end. Slip the other end under the unsealed part of the envelope's flap so that the paper inside is held between the needles. Turn the latter through a number of revolutions until the paper forms a thin cylinder round the needles, which are then pulled out and the contents of the paper become visible. The paper is returned to the envelope by reversing the process. All this can be done under a table top.

It is quite likely that before the first session of the Wilson experiments students would not know what the experimental conditions would be; but thereafter the five hundred or six hundred students would know what to expect, and any among them with a taste for practical joking could make their preparations accordingly.

The University of Hawaii is not the only seat of science and learning from which dubious ESP experiments have been ushered into print. Long before the Wilson affair, Dr. G. H. Estabrooks conducted a series of experiments at Harvard University. Thereafter, over a long period of years, they were discussed or mentioned with respect by J. B. Rhine, Whately Carington, J. G. Pratt and S. G. Soal, all men of great experience in the field. There is reason to believe that their appreciation was hardly justified.

In the course of several months Estabrooks tested numerous persons in the Harvard Psychology Laboratory. Some of them were personal friends of Estabrooks, but the majority were college students. Usually agent and percipient were personal friends—a point to be noted.

There were two types of experiment. In the first the agent sat at a table with Estabrooks, while his friend the percipient was placed in an adjoining room, with the communicating door closed. The experimenter drew a card from the pack, showed it to the agent, and by an electrical device signaled to the percipient in the other room, who then wrote down his impression of the target card.

A session consisted of twenty card trials made at intervals of twenty seconds. Eighty-three persons were tested, giving a total of 1,660 trials. By chance alone, the expected score for suits would be one quarter of the total, namely 415, but the percipients actually scored 473, an average of 28.5 per cent. For this score the odds against chance are 1,300 to 1. In terms of color of cards (black or red) the chance score would be 830. The actual score was 938, or 56.5 per cent as against 50 per cent expected by chance. The odds against chance are 8 million to one.

In the second type of experiment, Estabrooks and agent remained in the same room, but the percipient was removed to a room four doors and sixty feet distant. The scores were somewhat below what would be expected by chance.

The above is an outline of Estabrooks' report as published by the Boston Society for Psychic Research. Unfortunately for the facts of history, the author failed to print the most astonishing part of his experiments, which indeed he did not disclose to the world until twenty years later when he printed them in his book *Spiritism* (Dutton, 1947). He there recalled how he had "assumed fraud to be impossible," the conditions, he supposed, being "absolutely foolproof." And long after the report appeared, J. B. Rhine judged the conditions to be "excellent for excluding sense perception." Both authors were wrong.

Estabrooks now described how two sophomores whom he had tested for telepathy returned the next day and boldly told the researcher that they could make his "fraud-proof conditions look ludicrous." When he told them they were "talking nonsense" they bet him "the price of a supper" that they would do what they claimed.

Agreeing to the wager, Estabrooks for the first experiment put the percipient as usual in the adjoining room with the door closed. On this occasion he used the entire pack of fifty-two cards, the percipient apparently recording his guesses as red or black. "I felt sure of a free supper," Estabrooks recalled, and "I was keenly on the lookout for fraud . . . Then we compared results. To my utter consternation the mind reader in the next room had guessed the color of the cards—red or black—correctly the entire fifty-two times . . . [To] be tricked by a couple of college sophomores was a real blow to my pride. But the worst was yet to come."

He then put the youths through the long-distance experiment, which in this case meant that the percipient was in a room a hundred feet away with a hallway in between. "The sender allowed me to open the doors whenever I felt like it, examine him, in fact, do anything I chose." Yet once again the percipient got all fifty-two cards right. The chance odds for the whole evening's performance are a billion billion billion billion billion to one.

Estabrooks spent two days trying to think of schemes by which the youths could have fooled him. Completely baffled, he then persuaded them to confess their secrets—for the price of two theater tickets.

In both series of experiments the trials were of course numbered 1 to 52. The conspirators arranged that if in odd-numbered trials the actual card was red the sender would give no signal. Similarly for even-numbered trials if the card was black. But in trials where those specifications did not hold—e.g., if an odd-numbered trial was actually black—the sender would transmit a signal.

Two signaling methods were used. In the adjacent room experiments the sender "would clear his voice, or shift his chair or do anything to break the silence, but always in a perfectly natural manner so as not to attract attention." In the distant room experiments the secret of success was the presence of a third man. In those experiments Estabrooks and the agent sat at a table on which there was a lamp. Beyond the agent was a door leading to the hallway. There was a gap under the door. The lamp, when unobstructed, showed under this crack and could be seen in the hallway. The agent sat in such a way that normally the light was obscured from the crack. Then, as the unsuspecting Estabrooks recalled, "when the cards were coming as expected—red on odd, black on even guesses—he remained perfectly still. When not, he simply shifted his shoulder a couple of inches. This allowed a telltale beam of light to flash out under the door." The third man, some distance along the corridor and near the percipient's room, watched the gap under the door by looking through a pair of field glasses, and relayed the message by light tapping to the percipient.

Agent and percipient are not the only participants who may venture into cheating. As a British investigator, Dr. R. H. Thouless, has pointed out, researchers themselves "must also consider the possibility that other people may think the results are due to dishonesty on the part of the experimenter . . . It is unlikely that an apparently honest research worker will lie about his experimental results but the likelihood is not zero."

My wife (an ESP investigator for many years) and I were invited to act as observers in the telepathic experiments of two sisters. They were and remain (for reasons which will appear below) unknown to the world of psychical research. The percipient held an executive post in a business house. Her sister, the experimenter-agent, was much younger; she had apparently earned a fine reputation for accuracy in a minor professional post from which she earned her living.

Using Rhine-type ESP cards, for which the number of hits expected by chance is five in a run of twenty-five, they reported scores as high as twenty, which in terms of probability is out of this world.

Our own investigation took place in two rooms of the ladies' apartment. The connecting door was kept open, but with agent and percipient out of each other's field of view. In one room my wife supervised the experimenter as she looked at each card and recorded it. In the other room I watched the percipient, who lay on a sofa and called out her guesses, which were also recorded by the sister in the next room. What that young experimenter apparently did not know was that I too was making a record of the percipient's calls.

After about a dozen runs (several hundred trials) there was no sign of telepathy between the sisters, the score being close to chance. The experimenter-agent then suggested that perhaps the near presence of my wife (who, however, had been relaxed and friendly throughout) might be inhibiting the "phenomena": so would she care to move away? She did so—to a chair at the far end of the room—having previously noticed the experimenter's 100 per cent accuracy in recording the data trial by trial. The young lady was now of course free of supervision.

With the changed conditions the scores shot up miraculously. The hour being late, we had time for only four runs (a hundred trials), for which the chance number of hits would be twenty. In the very first run the recorded score was an incredible twenty-two, and for all four runs fifty-nine, for which the odds are trillions to one.

Returning home, I compared all the experimenter-agent's records of her sister's guesses with my own records. The outcome was disillusionment, for it turned out that so long as my wife was sitting beside the experimenter, and therefore confirming each guess, the two sets of records were in perfect agreement. But when, in the last four runs, the experimenter was unsupervised, a comparison of the two sets of records showed that in dozens of trials instead of recording her sister's actual guesses she had substituted bogus guesses to make them agree with the target cards. The seemingly high scores were altogether spurious.

A week later when we made a return visit and described the extraordinary contrast between the witnessed and unwitnessed records, the percipient, seeing the obvious implication pointing to her sister's faithlessness, was deeply distressed. The experimenter-agent never uttered a word.

In the March 1974 issue of his *Journal of Parapsychology* Dr. J. B. Rhine published a sensational article in which he wrote of numerous cases of fraud and deceit by parapsychology experimenters. A dozen of them seem to have occurred in the 1940s and 1950s. No names are given, nor how many of the frauds took place in his own laboratory. Four of them, he says, "were caught 'red-handed' in having falsified their results; four others did not contest (i.e., tacitly admitted) the implications that something was wrong with their reports that seemed hard to explain and they did not try. In the case of the remaining four the evidence was more circumstantial, but it seemed to our staff they were in much the same doubtful category as the other eight." He writes also of several more cases that seem to have occurred in more recent times.

It is desirable—indeed an imperative necessity—to know how many of those parapsychologists had published research reports before or after their particular frauds were unmasked. Where were they published, and when? If this is not made known, then students of our subject will try guessing the identities of the culprits. Human nature being what it is, gossip will develop and the finger of suspicion will be pointed at, perhaps, perfectly innocent men and women.

The ink was hardly dry on that number of the *Journal of Parapsychology* when Rhine had to write another article for the next number, revealing fraud by the director of Rhine's own Institute for Parapsychology in Durham, North Carolina. Rhine did not give the offender's name (denoting him as "W") but it was published in a long article in the New York *Times*. He was Dr. W. J. Levy, twenty-six years of age, who had previously printed quite a number of reports on his various experimental investigations.

The experiment that led to Levy's downfall was a highly technical one devised to detect the supposed power of mind over matter (psychokinesis) in rats. Self-recording electronic equipment was in use. Levy's co-experimenter was puzzled by his chief's behavior. As Rhine afterward reported, the colleague "observed W at the equipment table with his hand on the equipment at a time when the record showed a long string of hits on the paper punch tape, which was the official record of the experiment." Having communicated his discovery to two other staff members, he and they "planned for duplicate recordings of the test data," and for one of them "to witness from a concealed position the suspected manipulation of the equipment by W." As a result of these secret investigations, "the three men knew then that W had deliberately falsified the experimental results."

They reported their findings to Rhine. The latter confronted Levy with the allegations, which in a few minutes he admitted. He resigned his post. Soon afterward he was asked to resign from the Parapsychological Association, the president of which (Dr. Robert Morris) stated to the New York *Times* that "This whole thing serves as a reminder that you can't always take research findings at face value."

21

Psychosis in the Séance Room

HANS BENDER

Professor Bender, one of the world's leading parapsychologists, is a member of the Psychology Department of the University of Freiburg, Germany, and director of its Institute for Border Areas of Psychology and Psychohygiene. His many decades of research, teaching and publishing have recently been celebrated in a Festschrift, prepared by Professor Bender's colleagues in his honor, entitled Psi and Psyche *(1974). As a psychologist who is aware of the dangers of what he terms "mediumistic psychosis," Bender combines caution toward the dangers of spiritistic practices with tolerance toward the positive aspects of these and related activities.*

A German court once asked me to testify, as a specialist, in a trial dealing with "bodily harm" growing out of spiritualistic practices. The defendant was an elderly lady authoress who led a spiritualist home circle. One of the participants, a young woman, had suffered considerable psychological damage and her parents had brought the matter to court. On the basis of records kept during the various seances and through interviews with different participants, I was able to gain an exact impression of the prevailing atmosphere during these sittings.

At the beginning of the average sitting, the woman who led the circle and several of the other participants, handled a planchette. Messages that might be described as "wisdom for daily living" were first communicated. These were attributed to a "spiritual leader," a monk allegedly alive and residing on Mt. Athos, Greece. If any of these communications were unclear, the participants said "we have not understood this," and the communication was repeated. Eventually this cumbersome method was eliminated, as the leader of the circle, said that her "spiritual leaders" had instructed her to convey their messages orally.

The subject matter of the communications that followed were uplifting talks concerned with the alleged organization of the spirit world, comments on events in the lives of the participants, instructions on contacting the spirit world outside the circle, and medical advice by "spirit doctors" concerning illness. The circle was under strict discipline and those who did not abide with these arrangements were excluded from participation—in the name of the "spirits".

Participants who were trying to develop their mediumship were instructed to see spirits with their eyes closed, to hear spirit voices, and to let their hands be guided by spirits in automatic writings. One participant, a young woman who had recently been married, and who had joined the group with her husband, found herself in a dilemma. The instructions of the "spirit doctors" regarding the treatment of her sick child, she thought quite foolish, but her husband, who believed unswervingly in the reality of these experiences, wished to carry them out in every detail. Things came to a head when the leader of the circle expelled the young woman, thus sharpening the conflict in her marriage. The young wife, thoroughly confused, divided between faith and doubt, attempted to apply the mediumistic practices she had learned during the seance. She began to write automatically and suddenly heard voices demanding that she take her own life. She was barely prevented from throwing herself from a balcony while saying "it was a force that I had to obey." The spiritualist circle called a special session and asked the spirits to clarify the origin of this confusion. The reply was that the patient should not permit herself to listen to spirit whisperings for a period of three months. Her condition finally improved, and she separated temporarily from her husband to seek psychological shelter in the home of her parents.

Even convinced spiritualists, carefully judging a case such as this, would conclude that the alleged spirit messages must have originated, knowingly or unknowingly, with the leader of the circle. As a result of her key position, she had gained status and prestige; she fantasized her vernacular of the beyond; and almost literally infected the participants of the circle with her own psychological pattern. The uncritical use of spiritualistic practices such as "spirit writing" and "clairaudient transmission" created a transitory psychic disturbance in the young wife. The effective upheaval created by the misunderstood "experience of the beyond" was, in this case, linked with the training of dissociative capacities. This had led to a case of spirit obsession expressing itself in the hearing of voices and compulsive actions.

Such pathological conditions are occasionally referred to in the international psychic literature as "mediumistic" psychoses; in French they are known as *folie spirite*. These symptoms have a functional link with the "psychic automatisms" mentioned by a number of classical writers in the field of psychical research. Anyone familiar with the history of psychical research knows the manifestations of automatism. Few psychiatrists, however, take notice of this condition. Many confuse "mediumistic psychoses," which are hysterical disturbances, with schizophrenic psychoses. In view of the considerable following which spiritistic practices have today, it is difficult to see why experimental psychology and psychopathology have failed to utilize these practices for laboratory research. I had hoped that my dissertation, "Psychic Automatism," delivered at Bonn in 1936, would bring attention to this matter; others however, did not repeat or supplement my experimental work in this field. At the time of my original researches, I used a method known in Germany as "glass tilting." It is practiced as follows:

An upside-down water glass is placed on a smooth surface; a circle of letters of the alphabet is formed under this surface; participants are encouraged to place one finger on the glass, so that it can move from one letter to another. As letter after letter is touched, the indicator answers questions or produces spontaneous comments. By means of this "automatic" spelling, it is possible to produce intelligent personality traits on all levels of personality formation with reference to the conscious self.

Even those who are quite inexperienced at this sort of thing, are under the impression that the movement of arms and hands which causes the sliding of the indicator are taking place unconsciously. In cases of low-grade communication, the words spelled out can be identified by the automatist rather easily; where a deeper level of dissociation is reached and the automatist spells "blindly," a total amnestic barrier exists between the automatically produced results and the individual consciousness. Such self-contained thought processes are particularly impressive when the test person, who is writing or spelling automatically, simultaneously engages in some normal activity, such as telling a story or doing calculations. This shows that certain conditions permit two separate thought processes—one of them fully conscious, the other self-contained.

There are definite limitations to the work such simultaneous activity is able to support. If too much is asked, one of the two activities ceases, or the barrier between the conscious and unconscious system is broken. When this occurs, splinters of the self-contained thought activity may break through into consciousness or, conversely, fragments of conscious thought may appear as part of the automatic production.

These subconscious productions show a distinct tendency toward personification. Even with automatists who have no contact with spiritualism, such subconscious production often takes the form of outside intelligences usually behaving as "spirits." Naïve subjects are awed when the writing hand suddenly communicates a phrase such as "this is your dead father speaking. . . ." Even the most banal remarks are then regarded as of profound significance. This leads to further automatic writing, using every opportunity, day or night, to gain more "knowledge." Such misuse may lead to pathological results, particularly in the case of psychologically weak personalities. Several case histories which fall into this category will be summarized below.

Two married twin sisters, thirty-nine years old and residing in different towns, were brought to the psychiatric clinic at Freiburg within a few days of each other. In both cases schizophrenic tendencies seemed to be apparent. Both sisters had become familiar with table tipping and automatic writing through a mediumistically inclined relative who operated a spiritistic circle. Under the impact of their father's death, the two sisters took up these practices once more. One of them, whom we will call Frau Maria, instructed her sister, Frau Lotte, in automatic writing. During the first session, the pencil in her hand began to move; later it wrote letters and eventually full sentences. As she put it, "it seems as if my hand is being guided lightly; one doesn't know what one is writing." The patient was convinced that she was in touch with her dead father. Until late at night she continued to write, filling whole notebooks. In addition to instructions about conditions in the other world, came communications that showed extraordinary knowledge of her most personal affairs: early childhood experiences were described; the spirits—meanwhile other entities had joined her father—referred to unpleasant events, uttered accusations, and also gave her advice.

The actual writing grew faster and faster. Once, as she was instructed to underline a word, she heard it spoken loudly and clearly as if uttered by a strange voice. From then on she needed only to make lines with her pencil in order to hear the communication—each word being represented by one line. Eventually she heard spirit voices, not only while engaged in automatic writing, but everywhere all the time. These voices grew ever louder and more emphatic. They commented upon her behavior; gave her meaningless orders that she tried to resist; and alternated between quiet or vulgar and destructive tones.

When she entered the hospital, the patient at first refused to provide any information whatsoever. She maintained that the spirits had ordered her to remain silent. Also, at the behest of one spirit, the patient once tried to cut her wrist with a piece of glass. Later she reported "visions"—on the glass window of her door she saw her father with an annoyed expression on his face sorting out books. Simultaneously the voices told her that her careless reading, "origin of much misfortune," was supposed to be illustrated by this version.

Her twin sister, who had tried to commit suicide, was still at

home. She showed symptoms of a similar mediumistic psychosis.
These symptoms usually tend toward one direction: a growing in-
dependence of thought expressed in automatic writing, coincid-
ing with the appearance of the voices. The subconscious thoughts
which initially are reproduced by motor automatism, now appear
in a sensory manner as voices. The autonomic conflict, which in
the beginning is limited to the father personality, grows like an
avalanche and becomes the bearer of any number of suppressed
tendencies: feelings of guilt, thoughts of self-destruction, and
obscenities are able to manifest under the camouflage of spirits.

Both patients lost their symptoms after a few weeks of treatment. However, in the case of Frau Lotte, a woman of lower
vitality, two relapses occurred. Eventually, psychotherapeutic
methods enabled her to gain complete insight into the actual
character of her "spirit possession." At that point the voices
ceased and the compulsions disappeared. Years later both patients display completely normal personality traits. Their psychosis undoubtedly was not in the schizophrenic category.

In the case of a twenty-five-year-old teacher, I was able to observe the identical progress of a mediumistic psychosis. Inspired
by a spiritualistic tract, she began to practice automatic writing.
At first the spirit, calling himself "Bearer of Blessings," began to
communicate with rather excessively poetic verbiage. Next came
a well-known opera singer, with whom the patient was deeply in-
fatuated, and whom she erroneously considered dead. When the
singer propositioned her from the other world, the "Bearer of
Blessings" warned and finally advised her, through her writing
hand, that he was renouncing her. He could not condone her sinful behavior with the opera singer.

Suddenly the spoken and written words became simultaneous,
the voice independent of the act of writing. The patient was tortured by the necessity of absolving both herself and her discarnate admirer from their joint guilt. Eventually through hand mo-
tions in the air—with a signature of "God"—she was urged to
sacrifice her life. She gave one more lesson to her pupils, then she
followed the finger of her hand, unconsciously pointing in the direction of a river, ordering her to go into the water. She plunged
into the river and was rescued much against her will. This pa-

tient, too, was at first considered a schizophrenic case. Proper treatment was soon successful. The "personifications" disappeared; there remained, however, a sort of cordial *alter ego* which manifested itself in audible thought, and expressed concern about her wellbeing.

Fortunately, current spiritualistic practices lead to such substantial disturbances of psychic balance only in relatively rare cases. Specific traits of personality form the basis of such cases. Among these may be reactive lability; pseudo-hallucinatory disposition; disturbed contact with reality; rootlessness; lack of realization of one's own ideas; and a general personality weakness, which leads to disintegration of psychic functions.

The emotional dangers of spiritualistic practices should not be viewed entirely on the basis of these extreme psychotic reactions. I know many mediumistically gifted people who are so convinced of the reality of spirit communications that they consult the "other world" at every opportunity, giving great weight to the advice thus received. Whenever they receive messages that are clearly nonsensical, they attribute these to "interfering low entities." Often, however, they find themselves led astray by the suggestions of allegedly high level discarnate entities.

The fascination with such alleged spirit messages may become irresistible when spiritualistic practices bring paranormal material to the surface. A mediumistically gifted, intelligent woman received advice from her brother—who had died several decades ago—by means of automatic writing. One day he asked her to give support to one "Uncle Florian," said to be in pressing material need. With much difficulty the uncle was located, and it did turn out that he was completely without means. The medium could not remember ever having heard of "Uncle Florian;" he had been the main support of a football team of which her brother had been a member some thirty years before.

It is obvious that, with naïve people, such experiences create the convincing impression of actual contact with a discarnate personality. It is difficult to suggest that such extraordinary cases may be based on the medium's own ESP capacity; it becomes an almost insurmountable task to differentiate between the alleged spirit

communications and the medium's extra-sensory ability. During
my own work I usually do not provide a scientific explanation
when I deal with people to whom the conviction that they are
dealing with deceased loved ones provides strength and hope,
and where none of the known dangers seem to exist. Even if I
were to speak more freely, I would not exclude the possibility of
spiritual communication, but would prefer to speak of them as
unproven and probably unprovable; simple cases which require
consultation are best described as falling into the category of
wishful thinking.

22

Can Telepathy Make You Ill?

BERTHOLD ERIC SCHWARZ, M.D.

The idea that we are all, in some as yet undefined way, interrelated, has given rise to many concepts linking telepathy to illness. A Near Eastern and European tradition of "the evil eye" —suggesting that someone may not only wish, but by thought power bring about, another's misfortune—antedates modern medicine, psychosomatic research and parapsychology. From his viewpoint of a practicing psychiatrist, Dr. Schwarz has examined the possibility of symptoms that have telepathic origins, and he has coined the word "telesomatic" to describe their special nature. The presentation which follows is based on the paper "Possible Telesomatic Reactions," which originally appeared in The Journal of the Medical Society of New Jersey, *November 1967. Dr. Schwarz is the author of* Psychic-Dynamics *(1967) and* Parent-Child Telepathy *(1971), and of other books and scholarly papers.*

The psychosomatic significance of various illnesses is well established. It is thus relevant to explore the possible telepathic mediation of psychosomatic or "telesomatic" reactions.

Under controlled laboratory conditions, using sensitive mathematical methods, telepathic communications have been demonstrated principally by J. B. Rhine, in the United States, and S. G.

Soal, in England. Although many of the early investigators of telepathy were physicians, until the advent of psychoanalysis, psychiatry had relatively little to contribute to parapsychology. Since
Freud, there have been scattered psychodynamic studies. Notwithstanding considerable conscious and unconscious resistance
to this potentially revolutionary body of data, it is still a paradox
that comparatively little investigation by psychiatrists has been
undertaken. It has been suggested that parapsychology would
have more to offer psychiatry than vice versa.

Jule Eisenbud (Denver) has mentioned—in the *Psychoanalytic
Quarterly* (Vol. 15:32, 1946)—the likelihood "for a telepathic
stimulus to occasion an asthmatic attack or any other set of physiological events." Although he asserted that he had "seen several
examples of psychosomatic developments on a telepathic basis,"
he offered no examples. In a different detailed psychodynamic
study, I have noted how a patient's incapacitating psychosomatic
illnesses might have been induced (or at least strongly
influenced) by a "sick" relationship with a telepathic mother. Examples in this same study and elsewhere further show the tie-in
of psychophysiologic factors and telepathy.

Despite a handful of laboratory experiments, little has appeared concerning the practical clinical aspects: possible
telesomatic reactions. To date these essentially parapsychologic
studies emphasize (a) the use of physiologic measures to define
conditions under which ESP occurs, and (b) physiologic
measures used as a means of registering ESP responses. I noted a
series of 504 presumed parent-child telepathic episodes showing
many possible telesomatic and motor-acting-out responses. In
these, it looked as if the parent's or the child's thoughts caused
somatic motor (or autonomic) reactions in sender or receiver.

The usual criteria for telepathy are uniqueness, simultaneity,
actual or symbolic equivalence of thought and feeling, and telepathic tracer effects. Often it can be shown how the presumed
telepathic episode will recur in an almost predictable manner
when the psychodynamic-situational constellations are similar.
Psychiatric study techniques are involved in unconscious mechanisms, manifold nuances of interpersonal relations, and various
trancelike states of altered consciousness. Both psychiatric and

laboratory physiologic investigations suggest that telepathy offers an attractive hypothesis for the understanding of psychosomatic diseases. The following cases present some possible telesomatic reactions.

CASE ONE

"Last night, for the first time in years, I had a severe toothache. I told my wife about it at 7 a.m. and shortly afterward made an appointment with my dentist. At 10 a.m. my mother phoned to say she was having an extraction that day. Her last extraction was years ago. No one in my family knew about mother's trouble. When I saw my dentist later that day there was neither discernible disease nor reason for my complaint. I have had no recurrence since then. Could I have picked up and somatized my mother's repressed anxiety over her trip to the dentist?"

CASE TWO

The 38-year-old father of two children was awarded custody of them following his divorce nine years ago. Although the wife had left him on occasion in the past, she always returned and never threatened to take the children. During his psychiatric interview he said, "Even today, I don't understand it. At the time of our divorce things were at the worst. I was scheduled to work on Saturdays. One Saturday I left the house at 6:30 a.m. and got a third of the way to work when I suddenly became very ill. I had abdominal pain, and the cramps were so severe I couldn't drive. I rolled out of the car but when I turned around to go home the pain stopped. Because of this I decided to start for work again, but once again (for the second time) the pain returned. I then decided to go home. By the time I got to the house I had no pain, headache, or perspiration. It wasn't until the next evening that I discovered my wife's packed suitcases. I had no awareness of this at the time. She would not leave if I were around. I later learned that she had intended to take the children. I think it was because of this fact that I had the attack. She was most annoyed that I came home and was underfoot."

In this example the patient's security was threatened. He might have telepathically picked up this threat by his somatic reaction. Through being forced to return home he saved his children. The pains left twice, but only upon his decision to return home.

CASE THREE

A woman in her middle thirties with an old disability from polio-myelitis had been treated both in Holland and in the United States by the renowned Dutch healer and clairvoyant, Gerard Croiset, who has asserted that he could influence muscular contractions: eversion, inversion, and dorsiflexion of the right foot. In a light trancelike state, he indicated the patient's appropriate muscular reaction by the direction of his outstretched hands. The patient's eyes were not on his hands. In fact, Croiset was in another room and it was impossible for the patient to see whether (and in what direction) he was "stimulating" her. Unfortunately it was also impossible for the observer to check precisely when and how Croiset was stimulating.

This American woman (who was in close rapport with Croiset) was seized with acute "fast heart rate, abdominal cramps, diarrhea" and malaise in Tarrytown, New York. She connected her autonomic reaction "to Croiset" but did not fully understand it until four days later. At that time, following an interview with the physician, she learned that at the approximate time of her reaction Croiset had unexpectedly landed (from a paragnostic Australian crime-sleuthing trip) at John F. Kennedy Airport in a state of collapse, with severe abdominal pain and malaise. Although he was expected to arrive in America several days later than his actual arrival, this was not definite and was never confirmed.

The woman's somatic reaction was not related to any similar illness for any member of her family or friends. It can be conjectured that the woman's abdominal reaction and half-awareness of Croiset, which coincided with his acute distress and unexpected proximity, might have been telepathically mediated—a way of telling her that the man upon whom she had pinned such high hopes for help was close by and in danger. And in turn, Croiset, alone in America and acutely ill, in his desperation, might have thought of his kind friend and patient with the old disability.

CASE FOUR

A 10-year-old boy had a convulsion five years ago and nothing since. Because of this (plus an associated moderate, generalized dysrhythmia on the electroencephalogram) he had had yearly tracings and had been on anticonvulsant drugs in the interim. On the morning of his annual electroencephalogram, he had his second seizure. Contrary to their usual practice, the parents did not tell their son that they had planned to bring him from Atlantic City to Montclair for the electro-encephalogram. It was wondered, therefore, if these kind parents could, by their uneasiness, have triggered their son's seizure through subliminal, unconscious means, or possibly telepathic psychophysiologic stimuli. There was nothing unusual in the patient's immediate history to account for this seizure.

CASE FIVE

A thirteen-and-a-half-year-old girl with temporal lobe epilepsy was meticulously studied for eight and a half years and reported by my colleague, Dr. B. A. Ruggieri. My contact with the patient was limited to performing serial electroencephalograms. These all showed marked generalized dysrhythmia and right temporal focal sharp-wave changes. Once a typical seizure occurred during the recording. Clinically the patient had hundreds of major and minor seizures and had been difficult to manage with drugs and psychotherapy. The latter was given for depressive reactions. During one of the sessions, telepathic and telesomatic exchanges occurred between the patient and Dr. Ruggieri. For example, Dr. Ruggieri experienced a "severe but momentary abdominal cramp. The thought went through my mind, 'I hope she does not get a spell,' since her convulsive disorder frequently manifested itself as abdominal epilepsy. I had experienced the cramp as my own but mentally associated to my patient's problems. Immediately thereafter this girl began to stare straight ahead and make swallowing movements. When it was over, she described her feelings: 'It felt as though my stomach was about to blow up.' Later when the daughter described this incident to the mother, the latter asked, 'Did you tell the Doctor you had this spell?' and the girl reportedly answered, 'I didn't have to, he sensed it'."

Dr. Ruggieri continued, "One day, while I was talking alone with this girl's mother, I was surprised when she spontaneously told me that on several occasions through the years while away from her daughter she had sensed that her daughter was having a convulsion and, on checking the matter as carefully as she could, she had found that her daughter had indeed experienced a convulsive episode at that same time. From my interviews with the daughter it was apparent that she had some emotional problems with her mother. Repeatedly in the past the mother refused to see a psychiatrist for the benefit of her daughter if not herself. However, the mother's history and my own experiences with the patient made me wonder about the possibility of either the mother telepathically detecting her daughter's seizures, or telesomatically causing them."

A young Army wife was unexpectedly hospitalized for threatened abortion. Her mother (who was 56 years of age and hundreds of miles away) developed uterine bleeding at the same time. The older woman's last menstrual period had occurred eight years previously. She thought this was unusual because six months before this episode she had had bleeding when her second daughter, who lived more than one hundred miles away (and had no immediate contact with her) went into labor. The third episode of unexpected uterine bleeding occurred while the older woman was in New Jersey. At that time, her first daughter was in California. She had given birth to her baby seven weeks before the expected date. The older woman was not immediately aware of the relationships between her three bleeding experiences and her two daughters. She told her physician at the time because they seemed to be such strange coincidences. Twenty months after the last episode of bleeding, the older woman had a massive hemorrhage. Uterine carcinoma was diagnosed and she had a successful hysterectomy. Her episodes of pathologic uterine bleeding coincided with major obstetrical changes in the lives of her two daughters and might have unconsciously directed the older woman's attention to her illness.

The two grandchildren who were associated with the odd bleeding had congenital anomalies, and the earlier (the first born) grandchild also had anomalies. Possibly the grandmother had not developed her carcinoma at this time. Of the five grandchildren born during this period, the only one free of anomalies was also the only one *not* associated with the grandmother's bleeding. The last born was after the grandmother's hysterectomy—and of course, her incapacity to respond with bleeding—if there was any relationship at all. Detailed genetic investigation of both daughters and their families failed to uncover any reason for these four tragedies.

This woman's husband, a very successful businessman, came from a "telepathic" family and at times had himself been aware of his involvement in various telepathic episodes.

During his psychotherapy, a 36-year-old businessman had many physician-patient "telepathic" episodes. He had a sadomasochistic relationship with his alcoholic, hostile, competitive, domineering father, who was also his boss. After years of abuse, and threats of being fired or quitting, the patient surprised everyone by leaving his father's employ and seeking work elsewhere. He took great precautions so that his father would not know where he sought work and block him. Some prospective employers were doubtful about hiring him because of their knowledge of the father's precarious health, family loyalties, and so forth. Finally he obtained a new job at a marked increase in salary. Only his wife and the prospective new employer knew his secret. The new job involved much soul searching since it was with a competitor of his father's in a different state, hundreds of miles away, and would mean major changes in his life—the final manifest separation from the unhealthy destructive dependency on his father. He later learned that at the approximate time of his agonizing decision, and while awaiting the call from the new employer, his father had a second coronary thrombosis. The first such attack was nine years before. This event, so fortuitously timed, shifted all the complex relationships and at the "zero hour" the patient had a change of heart and returned to his family company. However, this time he was put in full charge, as his father was now forced, on his physician's advice, to retire. It can be wondered if the tyrannical father had an (unconscious) telepathic awareness of his son's major decision and responded somatically when no other response might have sufficed.

CASE EIGHT

While receiving psychotherapy for a depressive reaction, a 33-year-old physicist had many "telepathic" episodes with his physician. He also had some presumably telepathic dreams. A late afternoon dream vividly portrayed almost all the specific, detailed (censored) circumstances of his physician's anxiety over an unanticipated trip to a New York airport to see the acutely ill Croiset. The other dream apparently detected in surprising detail his physician's daughter's surprise birthday gift of an old-fashioned fourposter bed and canopy. A third episode was the physician's waking from a sound sleep in the early hours of the morning by the physicist patient's telling him telepathically, "I'm alright now—had abscessed tooth extracted." Earlier that day the patient telephoned the physician because of a toothache. His own dentist had previously examined him and told him there was nothing wrong with the tooth: the same advice he had received from a Midwestern dentist four months ago when he had a similar toothache.

The physician advised his patient to see another dentist, and no further thought was given this until the veridical nocturnal episode.

In his sessions the physicist was aware of some of the face-to-face patient-physician telepathy and contrary to the usual custom, these communications were explored in treatment. Because of his interest in telepathy, one day the physicist participated as a subject, in one of Dean's well-controlled laboratory tests for telepathy. The presumed episodes were monitored with the plethysmograph. On two separate occasions the physicist got attractive responses: pronounced transient tachycardia and change in vasoconstrictive states when a specific sender looked at a card saying (or symbolizing) "mother." It was hoped that with additional experiments a statistically significant result might be obtained. The patient had some deep-rooted problems with his mother. The telepathic response did not happen with other names.

During one of the experiments the successful sender was disturbed over some unanticipated extraneous sounds on his earphones. The patient, who was in a different part of the building and had neither earphones nor other connections with the sender, responded to this unpleasant intrusion in the same telepathic-physiologic way: "the biggest reaction . . . ever seen. It leads us to try better." With a different "cold, sourpuss sender" there was no evidence for telepathy.

In therapy the patient became aware of the superficial similarities between the successful sender and his mother. Both had a gushy, smiling effusiveness. Following the second successful telepathic-physiologic tests the physicist became depressed. He did not know why until therapy, when he recognized that he repressed his rage toward the successful sender who risked his life, on the trip back from the laboratory. The sender, in the physicist's opinion, was a reckless automobile driver. This dissociation of the sender's reckless driving was similar to the physicist's pattern of repressing all anger toward his mother's analogous behaviour.

This interesting laboratory and clinical datum justifies the speculation that with the passage of time various psychosomatic states could develop or be precipitated where there is an unhealthy parent-child telepathic rapport. That might apply, for example, to possible paroxysmal tachycardia, hypertension, hyperthyroidism, acute peptic ulcer, ulcerative colitis, and so forth. As indicated in the example of the physicist, all commonly recognized communications and those that occur on an unconscious, nonverbal basis could, *via* telepathic mediation, be vastly complicated by somatic shortcircuiting.

From these examples, it would appear that telesomatic reactions are part of a continuum of interhuman relatedness—physiologic expressions of telepathically sent thoughts, behavior, and affect. The process can be partial for any one of these areas or (as in these examples) complex. The telesomatic reaction occurs on an unconscious level and is almost totally out of the participants' awareness. Unless the data were carefully collected and scrutinized with a telepathic hypothesis in mind, the event could be entirely missed. Identification of telesomatic reactions is facilitated by the tracer effects which appropriately tag the events. Since the telesomatic reaction happened out of awareness clinically and also in one cited well-controlled laboratory test, it can be supposed that it might occur much more often than is commonly thought. Hence, it is worthy of serious consideration from both the practicing clinician and the researcher.

23

How Safe Is "Mind Training"?

ELMER GREEN, Ph.D., and ALYCE GREEN, B.A.

Courses in "mind training" or "mind control" have become immensely popular. This spreading phenomenon is analyzed by Dr. and Mrs. Elmer Green, noted biofeedback researchers at the Menninger Foundation, Topeka, Kansas. They are concerned about the dangers of commercially organized, often improperly organized courses, and they call for caution, better understanding, improved standards and a non-profit orientation. Their study, originally entitled "Mind Training, ESP, Hypnosis, and Voluntary Control of Internal States," was first presented before the Academy of Parapsychology and Medicine.

In order to sharply delineate my main points, it is convenient to first summarize the subjects of discussion and our understanding of them as follows:

1. Through hypnosis and through various training programs, including biofeedback, many persons can become aware of normally-unconscious processes.

2. Awareness of normally-unconscious processes is sometimes accompanied by spontaneous (and sometimes volitional) ESP phenomena.

3. Commercial mind training courses promising ESP powers are using hypnosis as the major method and, advertising to the

contrary, do not give biofeedback or brain wave training, nor are the subjects necessarily in an alpha brain wave state.

4. Commercial mind training "teachers" generally deny that they use hypnosis and by denying or ignoring the risks associated with hypnotic "programming" are inducing in some persons a form of paranoid neurosis or psychosis, often related to obsession or "possession."

5. Hypnotic programming for ESP bears a similarity to some of the methods used for development of trance mediumship, especially the "possession by spirits" of low grade mediumship.

6. Awareness of normally unconscious processes can be safely taught under the guidance of a counselor, without hypnotic programming, by methods which allow each person to develop according to his own inner needs.

7. Mind training procedures should be voluntarily modified by those interested in the subject to eliminate psychic hazards. If this is not done, government agencies may summarily ban many research and training programs that otherwise, if carefully developed, might become valuable adjuncts to our education and health systems.

8. The major problems are (a) to determine what techniques are safe as well as efficient for the extension of awareness, (b) to establish standards of qualification and responsibility of teachers, and (c) to offer the benefits of awareness training programs to the public through non-profit institutions.

Many psychologists in the last few years have become interested in research possibilities that a few years back were considered beyond the realm of science, namely, voluntary control of normally-unconscious psychological and physiological processes. The first medical approaches to this subject in the West, starting in about 1910, sprang from the researches and developments of Autogenic Training and Psychosynthesis, beginning with Johannes Schultz in Germany and Alberto Assagioli in Italy, respectively. At about the same time, Edmund Jacobson was beginning to develop in the United States his training program known as Progressive Relaxation. In other parts of the world, new interpretations of yoga were developing, such as the Integral Yoga of Aurobindo. His *Synthesis of Yoga,* for instance, is concerned with a program for enhancement of consciousness and for control of normally-unconscious processes. The newest development along this line of self regulation of mind and body and perhaps the most applicable to Westerners in general, has resulted from research in the area of biofeedback training.

The programs mentioned above deal with one's power to modify and control, through volition, one's own mental, emotional, and physiological states, without hypnotic programming by another person; and in all of these developments (except perhaps Progressive Relaxation, which deals primarily with problems of muscle tension) parapsychological events sometimes occur. These events are not, however, the goals of training. The primary goal is self mastery, and in Psychosynthesis and in Integral Yoga the primary goal is self mastery coupled with the development of awareness of what, in Zen, is called the True Self. Unless this aspect of Self is developed, it is said, psychic powers become an "ego trip." The attainment of psychic powers may follow safely *after* a degree of self mastery (ego mastery) is achieved, but if paranormal development comes first, psychological problems develop. Aurobindo's way of saying this focuses attention on what he calls the Overmind level of one's being. After achieving awareness of that, he says, one can explore in "astral" dimensions with a measure of safety. Otherwise, it is possible to become involved in psychic (psychological) entanglements and not be able to find one's way, through layers of mental and emotional confusion, back to one's center. The ancient Christian advice concerning these matters was to seek first the Kingdom of Heaven, which was within, it was said, and other things would follow in due course.

These considerations seem to have an especially important meaning today because we are bombarded by newspaper advertisements of entrepreneurs who (for a fee) will develop psychic powers in us, through hypnosis. It is denied that hypnosis is the technique employed, because hypnosis is a "bad word." Instead it is called "conditioning," "programming," "brain wave training," "alpha training," etc., but nevertheless, it *is* hypnosis. On this professionals agree, though they do not always agree on how hypnosis works. The "countdown" induction procedure used in commercial mind training "programming" is a classical hypnotic technique.

Hypnosis is an extremely powerful tool for control of physiological and psychological states. It is well known that through hypnosis painless surgery can be performed, people can be made to see things that are not there, and not see things that are there, but it is not generally realized, even by professionals, that through hypnosis parapsychological sensitivity can be enhanced. F. W. H. Myers, the British pioneer of psychical research, clearly summarized—in his classic *Human Personality and Its Survival of Bodily Death* (1901)—the major findings of hypnosis experimentation in the last century and showed that hypnosis and parapsychology are not necessarily two strange subjects. More recently, John Beloff, in *The Existence of Mind*, ventures the opinion that "hypnotism may not be just a psychological phenomenon but may have a certain paranormal component as well." Beloff, a psychologist, is the president of the Society for Psychical Research, London, England. The points being made here are that hypnosis *can* involve the paranormal, and the paranormal is being invoked by hypnosis in some of those who take commercial mind training courses, opinions of non-investigators notwithstanding.

The question might now be raised, "So what? What difference does it make?" This question can be answered in at least three ways, depending on whether one looks at commercial mind training (1) from a traditional *psychological* point of view, that is, treat the various phenomena that result from the program as figments of the imagination; (2) from a *psychosomatic* point of view, in which the power of mind over events inside the skin is accepted, but parapsychological events are considered to be figments of the imagination; or (3) from a *parapsychological* point of view, in which the phenomena of hypnosis are seen as consistent with research data from various psychological, psychosomatic and parapsychological studies.

But before these points of view can be considered, it is necessary to identify some of the phenomena that are claimed by commercial mind training teachers and by many of their students, namely:

(a) A person can "go down" into his own "unconscious", and

while in that deep "level", can program his own physiological and psychological processes so that various diseases in him that have not yielded to standard medical treatment can be brought under control, at least temporarily.

(b) While at his deep "level," a person can become aware of physical, emotional and mental states and diseases in other people, and can correctly diagnose ailments.

(c) While at his "level," a person can learn to manipulate the physical, emotional and mental natures of other persons, sick or healthy, and thereby modify their behavior.

(d) While at his "level," a person can learn to manipulate nature so that coincidences, "accidents," or lack of accidents, can come under his control. This is, essentially, a promise of psychokinetic powers.

Now from a traditional *psychological* point of view, the above ideas are sheer nonsense, some would say "sheer madness." From that point of view, the tens of thousands who have taken mind training courses and who are convinced of the reality of some or all of the above claims, have been programmed into a serious delusional system and can be expected sooner or later, if rationality is not re-established, to develop, in consequence, some degree of neurosis or psychosis.

From a *psychosomatic* point of view it might be acceptable to hypothesize that one could learn to manipulate certain normally-unconscious psychological processes whose physiological correlates are thereby brought under control, that is, item (a) above might be accepted, but items (b) through (d) would be considered to be belief in sheer nonsense, which, if persisted in, would probably lead to mental or physical breakdown.

From the *parapsychological* point of view, none of the items listed above are at variance with data accumulated in the last fifty years indicating that such events are possible or at least worthy of hypothesis testing, even though not statistically probable.

In an attempt to evaluate mind training, all scientists are not equally qualified. Scientists who subscribe exclusively to the traditional psychological or the psychosomatic views are in main those who either (a) have not studied the paranormal data and literature, (b) have had no spontaneous paranormal events in their own lives (that they admit, at least), (c) have not developed their own existential sensitivities and knowledge, or (d) all or some combination of the above. A probable example of this type of "scientist" is E. U. Condon, the former head of the National Bureau of Standards. R. A. McConnell, in his *ESP Curriculum Guide*, quotes Condon as stating:

"Flying saucers and astrology are not the only pseudo-sciences which have a considerable following among us. There used to be spiritualism, there continues to be extrasensory perception, psychokinesis, and a host of others . . . Where corruption of children's minds is at stake, I do not believe in freedom of the press or freedom of speech. In my view, publishers who publish or teachers who teach any of the pseudo-sciences as established truth should, on being found guilty, be publicly horsewhipped, and forever banned from further activity in these usually honorable professions."

Opinions from such scientists, who apparently have no adequate existential or experiential base, or who have not done their homework in the field of parapsychology, or who may (in some cases) have unconscious fears of the subject, are not appropriate here. The following is written, therefore, for those who can consider the parapsychological hypothesis without doing violence to their belief structure.

To continue then from the parapsychological viewpoint, the main questions that must be raised about commercial mind training programs are (1) judged by professionals rather than entrepreneurs, what is actually happening to students in regard to psychological, psychosomatic and parapsychological events and accomplishments, (2) what are the dangers of hypnotic programming for the purpose of enhancing psychic development, (3) what is the level of responsibility of program organizers and associated teachers, (4) what mind training techniques are safe as well as efficient in bringing a person to a level of psychic development that is not inappropriate for him, (5) what is the most responsible way of presenting mind training and its various benefits to the public, and (6) how is the mind training movement to be regulated in the interest of public welfare. Concerning these questions, the following comments might be made.

Hypnotic programming as used in the commercial courses has several defects, namely: (a) Many people are psychically catapulted, so to speak, into existential realms in which they cannot protect themselves from dangers arising either from within their own unconscious, or from psychic manipulation by other persons, or from "extrapersonal" sources (dangers inherent in so called "astral" dimensions). There is not time here to review the history of Spiritualism since 1848 and the psychic disasters that often resulted from dabbling in the area of trance mediumship, but mental hospitals, even today, contain many people who "hear voices." These people usually cannot turn the voices off, cannot separate fact from fiction, have lost their "reality testing" powers, and often are obliged to act out "against their will" instructions they are "given." (b) Commercial mind training students are often "programmed" in ways not appropriate to their own needs, nor at their own proper rates. What is proper for one can be disastrous for another. This hazard arises, because apart from the dangers of hypnotic penetration into "astral" levels of being, (c) many mind training teachers are incompetent to work with people in matters where psychological and physical health are at stake. For example, former salesmen who have had a few courses in hypnotic programming are not qualified to work in this very delicate area of the human psyche with its psychosomatic correlates. (d) And most seriously, psychic submission may be enhanced in "astral" dimensions rather than powers of self volition. This is the consensus of Eastern teachers who, it must be conceded, reflect much experimentation and experience over the centuries with training methods for self mastery. It is admitted that psychosomatic *self* regulation, achieved by any volitional method, is slow compared to submitting oneself to hypnotic instruction, i.e., turning the control of one's mind over to another person, but it is also maintained by the most accomplished teachers that the power of psychic self-determination is the *sine qua non* for safety in astral dimensions.

Concerning safety in "astral" dimensions, possibly the greatest specific danger associated with hypnotic submission in commercial mind training programs lies in the developing, or obtaining, of psychic "advisors." They are the male and female assistants who "know everything," who at the deep "level" of mind advise the student, and sometimes tell him what to do.

In the *mediumistic* version of the parapsychological paradigm, these advisors, however constructed or found, may serve as masks for "entities" who may attempt (now that the student has become amenable to suggestion at the unconscious level) to control the student's mental, emotional and physical behavior. The mediumistic concept will clearly be rejected by mind training teachers because, if accepted, it would imply that these teachers might be responsible for serious problems in the lives of some of their trainees. The physical frontiers of our planet have presented many dangers to humans, can it be safely assumed that the inner frontier has no corresponding perils? Is it realistic to accept the assurances of commercial mind training instructors that dangers that may be associated with "territorial invasion" by humans on "astral" levels are not possible? For those who accept the possibility of "entities," is it safe to assume that only good, nice, and safe beings (like humans?) are functioning in "astral" dimensions? This would be a truly Ptolemaic assumption.

Regarding the hazards associated with the all-knowing advisors found at the deep "level," some time ago we pointed out to an acquaintance that friends of his who were students of one of the mind training programs might consider being on guard against the possibility of mediumistic-like "possession" through the agency of the advisors. The upshot of this was that these students challenged their advisors, asked them to get out of their "psychic space." Eventually we received a letter saying:

"You may be interested in knowing that after I told my two close friends . . . the warning about the assistants . . . they both went down to their workshops and told their assistants to leave. In both cases a strong but eventually successful test of wills or something took place, with the assistants becoming very ugly and hostile in the process. However, they were finally forced to leave . . . The wife later told me that before I had talked to them about it she had been having increasing trouble getting to sleep at night or going down to her levels because of the appearance of hostile and ugly faces in her mind. It had become a serious problem. Afterwards she told me that since her assistants left she was no longer bothered by the faces, that they had disappeared. So perhaps it was fortunate for them that you gave your warning."

Along this same line, one of our friends in the Bay Area, a counselor on psychological and religious problems, reports that at least a dozen of his clients are suffering from paranoid neuroses as a result of taking mind training courses. Another acquaintance, a psychiatrist who took one of the commercial courses himself, reported to us that four of the thirty who went through the program became psychotic. Two of them had to be hospitalized. In part, he attributed this result to the psychic peculiarity of the instructor. Other students with whom we have discussed the "instructor effect" have reported similar events. Apparently a kind of psychic "transference" phenomenon can occur, a kind of "psychic pollution" can take place due to the unconscious receptivity of the subject to "extra sensory projection" by the hypnotist.

Another point: Mind training teachers often maintain that no harm can be done to another person by themselves or by their students, because they are programmed with the idea that if these "powers" are used for ignoble or selfish purposes they will be lost, but this is likely to be nonsense. Post-hypnotic suggestions are notorious for their impermanence, so if real psychic "powers" are developed in students it can be assumed that hypnotically-imposed restrictions on the use of such powers will not be long lasting.

The examples given above indicate that whether one chooses to examine commercial mind training methods from either the traditional psychological point of view or from the parapsychological point of view, there is risk involved for students. We do not presume to be able to answer all the questions raised, but when over one hundred thousand persons have already been processed through such mind training programs, some questions should be asked. In view of the hazards associated with hypnotic programming in commercial mind training courses, the present writers believe that hypnosis as a technique for inducing self awareness and parapsychological faculties is not adequately safe and should be discarded.

Does this mean that there is no use for hypnosis? Not at all, no

more than there is no use for surgery. But even as surgery has particular use in *acute* situations, where something must be done or
else unbearable pain, or permanent damage, or death may occur,
so also with hypnosis. For *chronic* situations, however, those
which are characteristic of most psychosomatic diseases, non-
hypnotic volitional training programs such as those employing
biofeedback are more desirable. For exploring in psychic
domains, new and safe training methods are being developed by
Dialogue House and Psychosynthesis, for example, and through
research in brainwave training. Other safe methods also exist, as
is well known, such as the various forms of yogic meditation. In
all of these methods, both old and new, accent is placed on learning to handle psychological and physiological problems through
voluntary control at a rate consistent with one's capacity for self
protection.

Spiritual teachers concerned with the development of inner
awareness have always excluded hypnosis as a technique, both in
the East and in the West, not because it was not understood, but
because it *was* understood. Self development and programming
by another were considered antithetical. There is no logical
reason to assume that things are now different merely because we
are in the twentieth century and people are in a hurry, wish to
have immediate results and perhaps even hope to get something
without effort. Hypnotic programming (like LSD) has convinced
many people that an inner terrain exists, and in this way it has
been instrumental in drawing attention to an important dimension of human life, but it is also important that we now look at the
entire area of "inner exploration" and, in as balanced a way as
possible, evaluate the many programs that are being offered for
penetration into hitherto arcane dimensions of the psyche. Commercialism should not enter into such a vitally important matter.
Commercialism often results in (a) false and misleading use of
scientific terms, such as "alpha and theta brainwave training,"
and distortion of what is actually accomplished by such training,
(b) exaggerated claims for "powers" that can be obtained by anyone who pays the price and takes the course, (c) stressing of
powers not appropriate to certain persons, such as the ability to
diagnose and treat diseases, (d) undue emphasis on large enroll-

ment in courses in order to earn more money, rather than to be of service. Large enrollment interferes with one-to-one contact between teachers and students so that whatever problems arise are unlikely to be properly handled even if the teacher had the necessary skill.

In short, commercialism in the mind training field does not lead in the direction of high responsibility and service, and this raises the very important question about the manner in which regulation can best be established in the mind training movement. We are of the opinion that if responsible control is not established quite soon by those already involved, government agencies will step in and provide regulation in the interest of public welfare.

In our estimation, a list of positive guidelines to follow in establishing an "ideal training method" might include the following items:

(1) Make it possible for each person to discover "himself" at a proper rate, that is, penetrate into the unconscious at a rate consistent with his ability to keep his feet on the ground, keep his reality testing powers intact. This means that those for whom psychic unfoldment would lead to destructive neuroses or psychoses should obtain only those insights and awarenesses which, in the usual therapeutic sense, would help integrate and bring under control various discordant sections of the personality.

(2) The student should be shielded by the training method from imperfections of the teacher that might otherwise become part of the student's "psychic atmosphere" and hinder his progress.

(3) Teachers should be ranked or evaluated according to their level of insight and awareness so that as each student progresses existentially he has a properly qualified *human* advisor with whom to talk.

(4) The student should be passed on from teacher to teacher, so to speak, as rapidly as his experiences require more advanced advice or suggestion (not analysis or programming).

(5) Training centers for self awareness should be located within access of anyone interested in participating in the program and should be established on a *non-profit* basis.

24

I Have Been a "Ghost"

VINCENT H. GADDIS

A veteran writer and psychic researcher gives a balanced appraisal of the "out-of-the-body experiences" that were pioneered by his old friend, Sylvan Muldoon. But an astral traveler may encounter dangers and horrors, such as "the dead man glaring at me like a maniac," with whom Muldoon wrestled before he could escape back into his physical body. Vincent Gaddis is the author of many books, including Invisible Horizons (*1965*), Mysterious Fires and Light (*1967*), The Wide World of Magic (*1967*) and Courage in Crisis (*1973*). In collaboration with his wife, Margaret* (see: "*Teachers of Delusion*"), *he also wrote* The Strange World of Animals and Pets (*1970*) and The Curious World of Twins (*1972*).

The belief that man is composed of two counterparts, a physical body and a psychic body, the latter being the vehicle of the mind and consciousness, has been universally accepted for centuries. This second body of tenuous composition normally coincides with the physical body. It has been given many names, the better known being the astral, psychic, mental, and more recently the parasomatic body. It is a duplicate of the physical body and is complete, that is, if a physical limb is lost the astral limb remains, which may explain the "phantom limbs" experienced by amputees.

The astral body can leave the still-living physical body and return to it. The projected body is at all times in communication with its earthly counterpart by means of a line-of-force, a sort of elastic cord akin to the umbilical cord of physical birth, across which flows an energy maintaining life in the unconscious body. This cord, though capable of infinite expansion, may not be severed during a projection without causing instant death to the physical body.

There are involuntary projections that may, or may not, be consciously experienced. They can be caused by anesthetics, shock, certain drugs, extreme illness, accidents, hypnosis, and suppressed desires. There are also voluntary self-projections brought about by certain exercises and practices. Both types are now known as "out-of-the-body experiences" or OOBEs.

OOBEs have been reported by persons in all walks of life. Novelist Ernest Hemingway experienced his projection in the trenches of World War I when a mortar shell exploded and he suffered leg injuries. He said he felt his spirit coming out of his body ". . . like you'd pull a silk handkerchief out of a pocket by one corner. It flew around and then came back and went in again and I wasn't dead any more." Later, in writing *A Farewell to Arms*, he had his fictional hero, Frederic Henry, undergo a similar experience.

C. G. Jung, the philosopher and psychoanalyst, tells of his OOBE after suffering a heart attack. In his book *Memories, Dreams, Reflections*, he writes that he was high up in space and "far below I saw the globe of earth, bathed in a gloriously blue light . . . The sight of the earth from this height was the most glorious thing I had ever seen." He stressed his belief that the experience was not the product of imagination. "The visions and experiences were utterly real," he insisted. "There was nothing subjective about them; they all had a quality of absolute objectivity."

The remarkable OOBE of William Seabrook, the late American writer, which occurred while he was on board a yawl with its owner, Harrison Smith, the New York publisher, will be found in his book *Witchcraft*. Two women: Cora L. V. Richmond, the early peace advocate, and Caroline D. Larsen, noted for her Danish short stories, have reported projection experiences. Similar accounts have been published by the American writer Gail Hamilton, and British authors Sax Rohmer and William Gerhardi.

Cromwell Varley, the inventor who contributed so greatly to the success of the Atlantic cable, reported his OOBE before the Dialectical Society in England. While doing some work on pottery, he inhaled the vapor of hydrofluoric acid, which resulted in spasms of the glottis. His physician advised him to keep chloroform on hand in case relief was necessary from night attacks.

One night he fell back on the bed unconscious with the sponge still applied to his mouth. His wife was in the room above. He continues: "At the end of some seconds, I became conscious again. I saw my wife above, and myself lying on my back. I had an absolute inability to make any movement whatever. By force of will, I conveyed into her mind the vivid idea that I was in danger. She arose, under the impulse of a sudden alarm, came down, and hastened to remove the sponge. I was saved."

OOBEs have become a subject of increasing interest to psychical researchers and students of parapsychology in the last decade. Until recently the major available work on this subject was *The Projection of the Astral Body* by my friend of many years, the late Sylvan J. Muldoon, and his editor, the late Hereward Carrington. Today some of the classics, such as Oliver Fox's *Astral Projection,* have been reprinted and new studies have appeared, both scientific and occult. These include *Altered States of Consciousness,* by Dr. Charles T. Tart (John Wiley and Sons, 1969); *Out-of-the-Body Experiences,* by Professor Celia Green (Institute of Psychophysical Research, England, 1968); and the many books of case histories written by Dr. Robert Crookall, especially his *The Supreme Adventure* (James Clarke and Co., Ltd., London, 1961).

Publicity has been given to the experimental work at the American Society for Psychical Research (ASPR) in New York and at the University of California at Davis. Other experiments are being carried out at the Psychical Research Foundation, Durham, North Carolina. Robert A. Monroe's rather startling book *Journeys Out of the Body* (Doubleday, 1971) has had a wide sale.

There are a number of paperback books on the subject. There are even several mail order courses.

All this growing interest, naturally, will result in individual experimentation in voluntary conscious projections. Along with successful achievement, there are risks. The neophyte is entering a Great Unknown. He is at the border of a realm that is seemingly limitless. Evil as well as good exists in its vast expanse. One does not set sail without a knowledge of navigation, and the beginner should have a knowledge of how earlier experimenters solved the problems they encountered.

With the exception of Oliver Fox and Prescott Hall (whose information came through the mediumship of Mrs. Keeler), the first detailed study of projection techniques was Sylvan Muldoon's *Projection of the Astral Body*, first published in 1929. As a result of this and his later books, he received almost a thousand accounts of experiences from readers.

After a crisis in his personal life, Muldoon spent an entire summer in my home at Winona Lake, Indiana. In later years we visited back and forth between Winona Lake and his home in Darlington, Wisconsin. My approach to this subject is personal as well as academic, for following Muldoon's instructions (combined dream control and desire stress methods) I was a projector. In short, I have been a "ghost."

It is an awesome experience. To see one's physical body from the outside, feel the buoyancy of the externalized body, and see the milky pellucid astral light, also known as the etheric web, are sensations marvelous as well as fascinating. You are in a mental realm, and thought travel leaves one with a sense of wonder that is overwhelming.

History fascinated Muldoon and his first and only non-psychic book was a biography of Alexander Hamilton's pioneer son. As we drove through the Hoosier countryside searching out scenic and historic spots, then spent the warm evenings on the porch and along the lake shore, we discussed many things during those three months. One was the risks involved in practicing voluntary astral projection. We came to the following conclusions:

There are physical dangers. Muldoon's lifelong poor health probably contributed to his natural projection ability, but the nature of his complaints presented no danger. However, individuals with high blood pressure or a heart condition should not attempt these exercises. My friend and fellow writer, D. Scott Rogo, who has voluntarily projected, said in *Fate* magazine (May 1973) he agrees with Robert Crookall that conscious experimentation with projection is dangerous, not because of the possibility of "possession" or because it may cause death, but because of very basic physical and psychological hazards.

"For example," he writes, "rhythmic breathing exercises that may favor projection also can upset the blood pressure and put abnormal stress on the heart. Staring into a mirror can cause dissociation or even psychotic disorders. Conscious control of the heartbeat can backfire and throw the heart off its normal rhythm so that it beats sporadically, too quickly and completely out of control (as I can testify from unhappy personal experience). Other techniques can affect the oxygen supply to the brain. I should think these physical dangers should warn off most persons."

Involuntary projections, particularly unconscious ones during sleep, appear to have built-in protections. Rogo says that persons who have "a natural history of this fascinating experience" should cultivate the ability as this can lead to breakthroughs in our scientific study of the phenomenon. "If not, I suggest the would-be experimenters analyze their motivations for undertaking so risky a practice."

Ingo Swann, the noted psychic whose astral abilities have been studied by the ASPR, was asked about projection dangers. He replied: "We know that people sometimes have out-of-the-body experiences when they're in crisis situations, when they're very ill or under drugs. And all of these can be very taxing on the body itself. So I would caution them against drastic methods of trying to achieve it, though the out-of-the-body experience itself is a natural heritage of man." (*Psychic* magazine, April 1973)

Some projectors never notice the cord or only feel its pull. This usually occurs as the two bodies violently coincide causing a "repercussion" or falling dream. During sleep the two bodies are slightly out of coincidence, and a sudden light or other disturbance results in the repercussion.

The operating control in a projection is what Muldoon called the "crypto-conscious" mind. On one occasion he awakened to find his body in a twist with the astral cord around his neck. He was unable to move. After several anxious moments, his crypto-conscious mind took over and he was tossed into the air and spun around, with the cord resuming its usual position. Actually there are several kinds of projections involving the astral and vital bodies of man, and the cord position varies as attached to the bodies according to the type of exteriorization involved.

Projections have been reported under the influence of various drugs, including LSD, peyote, hashish, yaye, opium, and telepatina. It should not be necessary to warn readers against their use. They act to disturb the consciousness and induce hallucinations instead of sober, clear vision. In most instances I've heard about, the experimenters had "bad trips." Moreover, as Dr. Tart points out, there is quite a difference between inexperienced amateurs in our culture playing around with psychedelic drugs, and their disciplined use in Carlos Castaneda's *The Teachings of Don Juan* for specific goals with an age-old knowledge of their nature.

In some OOBEs sex is a factor. One of Muldoon's correspondents was a John H. Watson, who has had a number of projections. He wrote: "In most instances, immediately after recoinciding with my physical body, I experience a powerful influx of sexual energy. And in connection with this I can well understand the warning of many theosophical writers that if one be not continent, and yet attempt occult development, he is liable to excessive sexual indulgences. Perhaps, and it seems quite likely to my mind, there may be more than the elements of Hindu mythology behind the Yoga concept of the psychic centers known as chakras. May I not, quite unconsciously, have stimulated the region corresponding to the Svadisthana chakra?" Watson's account of his OOBEs appears in Muldoon's *The Phenomena of Astral Projection* (Rider, 1951).

Robert Monroe (*Journeys Out of the Body*) says he has had strong sexual drives while projected. He points out that in scientific studies of dreams and sleep, it was noted that during REM (rapid eye movement indication dreaming), male subjects had a penile erection. A dream with non-sexual content still produced this effect. He mentions this because his most consistent physical reaction when returning from a projection is a penile erection.

Monroe, whose book is startling even to the well-informed, tells us that sexual relations are different in the astral world. There is no male-female interpenetration. Instead the couple move in close or embrace and "There is a short, sustained electron (?) flow one to another. The moment reaches unbearable ecstasy, and then tranquillity, equalization, and it is over."

In most OOBEs the subject remains on the physical level among the earthly things and places he knows. Usually he will find he will not be able to retain his normal consciousness and penetrate the fog or vibratory barrier separating the physical world from the higher spheres where dwell the so-called dead. He will see spirits of the dead from time to time who have returned to the earth's atmosphere or who have just passed on, but most of the time he will be alone. But occasionally sublimated projections do take place.

"Some of those I meet in my projections," Muldoon said, "are people known to me who passed over some time ago. Others are strangers—some helpful, others distinctly evil. The places I visit during my astral excursions are almost invariably places well known to me, though I have occasionally been transported to distant scenes and even distant lands. But all these are on the earth-plane, and certainly material and existent. It is rarely indeed that I am transported into any of the astral realms, entirely disconnected from the earth-plane."

The greatest danger is the projector's own mind. In this realm where thoughts have such awesome power, character development determines one's environment. Monroe said he had to change his attitudes and ways of thinking completely. Those having weak characters and wills or uncontrolled lives are liable to be influenced by outside, evil entities, opening the door to attack and possible "obsession." If the projector passes beyond his immediate physical surroundings, stray negative thoughts or improper motives can turn astral journeys into nightmares.

Back in the 1920s a neighbor of Muldoon's died of cancer. About four days after the funeral Muldoon overheard a conver-

sation between the dead man's wife and his mother. According to
the wife, her husband had been a brute, practically a sadist, so
much so that Sylvan was angered. "My blood boiled with rage
against him," he said.

About two hours later he went to bed and experienced a
OOBE. "My eyes encountered a terrifying sight," he said. "There
stood the dead man glaring at me like a maniac. I knew he meant
revenge. Before I could do anything he leaped upon me. We
fought for a few moments—he getting the better of me, as he
cursed and beat me with all his might."

Then his crypto-conscious mind came to the rescue. He was
pulled back toward his physical body, the man clinging to him,
then raised into the air and literally dropped into his physical
body. He said it was the most severe repercussion he had ever experienced.

Close to and partly interpenetrating our physical world are the
astral hells. Here the earthbound, gripped by vices, try to enjoy
vicariously the material pleasures now denied them. They are
said to congregate around saloons, dope dens, brothels, and mas-
sage parlors. But on a different level or plane are the haunts of the
truly evil. The inhabitants, as Monroe puts it, "are insane or near-
insane, emotionally driven beings." The unlucky projector who
happens to enter this realm is subject to torment and attack.

There are also beings on the lower astral that for want of a better word are called elementals. They are said to be native to this
realm and they like to play tricks. The French writer Yram (*Practical Astral Projection*) tells of being hallucinated by these beings
by being surrounded by four walls. As he would break through
one wall, there would be another four walls. With an act of will
he ended the charade.

Robert Monroe tells of being pestered by small humanoid entities that clung to his back. They weren't vicious, just troublesome.
When he tried to pull them off his back, their limbs would stretch
like rubber. If he succeeded, they fought to get back on him.
After several weeks the annoyances ceased.

This is the negative aspect of OOBE. There is a positive side.
And there is the wonder of it all.

Harold Sherman, in his book *You Live After Death* (G. and R.

Anthony, 1949), tells of his late friend Harry J. Loose, who lectured on criminology on the Redpath Chautauqua Circuit. Later he was in charge of security for the Chicago *Daily News* and at Hull House. In retirement in California, he told Sherman that he and John Carlos, a Roman Catholic priest living in South America, had occasionally visited each other while projected for many years.

Stuart Harary, a Duke University student and research assistant at the Psychical Research Foundation, Durham, North Carolina, projects to the bedside of a friend, helps him to project, and together they visit an old friend of Harary's, an elderly woman living in Maine. Although there had been no contact for some time, she knew they were coming and had projected herself to meet them.

How many ethereal meetings throughout the world will take place tonight? How little do we know of little-suspected events and activities occurring just beyond our ken?

And there is the underlying oneness of all minds, affinities that so strangely link us in love and brotherhood, greater than time and space. You leave your body. You think of a loved one at an unknown location. Almost instantly you are in the presence of the one you seek. And there is the unity of all life and nature.

As quoted in Raynor Johnson's *Watcher on the Hills*, one percipient wrote: "It was a night in October about 11 P.M. I suddenly found myself out of the body floating over a Highland moor, in a body as light or lighter than air. There was a wood at the side of the moor, and a cool fresh wind was flowing. I found that I didn't mind the wind as I should have done had I been in my physical body, because I was *at one* with it. The life in the wind and the clouds and the trees was within me also, flowing into me and through me, and I offered no resistance to it. I was filled with glorious life."

And there are those fortunate occasional projectors who pass beyond the habitat of elementals, the astral hells, into the upper realms; and they return with wondrous tales of beauty and peace. Here, as below, like attracts like; birds of a feather flock together. We are told there are buildings and scenery created by the minds of the inhabitants, that there are visions beyond words to describe. For those who live as they should, it is heaven.

Someday, after the tilling, the sowing, the growing of our lives, the harvest will be at hand and we shall go forth to live in these spheres. It will be the permanent projection.

25

"Let Me Tell You: There Is Black Magic!"

NANDOR FODOR

The crossroads of psychology and psychic phenomena were the particular study area of Dr. Nandor Fodor (1895–1964). Born in Hungary, he spent many years in England, where he served as director of the International Institute for Psychical Research. From 1938 on he lived in New York City, where he was a practicing psychoanalyst. Among his many published works is the Encyclopedia of Psychic Science.

Of all archaic fears of humanity, one of the greatest is the fear of the devil. This is as old as the belief in God. In fact, in the pre-Christian era, the line of demarcation between the powers of light and of darkness was not clearly drawn. Prayers and evocative rituals were not distinctly set apart. With the advent of Christianity, the power of God, particularly for the uneducated, would have been far less dramatic without the contrasting presence of the devil. An emphasis on the perils of the soul was indispensable for the seeking of salvation.

Today, the worry about our immortal soul is far overshadowed by the worry about our mortal body. The devil has become historical, as dead as Faust, and is fast fading even from literature. But as an archaic idea, it is deeply imbedded in the unconscious. Stirring it into life may still prove dangerous.

This was the lesson learned by a strange woman I knew in London. Because of her odd crusades, she was often mentioned in the newspapers, but not in complimentary fashion. Her business talent had made her a millionaire, a fact about which she boasted whenever she had a chance. In many ways, she was a totally incredible person: of Cockney birth and speech, entirely uncultured, she had an excellent brain, tremendous will power, and a hypnotic personality. A thin cloak of generosity and goodwill failed to hide her extreme possessiveness and utter egotism. She could hate with a passion that flared like a fierce flame. Fundamentally, she was cruel and exceedingly narcissistic. I met and spoke to her for the first time during a drawing room discussion of "black magic." As I protested against consideration of such nonsense, I was met with a steady gaze from a pair of eyes that glowed like coals of fire.

"You speak unwisely," she said, a warning note in her voice. "Demonology is not to be laughed at."

I found that she had a passionate interest in demonology and had collected an extensive library on the subject. She admitted that she had always been fascinated by the devil. As a child, she said, she had prayed to the devil and not to God. Her parents had grown frightened and cast her out, she added, but her interest in demonology had increased. She feared nothing. Observing the look of ruthlessness in her eyes as she spoke, I could well believe her. Her vibrant voice suggested tremendous strength and a character that shirked nothing to achieve her ends. Nevertheless, I was unprepared for the story she told.

"Some years ago," she began, "I had a young boy staying with me who was a good hypnotic subject. I drew a magic circle, put him inside and sent him into hypnotic sleep. Then I commanded him to go to hell and bring up the Devil!

"The boy writhed and cried. He was afraid.

"I ordered him to obey, saying I would give him power.

"Nothing happened in the first five hypnotic sessions. But the sixth time something did, and it frightened me out of my senses.

"In the magic circle a light appeared. Out of a luminous haze, two eyes—as big as eggs—looked at me with an awful, penetrating look, a horrible expression. I asked hoarsely what it was. The boy

answered—in a totally different voice—'The Evil that you conjured up speaks to you.'

"There was an earthy smell in the room, an icy cold, and a
dreadful breathing sound, as if the whole room were taking a
choking breath as a living thing. I was so scared that I shrieked,
'Go back, never come again! I will not permit you, I don't want
you!'

"The light disappeared with a rushing sound, and things returned to normal. But I was white as chalk and for days afterward
I felt that all the strength had gone out of me. The boy felt the
same. Four or five times he felt that a power had tried to gain
control of him.

"I never tried the experiment again. I was too frightened. But
let me tell you: there is black magic."

Later, I paid many visits to the home of this woman. In her
desire for power, she overrode any opposition. She was vindictive
to the point of evil and I came to the conclusion that she was
definitely dangerous.

I did not doubt that she had tried to evoke the devil, but I did
not believe that he had appeared to her. She had pushed the boy
too far and had been caught in a net of her own weaving. In an
act of self-defense, the tortured boy's unconscious may have risen
to the occasion, producing a set of visual and auditory hallucinations that fully confirmed what she had read about demonology.
Perhaps by some manner of mental acrobatics, the hypnotized
boy had succeeded in turning the tables on the hypnotizer.

Scared as she had been, the experience did not deter her from
trying to impress people with her knowledge of the black arts.
Some time before, some silver spoons had been stolen from her
home. She suspected a discharged cook, and in her anger she uttered a curse: "I wish that whoever stole the spoons would drop
dead—then I would know!" There was a church clock in front of
her window, and as she looked out she saw that the time was 11
A.M.

The following day, as she was being driven in her car through a
quiet street, her chauffeur turned to her: "Did you know,
Madame, that your old cook dropped dead at this spot yester-

day?" She made inquiries and found out that the time of the death had been 11 A.M.

I am not inclined to take much notice of such stories. There is too much emotion connected with them, too little evidence, too much possibility of coincidence. But it was not the first time that I had heard of the demonic power of the death wish. A fierce outburst of passion appears to be its chief component. Another woman, interested in psychic matters told me of occurrences of this type in her life and said they had seriously frightened her. Once, as she entered the home of some friends, their Great Dane leaped upon her. The dog was friendly, but this manifestation of its affection was so sudden that she was terrified, and cried: "God damn this dog!" As if it had succumbed to her curse, the dog was found dead the next morning. Her friends told her never to visit them again.

I first began to wonder about the effectiveness of such death wishes when I met a man who had been tried for high treason in Canada during World War I. I will call him X. He had duped a ring of German secret agents and had got away with a packet of $50,000—which he had not turned back to the Canadian government. Government agents suspected him, and had they located the money, he would undoubtedly have been found guilty of treason. As agents searched him and his personal belongings in a railway compartment, the money lay snugly in another suitcase in the baggage car. Then the identity of his accomplice in the theft was discovered. It was either his neck or that of his accomplice. So X concentrated on his associate in guilt, mentally willing him to commit suicide.

On the following day, X was arrested on a charge of murder. The psychic experiment had succeeded too well. The victim had walked into the house of my traitor acquaintance, took a revolver from his desk, and shot himself, making X a prime suspect in his death. X was saved, however, for he was able to show at the trial that his friend had had free entry into his house. The jury was unable to reach a unanimous verdict of guilty, and he was freed.

"But if there is such a thing as psychic murder," X told me in a burst of candor, "I was certainly guilty of it."

This man was a weird creature. He was convinced that he had a familiar spirit always ready to do his bidding. I certainly did see some queer phenomena in his presence that I could not explain.

The "psychic murder" I have described and the fatal curse that "struck" the cook would be much less mysterious if experimental evidence could be collected on the nature of the impact which a telepathic message makes on the recipient's mind. Whatever the scientific evidence, they correspond to reports of the powers of black magic in old-fashioned witchcraft and in primitive tribes today.

All this has bearing on a further story concerning the woman preoccupied with demonology. I accepted a Christmas invitation to her country home and took my wife and daughter along with some misgivings. I did not like the fascination that my hostess had shown for my wife, I felt she was becoming hostile to me, and besides, there was no telling what queer experiments she might have in mind. I hesitated to expose my family to such an atmosphere. However, it was nearly impossible to say no to this lady and we found ourselves in the country as her guests.

Two things happened of a rather disturbing nature. The first occurred in her playroom. We played darts. They were so weighted that if dropped they landed invariably with the heavy metal point downward. Apparently by accident, our hostess dropped one of these heavy darts on my daughter's instep. Miraculously there were no ill effects, but I was considerably upset. My daughter was a ballet dancer at Sadler's Wells. Her career depended on the fine condition of her feet. The heavy metal dart could have easily inflicted a serious injury.

I accepted our hostess' apologies, but my wife could not shake off the impression that the dart was dropped with evil intent. Her anxiety reached a new height the following day. As we were about to leave for home, my daughter could not find one of her shoes. It had simply disappeared. The servants could not account for it, nor could we. One does not lose a shoe in a guest room. Our hostess tried to reassure us; the shoe would turn up somewhere, she said.

It did. Several days later it was returned to us in the mail, with no explanation as to where it had been found. A few days later my daughter had an accident: she broke a cartilage in her left instep which incapacitated her for almost a year. Her foot was in a plaster cast for a month. Shortly after the accident we were telephoned by our former hostess—by now I was calling her the Devil's Disciple—and, in the course of the conversation, she inquired after my daughter. When I told her of the accident, she remarked, "I thought so."

This was a very strange statement, and perhaps a stupid giveaway of an experiment in malignant telepathy. My wife was now convinced that she had purposely stolen the shoe and had practiced her black art on it in order to vent the hostility she felt for me. My wife assumed that my daughter had been chosen as the weakest link in the family chain.

Of course, I do not believe that my wife was right. But psychologically the developments were extremely interesting. The night after my wife reached her conclusion about the malignant attack against our daughter, she fantasied or dreamed that she had visited the woman, had blinded her and slashed her face with a whip. The next night my wife dreamed she had made our Devil's Disciple stand on the swinging branch of a tree; the magician fell and broke her ankle.

In these retaliatory fantasies, three separate acts of aggression are portrayed: blinding, slashing the face, and breaking the ankle. The blinding is suggestive of self-defense on the primitive assumption that without eyes the magician would be unable to see her victim, and unable to hurt her again. The whipping is revenge with intent to degrade and humiliate the enemy, the breaking of the ankle is punishment by Mosaic law: an eye for an eye, a tooth for a tooth.

I did not like these dreams because I feared that by indulging in them my wife had unwittingly strengthened the hold of magic on herself. They implied an admission that the Black Magician was dangerous. By defending herself against magic, my wife exposed herself to it.

I was right. It took my wife a year to shake off the effect of these cumulative defensive self-suggestions, a year during which

I was careful to keep her from all contact with the "Devil's Disciple." This is how the release was indicated to her in a dream:

"I made an entrance in my beautiful red velvet cape in a night club. The 'Black Magician' walked beside me and looked like a twin sister. I thought the boys did not know which one was me, so I tore off her cape and shouted to them: 'I am not that one. She only has my cape.'

"There stood the Black Magician—exposed, bejewelled, glittering. I told her: 'If I don't give you my cape, you cannot do anything.' I touched the cape with a fan, and lo! the cape disappeared."

This dream is a beautiful statement of how thoughts of the "Black Magician" had been integrated into my wife's personality. She had been made into a twin, into part of my wife's self, and as long as she was residing within my wife's psyche, the magician was dangerous. But my wife took back the cape, the symbol of identification, the mantle of magic—and, on making the cape vanish, had released herself from the evil influence.

The point this story makes, it seems to me, is that fear works like bad magic—a secret known to witch doctors and medicine men for ages past. The fear may be so deeply imbedded that no counter-persuasion can reach it. We do not believe in the bogey man, but we can still be afraid of the dark.

A medical man who came to me for help was so frightened of his father's snoring that he had to stuff his ears with cotton and have several drinks each night before he dared to go to bed. He did not know that, to an early level of his mind, his frail old father was an ogre, the man-eating giant whom tiny Jack killed in the fairy tale. His father had done a terrible thing when my patient was a year and a half old. In order to intimidate his wife, he tore the child from her breast and held him out of a third-story window threatening to drop him if his wife would not put the child out of the conjugal bed. The drunken rage of the father and the shriek of the mother conveyed murderous intent to the infant, and ever since the child had been overwhelmingly frightened of his father. Clutching, ghostly hands seemed to reach for him in the dark, he could never lean out of windows at any height, and the sight of window cleaners at work caused him severe anxiety.

It took almost nine months of analytic treatment to release my patient from this awful trauma. After treatment, he still disliked his father's snore—but now he could bear it. He continued to have misgivings, however: Would he be able to face the darkness if he had to sleep all alone in a house? Usually he slept with his dog in the room, from which he took comfort and courage. But he was going on a trip and could not take the dog. I suggested a very simple remedy: if bogeys were waiting for him in the dark, he should visualize his dog preceding him and chasing them out. That meant placing the dog on the same mental level on which existed the remnant of his fears.

The trick worked. Counter-magic is the proper answer to "black magic."

Strangely, the instinct of self-protection by counter-magic and the ability to devise mental defense measures is stronger in psychotic people than in normal individuals. The probable explanation is that a normal man believes in magic only with a small part of his mind, whereas the psychotic surrenders to it. Here is how a paranoid patient protected himself from persecution by wearing imaginary glasses:

"This morning, I felt a drawing feeling on my brow. I put on an imaginary pair of glasses and the voice said: 'All right, I am licked again.'"

The "voices" that this patient heard claimed that glasses prevented them from sharing visual experiences with him. But the glasses were imaginary (as were the voices), and stymied them. The patient explained that the shape of the lens acted as a magic circle, and then added the really significant association: his mother used to wear glasses. It was she who protected him.

Love is the greatest answer to fear. He who learns that lesson, and feels himself loved, need have no fear of the power of darkness, of malignant telepathy, of black magic, or of the traditional spells of the devil.